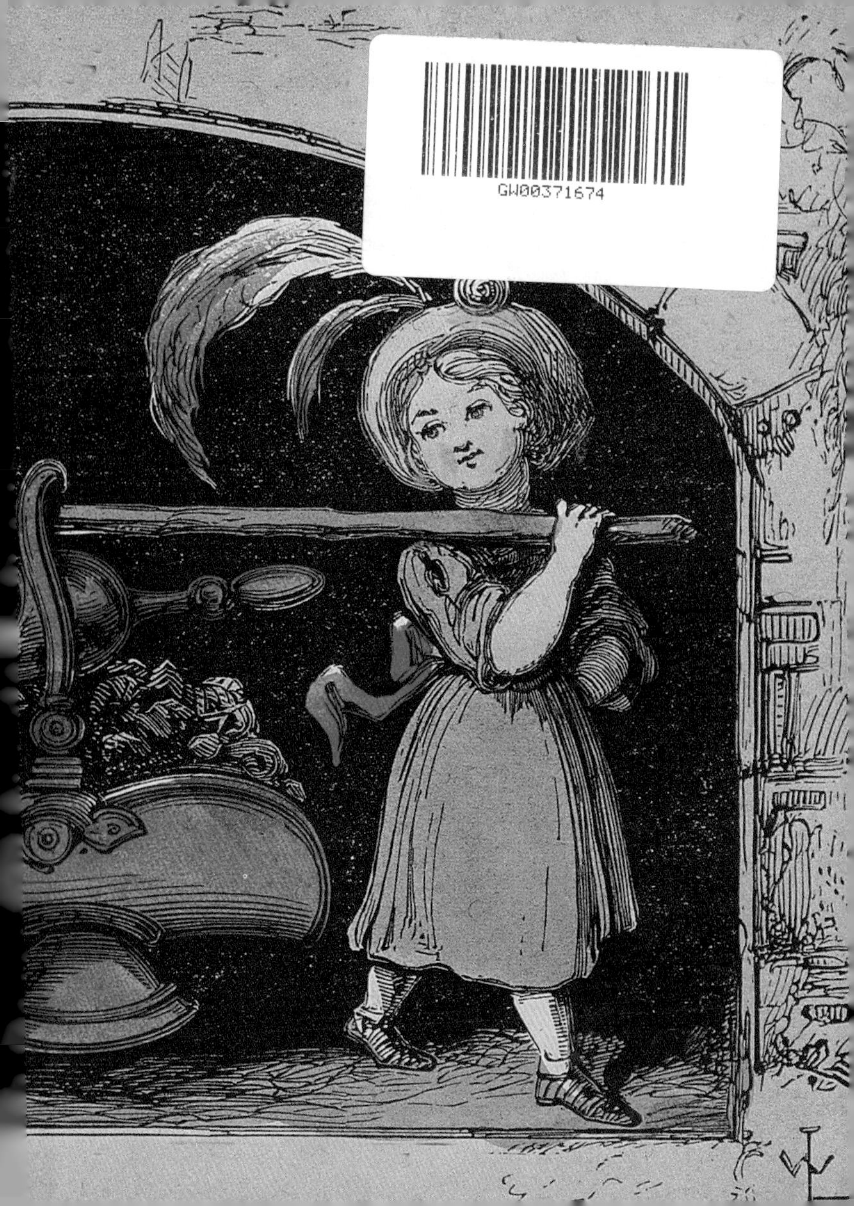

A little book for you
to pick up and read when
ever you get a moment to rest

Love from Marion & Jeff

Fireside

A FAMILY COMPANION

MQ Publications Limited
12 The Ivories, 6–8 Northampton Street
London N1 2HY
Tel: +44 (0) 20 7359 2244
Fax: +44 (0) 20 7359 1616
email: mail@mqpublications.com
www.mqpublications.com

ISBN: 1-84072-723-3

10 9 8 7 6 5 4 3 2 1

Printed and bound in Italy

Fireside

A FAMILY COMPANION

JANICE ANDERSON

MQP

Contents

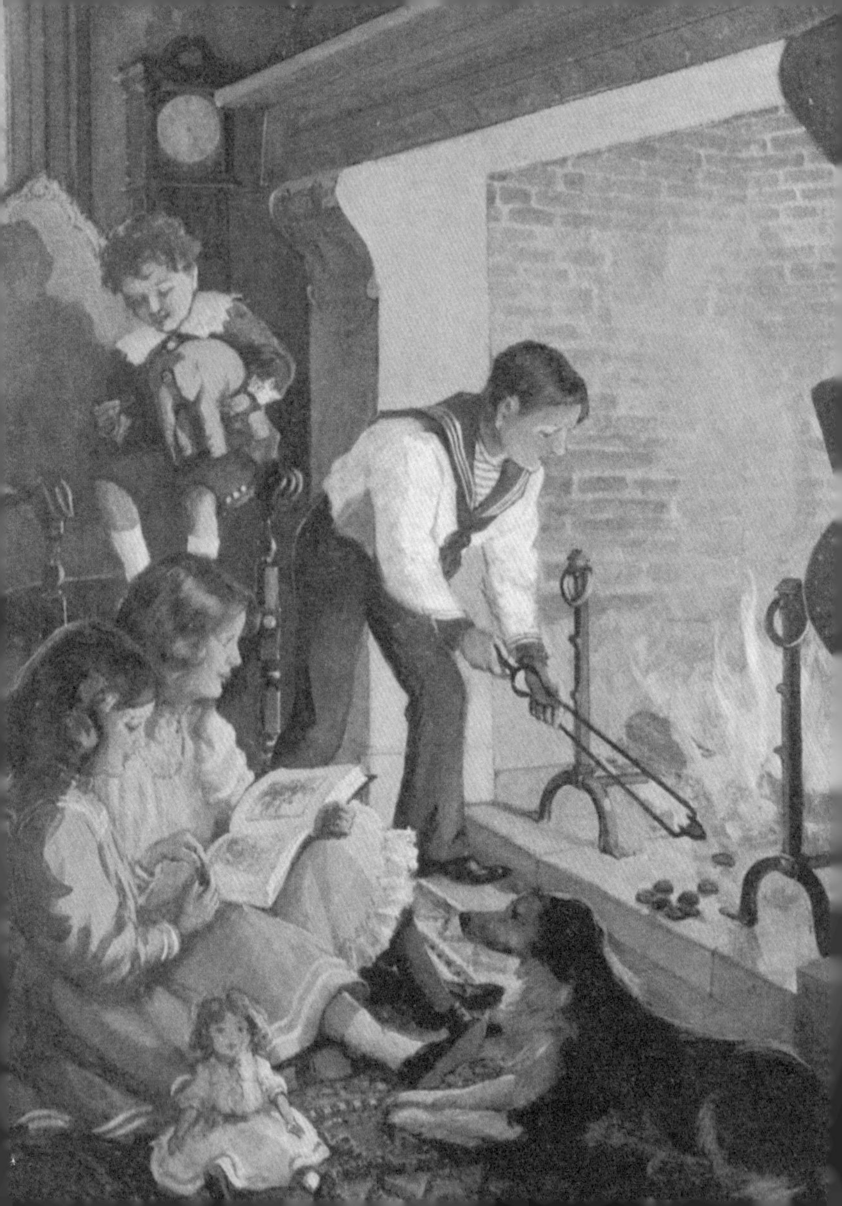

Introduction

After a hard day what bliss to sink into the comfort of a favorite chair, kick your shoes off, and let yourself relax by the fireside! It's a wonderfully warm and cozy place where you can slow down, be peaceful, and quietly gaze into the flames for a while. Forget all life's pressures, and sip a hot, comforting drink while you explore the pages of *Fireside: A Family Companion*. And what varied pleasures await you here as you happily immerse yourself in this captivating collection of fireside lore.

An artfully assembled miscellany, *Fireside: A Family Companion* creates a unique world of its own. The fireside—the earliest place where we humans gathered together—is a legendary kingdom in itself; a fascinating, curious realm evoked by quirky facts, stories, myths, rhymes, and quotations from poetry and literature from around the world. You'll be visually enchanted too—each page reveals one amusing, amazing delight after another in an eclectic mix of evocative paintings, illustrations, engravings, and photographs.

Fireside: A Family Companion entertains and informs everyone, young or old. As children, we spent hours by the fire—reading stories, playing games, and listening to songs, fairy tales, and nursery rhymes—and they are here to charm and enchant. There is also much to satisfy the curious mind, as well as projects to occupy a practical hand. Learn all about chimney sweeps; discover the best kind of wood or coal to burn, how to keep the hearth clean, how to roast chestnuts, make popcorn, and fix a hot toddy! Try your hand at knitting a cozy throw, or making a christmas stocking to hang from the mantlepiece.

Fireside: A Family Companion is a book of timeless treasure, an illuminating and evocative portrait of the haven that is the hearth. Keep it on your fireside table as a perfect companion, to enjoy on your own, and with your loved ones.

Radiant Cozy Heat

At the hub of every house, there was always a fire. It was a place for drying damp clothes, thawing frozen bones, or spinning yarns by firelight. The hearth or stove was the emotional and physical heartland. We were instinctively drawn to the flame: it made us feel warm and secure.

Now, why not install a fireplace or stove? Pieces with past lives rescued from salvage yards tell their own stories. Most old stoves and hearth surrounds are made from rustic textural elements: wood,

stone, wrought iron, brick, and tile. Use an old wooden beam or choose local stone for a mantlepiece. To enhance the warm, glowing atmosphere, group dozens of lighted candles in the hearth or in one spot in the room.

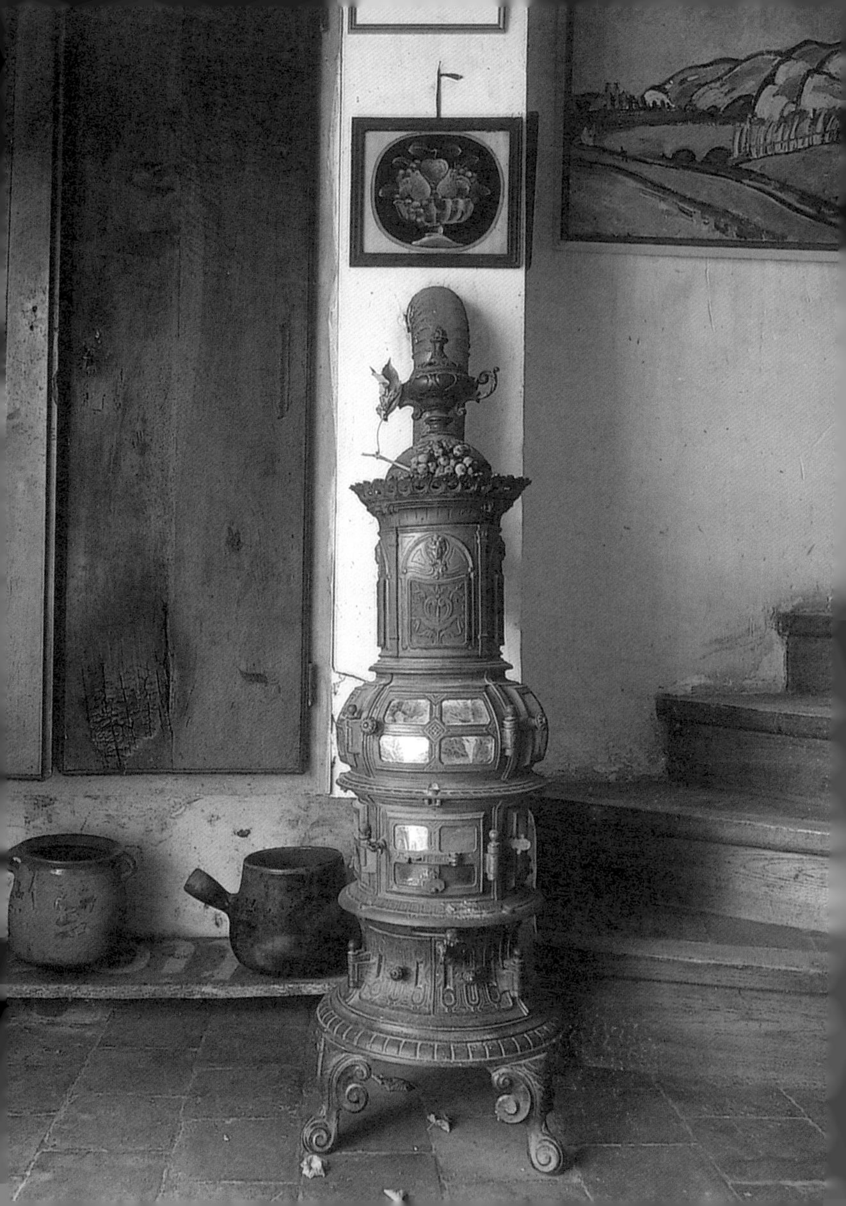

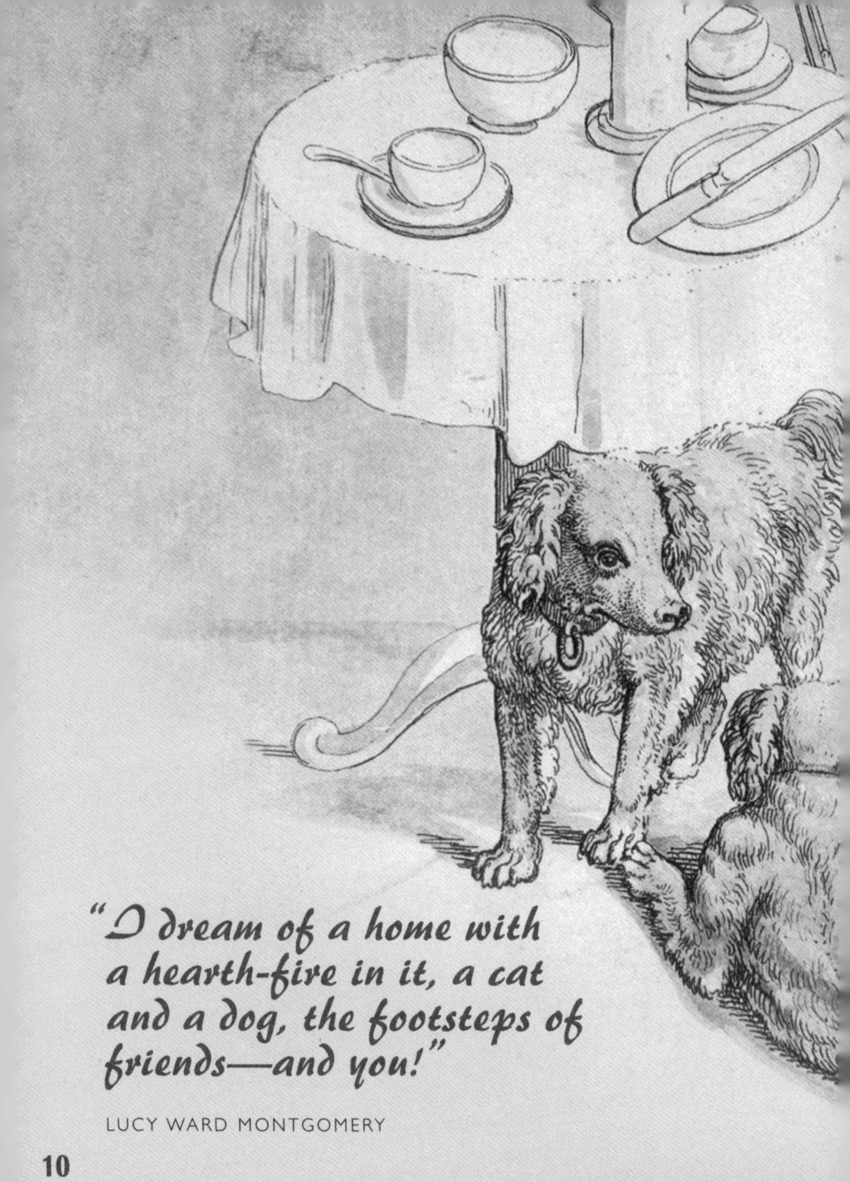

"I dream of a home with a hearth-fire in it, a cat and a dog, the footsteps of friends—and you!"

LUCY WARD MONTGOMERY

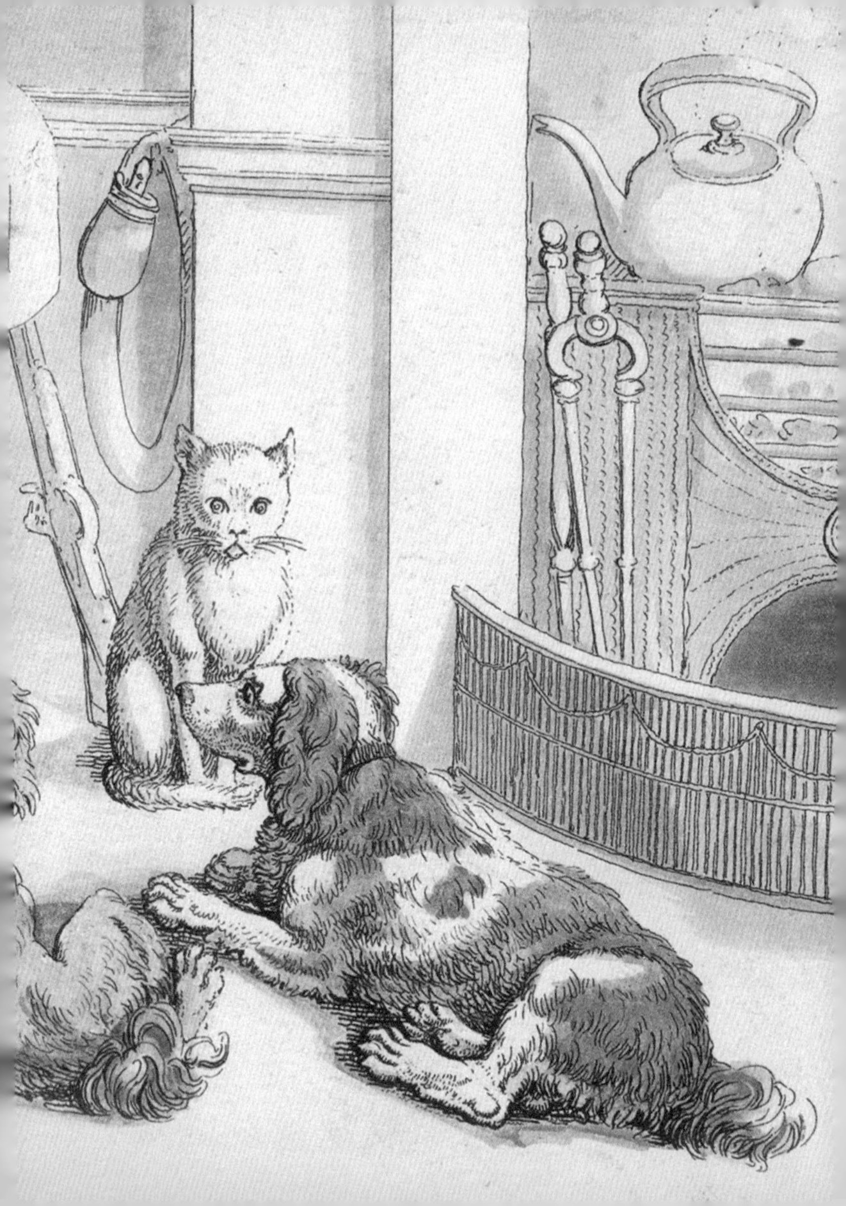

Hot Tips

If you have an old hearth and chimney, before you even think about putting match to wood for the first time, have the chimney inspected by a qualified professional. Smoke will only escape up a chimney if it is hotter and lighter than the surrounding air. A damp, cold draught or blockages caused by soot or loose bricks stop the smoke spiraling upwards, and instead allow toxic smoke and gases to waft right back into the living room.

Chimneys in older houses may sometimes need relining. One possible technique, "cast-in-situ" (where concrete is poured into a tailored mold around the existing structure) also adds strength to structurally dubious chimneys. Other indoor-smoke eliminators include proper fire ventilators, such as a flue with a smoke shelf and air damper, and an under-floor duct in front of the fire. You should also remember to have your chimneys professionally swept twice yearly to prevent hazardous tar buildup.

Bear in mind local regulations. In the United States, the Environmental Protection Agency has introduced controls on all emissions, and in Great Britain most urban areas are smoke controlled. Generally, clean air laws in built-up areas state that only smokeless solid fuels (such as smokeless coal, gas, or electric fires), or woodstoves with secondary burners (a second stove reignites and burns off solids produced by the original fire, consequently reducing emissions to a minimum) are permitted.

Gas fires have the environmental thumbs-up and have thankfully progressed since their 1970s heyday as living flames. Now outputting warmth as well as mimicking nature's own blaze, gas fires are often more fuss-free and better cost-wise than real fires. ☞

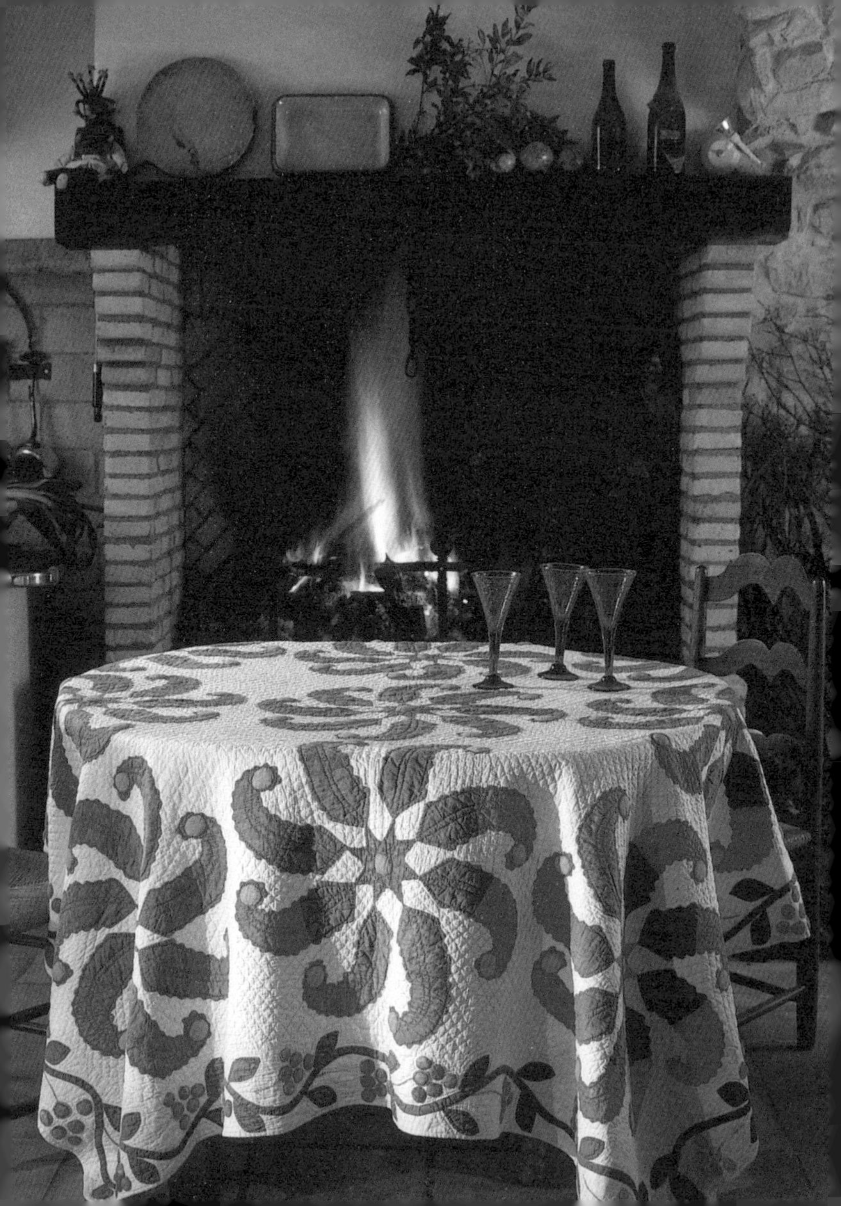

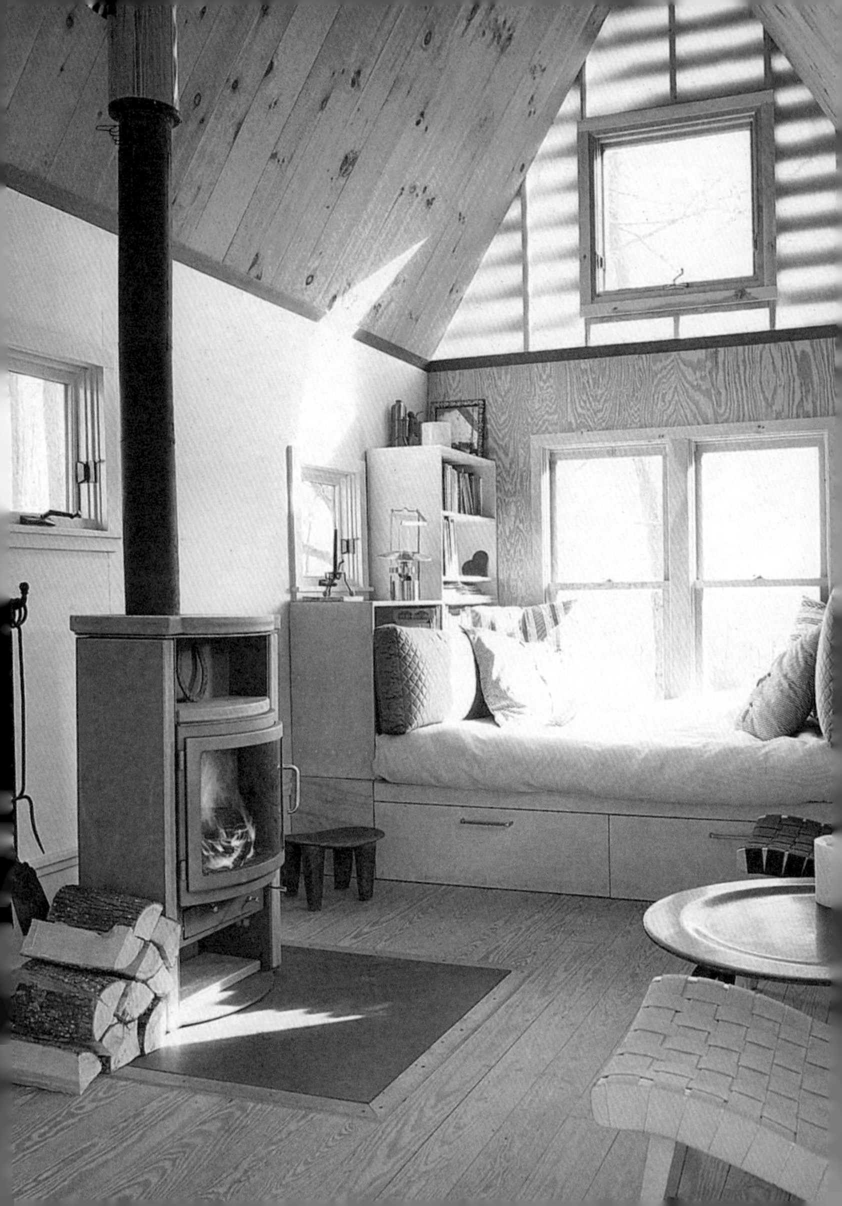

Nothing is quite so seductive as the hiss and crackle of wood burning on your fire. Attaining the rustic idyll, however, requires forethought—wood fires are exremely labor intensive. When trees are freshly felled, the wood comprises fifty percent water and consequently requires seasoning (air-drying) for up to twelve months before it can be burned. If the rules of wood seasoning are not strictly adhered to, burning wood deposits highly flammable tar residue on chimney walls, which, unsurprisingly, can spark chimney fires. As always, safety should be your first priority.

Wood is a renewable resource, but there is no excuse for felling healthy trees. Instead use timber from dead, terminally old, or diseased trees. Coal is perhaps a better alternative: With a high heat content in relation to its weight, it is more efficient than wood, burning evenly and becoming, as the cliché goes, a glowing ember.

Remember that what looks hot can be deceptive. About ninety percent of a fire's heat disappears up the chimney with the smoke, rather than heating up your home. So maximize warmth by installing a convector system. Air is drawn in through a vent at the bottom of the hearth and passes up through a chamber at the back of the fireplace, heating up as it travels. It then crosses through another convection chamber fitted into the roof of the fireplace, and the hot air is expelled into the room.

If heat is your priority, opt for a high-performance airtight stove (fires burn hotter when the door is shut tight), fitted into an existing chimney. These stoves can be as attractive as a traditional open fire, but they give off much more heat. For convenience, most of these models are built to allow a jet of cold air to run in front of the window, ensuring the glass won't be covered in soot, so your view of flickering flames will not be obscured. Central heating systems can also be run off stoves, so once you walk away from the fire, you won't freeze.

Mark Twain's Fireside

"I know the look of an apple that is roasting and sizzling on the hearth on a winter's evening, and I know the comfort that comes of eating it hot, along with some sugar and a drench of cream...I know how the nuts taken in conjunction with winter apples, cider, and doughnuts, make old people's tales and old jokes sound fresh and crisp and enchanting."

MARK TWAIN

As is clear in the above extract from his autobiography, the great American writer Mark Twain (a.k.a. Samuel Langhorne Clemens) was well aware of all the comforts and pleasures of the fireside. His fondness for hearth and home—and for relaxing in front of a warm fire was also confirmed by the following letter written by Mr. R. J. Burdette after a visit to Twain's home in 1881:

"The pleasantest view I had of the city was from the cozy fireside in that wonderful home of Mr. S. L. Clemens, who was my host during my stay in Hartford. I am not a man addicted ☞

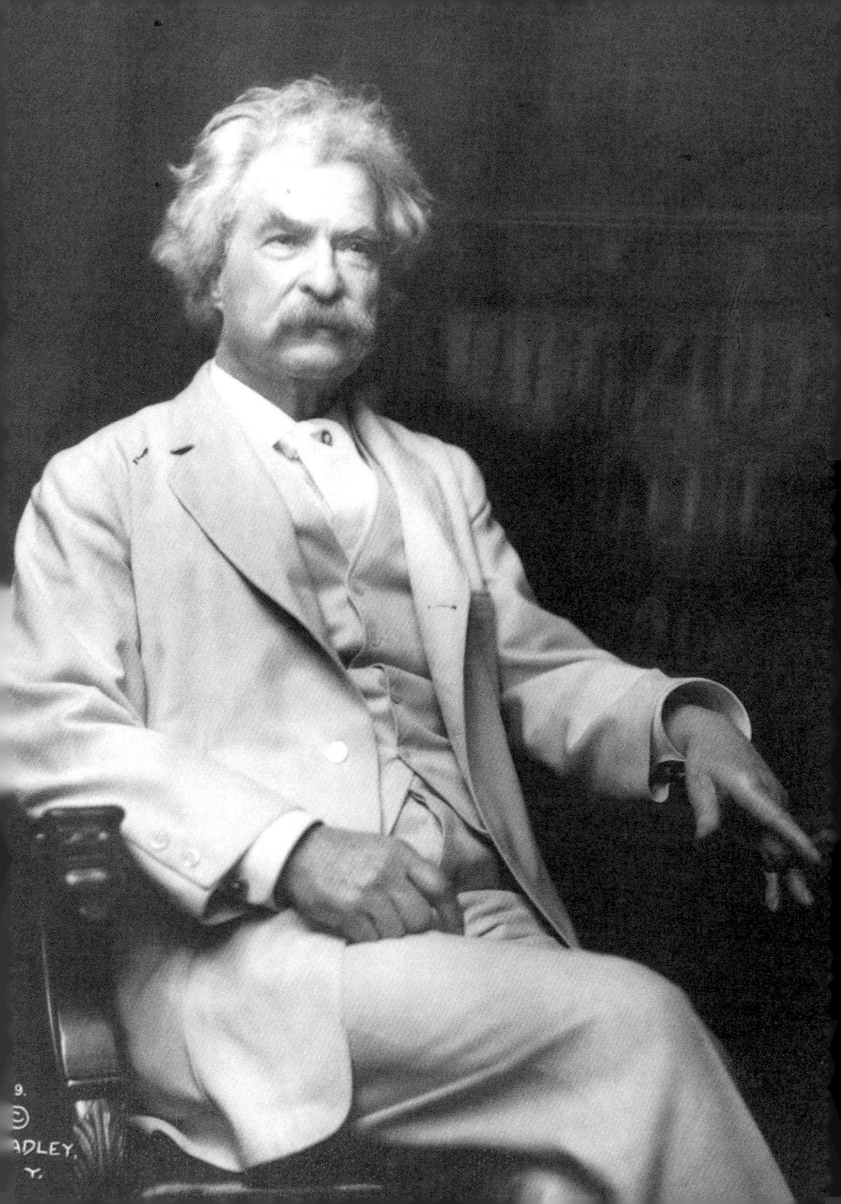

to cold weather. I am not sufficiently 'British' to wander through December and January in short checked coat and no ulster. I am given to much wrapping up when I do go out in the snow, and to very little going out in the snow at all. I begin to shiver with the first frost, and I keep it up until the following April. And so when I can sit down before a bright wood fire, and burn up cigars while somebody entertains me, I love the icy Winter.

"I think I have never been in a home more beautiful home-like than this palace of the king of humorists. The surroundings of the house are beautiful, and its quaint architecture, broad East Indian porticos, the Greek patterns in mosaic in the dark-red brick walls attract and charm the attention and good taste of the passer by, for the home, inside and out, is the perfection of exquisite taste and harmony. But with all its architectural beauty and originality, the elegance of its interior finish and decorations, the greatest charm about the house is the atmosphere of 'homelikeness' that pervades it.

"Charmingly as he can entertain thousands of people at a time from the platform, Mr. Clemens is even a more perfect entertainer in his home. The brightest and best sides of his nature shine out at the fireside. The humor and drollery that sparkle in his conversation is as utterly unaffected and natural as sunlight. Indeed, I don't believe he knows or thinks that most of his talk before the sparkling fire, up in the pleasant retirement of his billiard-room study, is marketable merchandise worth so much a page to the publishers, but it is. And it is not all drollery and humor. He is so earnest that his earnestness charms you fully as much as his brighter flashes, and once in a while there is in his voice an inflection of wonderful pathos, so touched with melancholy that you look into the kind, earnest eyes to see what thought has touched his voice. And he has a heart as big as his body; I believe there does not live a man more thoroughly unselfish and self-forgetful. Two little girls and a boy baby, bright-eyed, good-tempered, and with a full head of hair as brown as his father's, assist Mrs. Clemens to fill the heart of the reigning humorist, and they do it most completely.

"Personally, Mr. Clemens is, perhaps, a little above the medium height, of good symmetrical physique, brown hair, scarcely touched with gray that curls over a high, white forehead; friendship in his eyes, hearty cordiality in the grasp of a well-shaped white hand, strong enough and heavy enough to be a manly hand; his age is 40 something, and he looks 35; in the evening after the lamps are lighted his face has a wonderfully boyish look, and he loves a good cigar even better than Grant does."

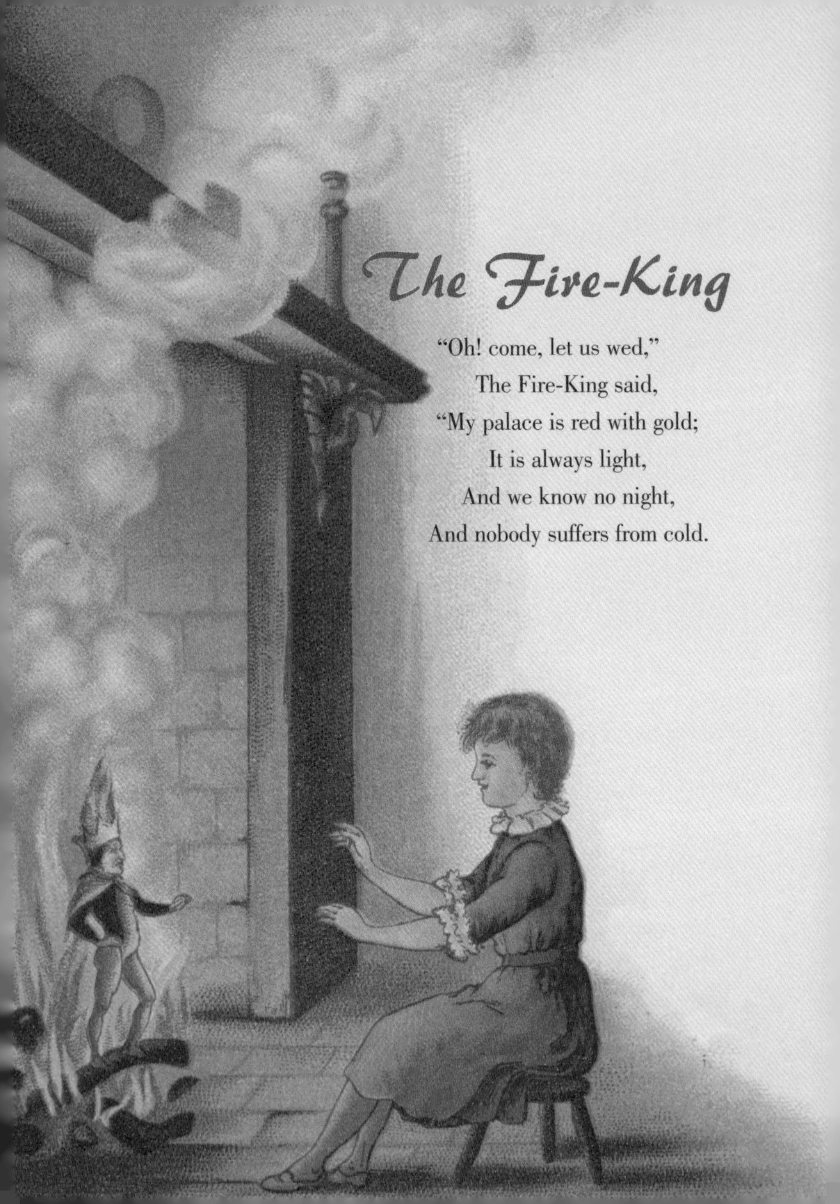

The Fire-King

"Oh! come, let us wed,"
The Fire-King said,
"My palace is red with gold;
It is always light,
And we know no night,
And nobody suffers from cold.

"The glowing heat,
Of coal or peat,
Shall never be known to fail:
And we'll play at ball
With the sparks that fall,
And on the smoke we will sail.

"When we laugh and shout
The people cry out,
'What a noise that fire is making!'
But little they know
(They are stupid and slow),
How we mock them, with laughter shaking.

"My palace so gay
Is changing alway,
The coals are for ever dropping:
And the ashes grey
We shovel away,
And work without any stopping.

"Then oh! Let us wed,"
The Fire-King said,
"Let us wed, little mortal, to-morrow
My fame you may see,
If you'll but look at me,
And in Fireland we know of no sorrow."

Whiskey Sour

Sour by name, sour by nature, this is one of the simplest, classic fireside drinks available. It is the quintessential gentleman's drink and it is best enjoyed on a quiet evening in front of a roaring fire. A Whiskey Sour was traditionally made with Scotch whiskey, such as Dewar's, but Bourbon is now often preferred. Bourbon was first made by Scottish and Irish colonists in Kentucky, America. Unable to exactly reproduce the fireside dram of their homelands, they created new Bourbon and rye whiskeys, which many people believe are just as good as the original.

Ingredients:

2 parts whiskey, preferably Bourbon or Scotch
1 part freshly squeezed lemon juice
1 tsp sugar
lemon peel, to garnish

1 Put all the ingredients together in a cocktail shaker and shake vigorously with cracked ice, until foamy.

2 Pour into a chilled, old-fashioned glass. Garnish with a twist of lemon peel.

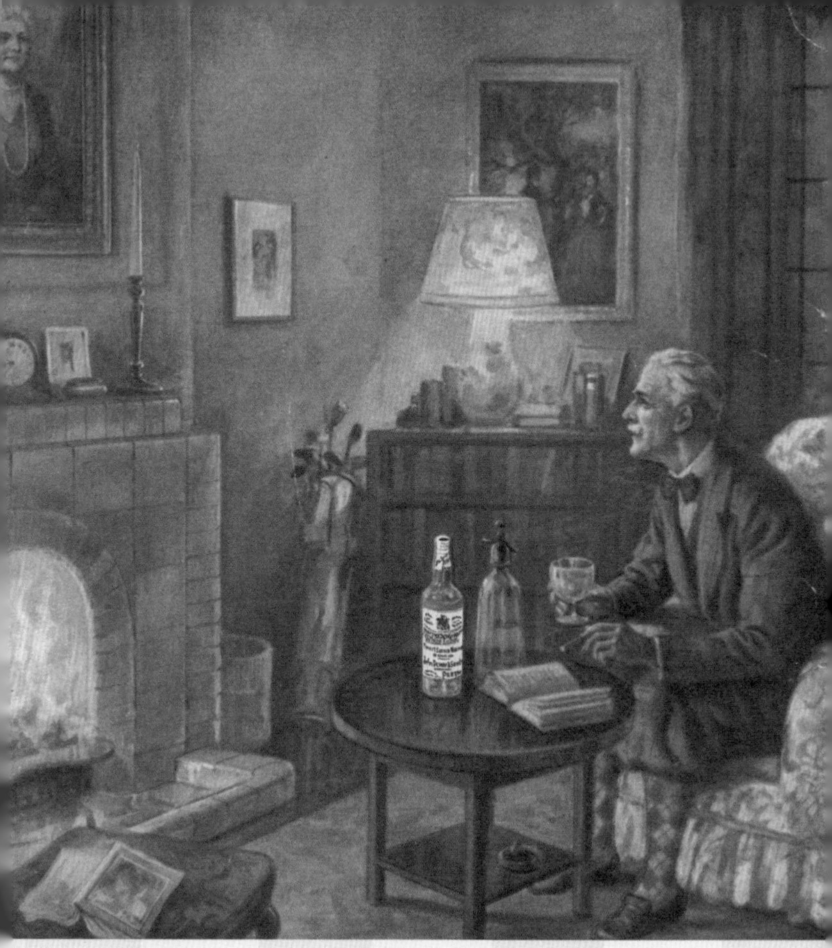

"When she's away from Home
DEWAR'S
is a real consolation"

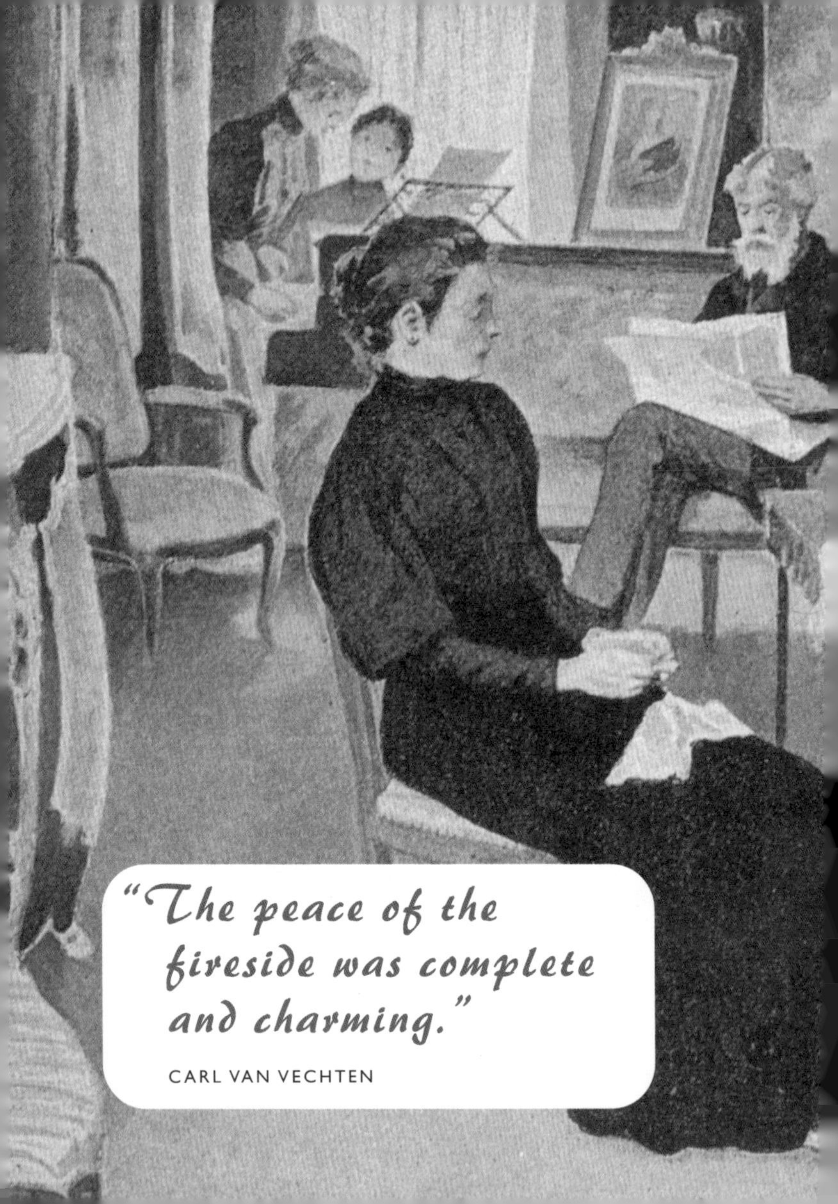

"The peace of the fireside was complete and charming."

CARL VAN VECHTEN

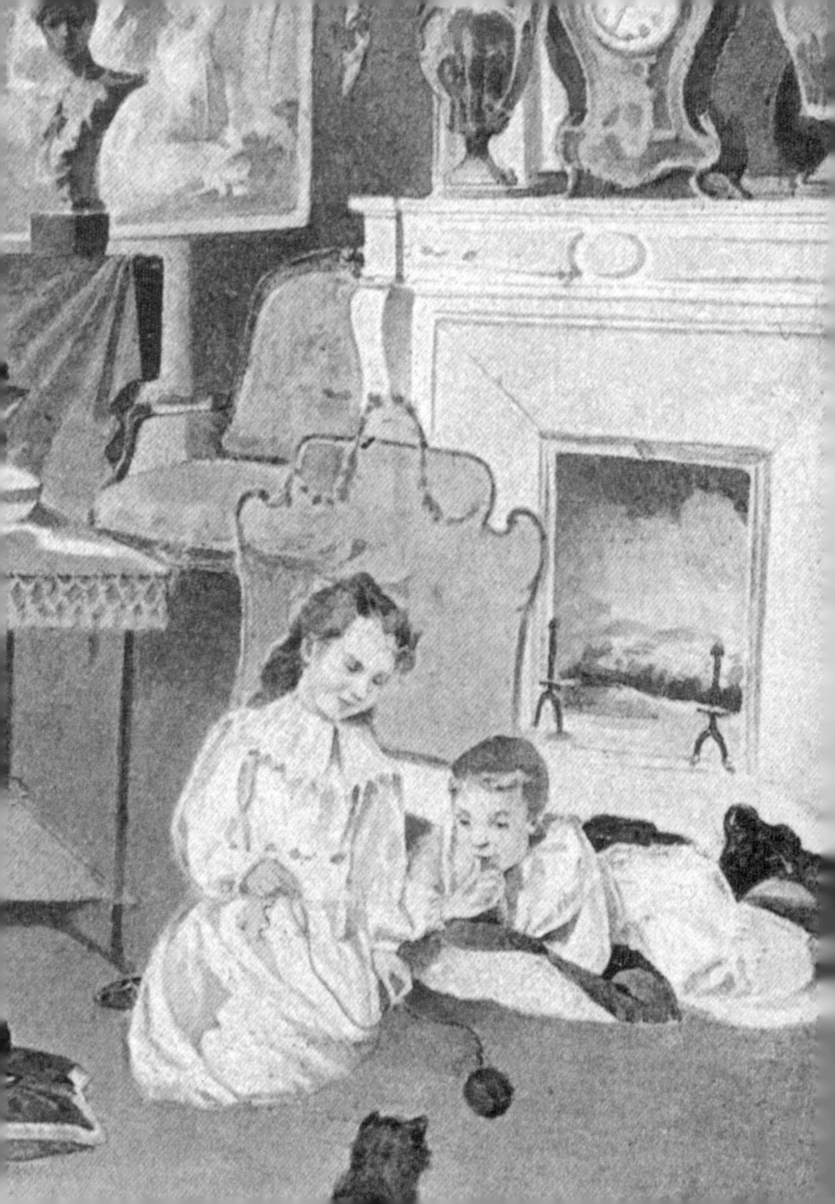

Fireside Games

Children cooped up inside on a rainy day need more than just a bright fire in the grate to keep them entertained and prevent boredom from sinking in. Board games and jigsaw puzzles that can be enjoyed on the hearthrug have long been the answer. Two of the most popular games are Ludo and Snakes and Ladders.

Ludo is a simplified version of the ancient Indian game *Pachisi* (Parcheesi), which was introduced to Britain in the late 1800s. Snakes and Ladders also derives from a game played in India many centuries ago. In America, it is better known as Chutes and Ladders, which was the name given to it by Milton Bradley when it was introduced there in 1943. Whatever name you know it by, it is essentially a game about morality—land on the right square and you successfully climb up a ladder; land on the wrong square and you sink back down a snake (or chute!).

The jigsaw puzzle, best played on a table or, if on the floor, on a couple of trays, can be dated much more precisely. It was invented as an educational aid by Englishman John Spilsbury in 1767. Spilsbury used a jigsaw to cut a map of the world pasted on wood into many small, oddly-shaped pieces that could be fitted back together again to make the picture.

Spilsbury thought his "dissected map" would be a useful

aid in teaching children "the use of the globes," the eighteenth-century phrase for geography. He soon followed up the world map puzzle with jigsaw puzzles based on smaller areas of the globe. The jigsaw puzzle became very popular in the nineteenth century and began to be produced with countless subjects and in many sizes. Today, jigsaw puzzles are still very popular all over the world with adults and children alike. There are jigsaw clubs with a worldwide membership and regular international competitions and championships. Like many board and card games, it can even be played on computers.

Ludo and Snakes and Ladders have also been moved out of the nursery and living rooms and have been enlarged to play in backyards and school playgrounds. There are, not surprisingly, computer versions of both of these games, too.

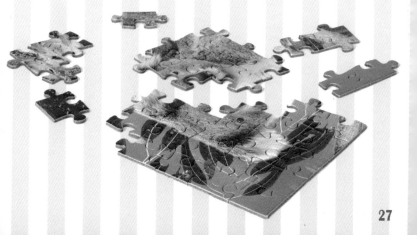

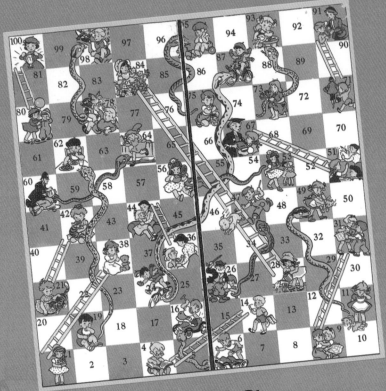

SNAKES
and
LADDERS

LUDO

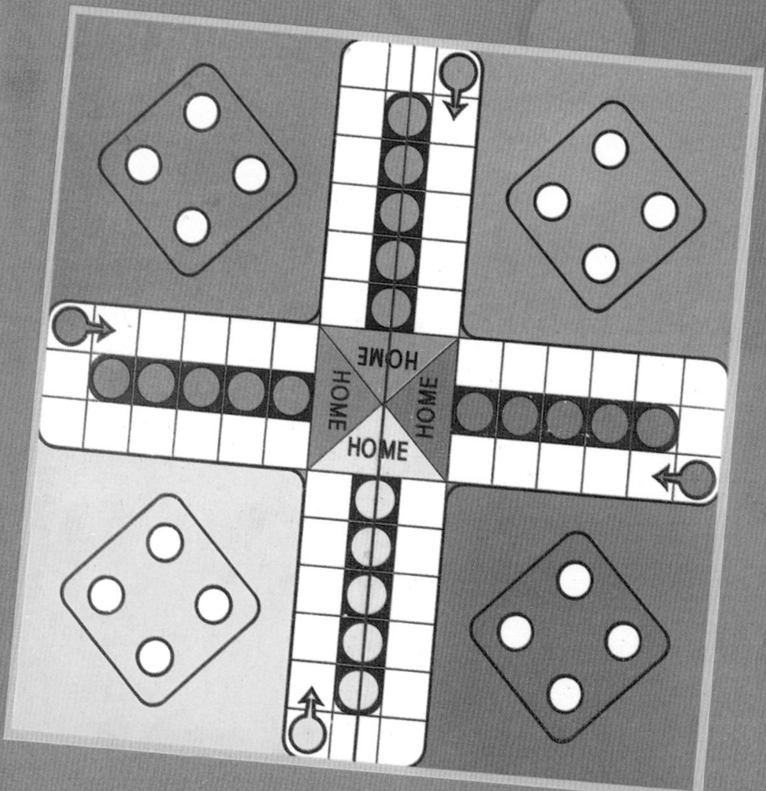
HOME
HOME
HOME
HOME

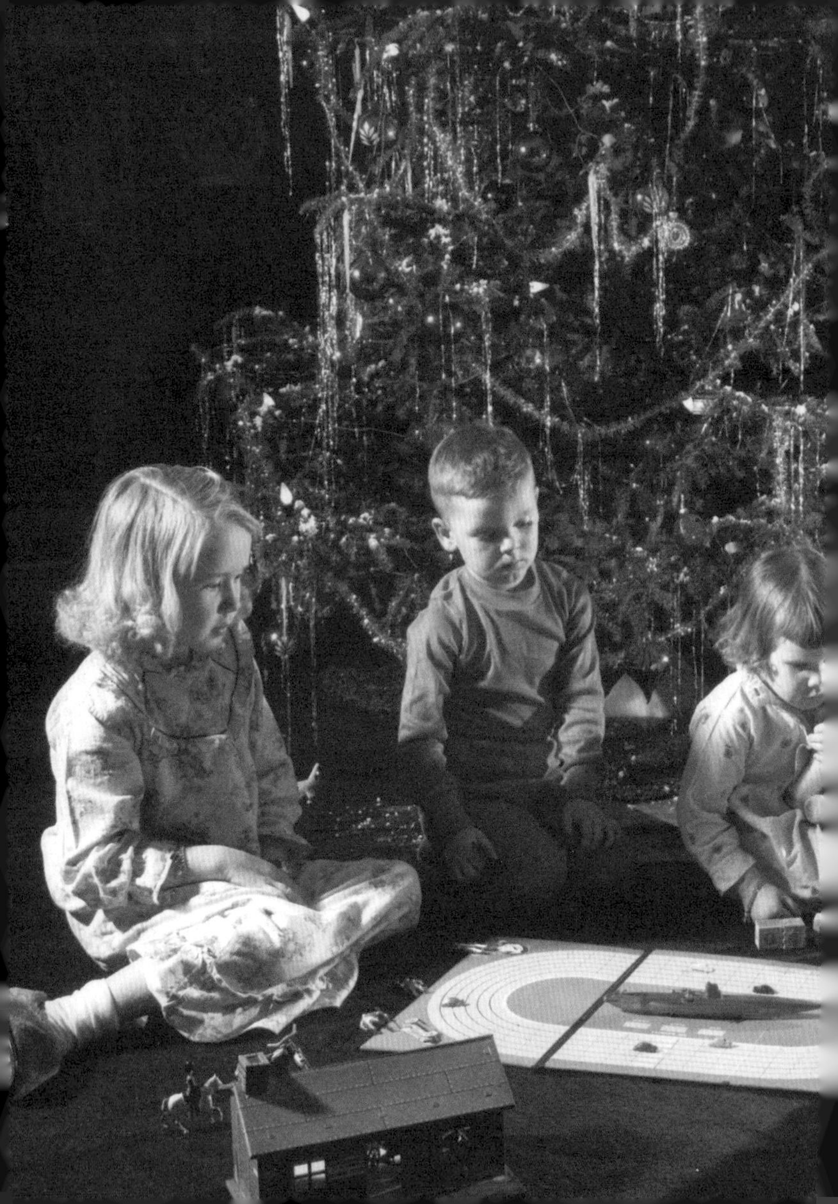

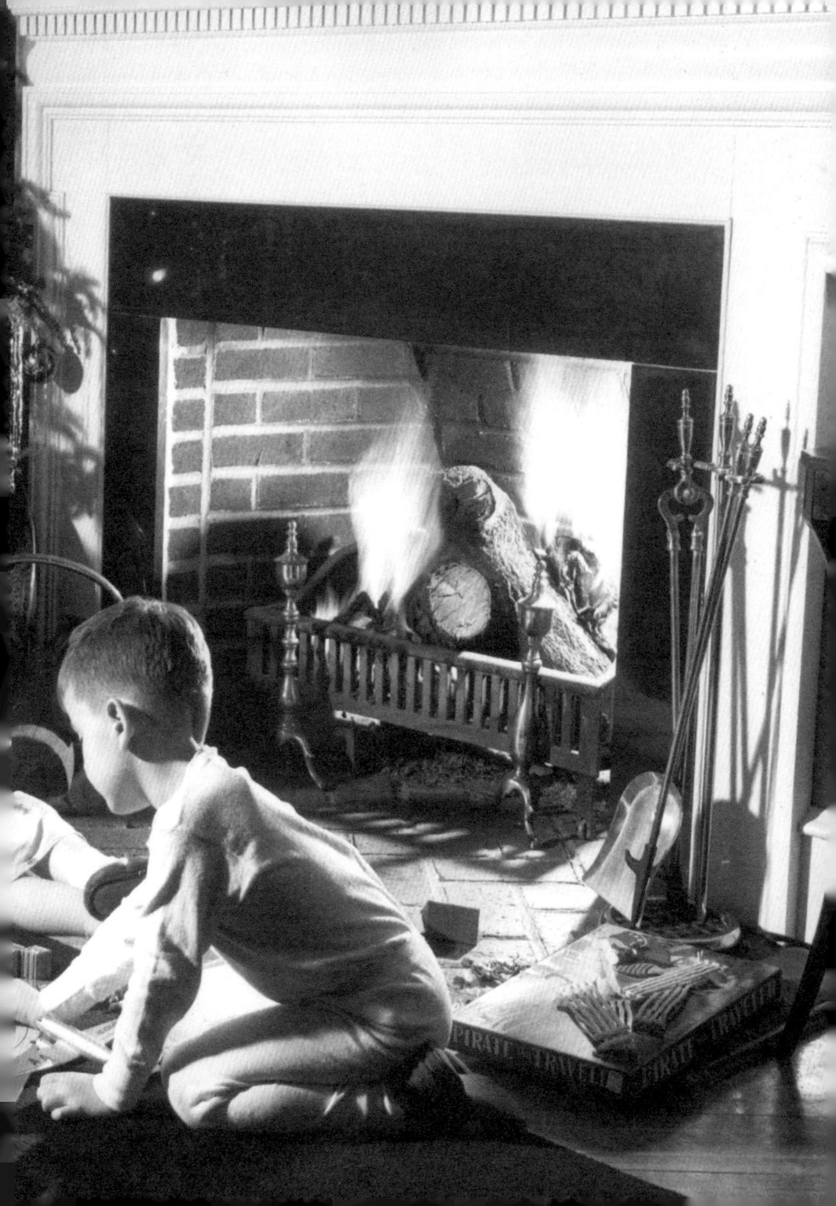

Pencil and Paper Games

There are many great games for children—and adults—to play on a rainy afternoon in front of the fire, perhaps after a good lunch or afternoon tea that has left everyone feeling pleasantly relaxed. Here are a few examples of simple fireside games, for which all you need to play are paper, pencils, and, in the case of Beetles, a dice.

Battleships

This game is best played by two people, because the players are working on one piece of paper. The object of the game is to make squares by joining up dots. The player who makes the most squares wins the game (or the round, if you decide to play a "best of 5 or 10" game).

To begin the game, draw up a rectangle or square of dots in neat rows and columns on a sheet of paper. Each player takes it in turns to join up two adjacent dots, horizontally (straight across) or vertically (up and down), but not diagonally. As the game progresses, it becomes easier to join up dots that will make the fourth side of a square. As a square is completed, the player puts his or her initial in it. A player who completes a square has another turn. This means that a vigilant player may complete several squares in one turn.

When all the dots are joined up as squares, the initials written in them are counted up, and the winner is the player who has made the most squares.

Beetles

This game was once so popular that whole communities would get together to hold Beetle Drives. Unlike Whist Drives, which were also very popular at one time, there is no skill needed to play Beetles, which is a game of pure chance. A sheet of paper, a dice, and a pencil for each player are needed.

The object of the game is to draw a beetle, complete with body, head, six legs, two antennae, two eyes and a tail. Since this is not an anatomically correct beetle—real ones don't have tails—the number of legs may be reduced to four to speed up the round.

Players take it in turns to throw the dice and cannot start drawing a beetle until they have thrown a six. With a six, they can draw the beetle's body. To add on other parts of the beetle, the dice must show these points:

> *Head* – five points
> *Each leg* – four points
> *Each antenna* – three points
> *Tail* – two points
> *Each eye* – one point

The first person to complete a beetle gives a loud shout of "Beetle!" and wins the round. Assuming the beetle has six legs, the player will have had to throw the die at least thirteen times to win.

Consequences

For this very popular party game, you will need pencils, paper, and a wacky imagination! The object of the game is to end up with as funny a story as possible about two people, usually a man and a woman, and the ridiculous situations they get into. If children are playing it might be fun to use people they know, such as their parents, grandparents, teachers, or favorite film stars. Each player takes it in turns to contribute a phrase or sentence to the story without knowing what another player has written on the paper before him.

To begin, the players sit in a circle. Each player, starting at the top of a sheet of paper, writes down one or two adjectives. The player then folds over the paper so that what he has written is completely hidden, and passes the paper on to the person sitting to the right. Each player then writes down the name of a man (or a boy), on the paper he has received, folds this new sheet of paper over again and passes it on. The game continues with more words being added to the paper by each player, but without them being able to see what was written before. By the time the game has ended, the following items should be on each piece of paper, in this order:

1. Two adjectives, perhaps joined by "and" or "but"
2. The name of a man or boy
3. Another pair of adjectives
4. The name of a woman or girl
5. A place where the two met

6. An object the man gave to the woman
7. What he said to her
8. What she said to him
9. The consequence of this
10. What the world said

When each player has written down item ten, the paper is passed on one more time, and the player who receives it unfolds it and reads out the often very funny story that has been written on it.

Key Words

This is a game in which the rounds are over very quickly. You will need just a pencil and some paper for each player, and some kind of timer. The best timer to use is something with a loud buzzer, which will add to the fun and tension of the game.

When the players are ready, pencils poised over their papers, a three-letter word is called out. The players then have three minutes to write down as many words as they can think of that have the three-letter word in them. With "cat," for instance, players might write down scat, catty, scatter, scathing, catalyst, catastrophe, scatological, category, decathlon, and many other words.

The player who has written down the most words when the three minutes are up is the winner. It may be a good idea to have a dictionary on hand to check some of the more outrageous offerings!

Children's Fireside Game

"Hunt the Slipper" from *Kate Greenaway's Book of Games* is a wonderful traditional fireside game. It is very easy to play and requires just a comfortable place to sit and a single slipper. These rules by the popular nineteenth-century British illustrator are very simple to follow:

"The children sit on the ground, or on low seats in a circle, with their knees raised. One has been left out, she brings a slipper, and

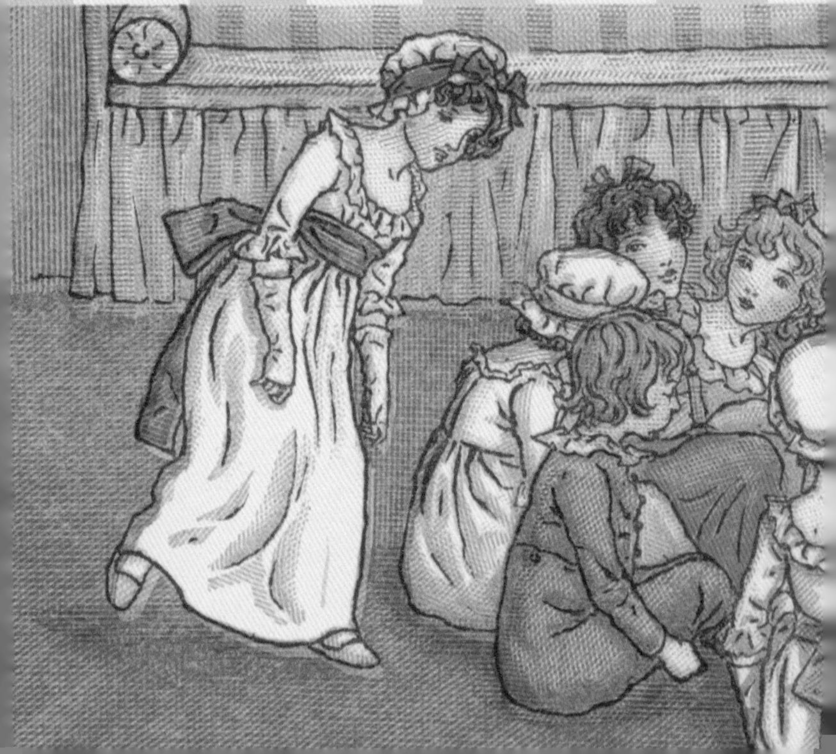

giving it to one child says: 'Cobbler, cobbler, mend my shoe, Get it done by half-past two.'

"She goes away, and comes back in about a minute and asks if it is done. (During this time the slipper has been passing round.) The child answers, she thinks her neighbor has it; so the seeker passes on to her, and getting the same answer she has to go round till the slipper is found. If she is a long time finding it, the slipper may be thrown across the circle."

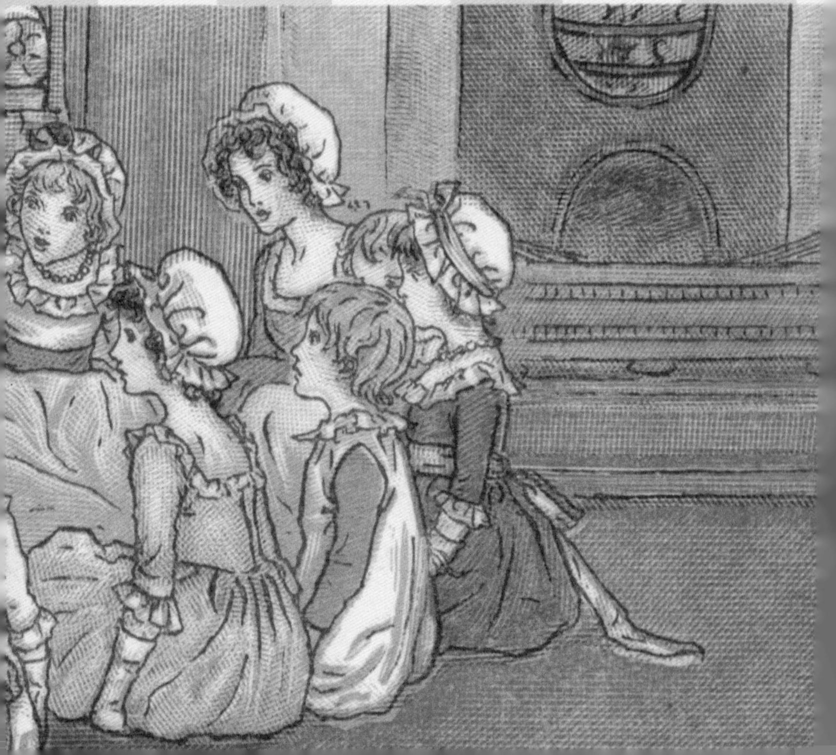

The Corn's a Poppin!

One of the earliest ways to make popcorn was by toasting it over an open fire or even throwing the cob directly into the fire until it began to pop. Popcorn lovers also held a covered clay or metal cooking pot containing oil over a fire, much as we do today. It wasn't until the eighteenth century that popping in oil really became the preferred method. The result—crisp corn with a delicious flavor—was so superior that popping corn in oil became the only way to do it.

Homemade Popcorn

This is such a simple fireside treat. Just remember that 1 cup/240ml of unpopped kernels yields about six cups/1.5 liters of popped corn. Use a heavy-based lidded pan made out of stainless steel or iron. These are best because they distribute heat evenly.

1 Begin by heating 3 tbsp of vegetable oil over medium-high heat in the pan.

2 Add three popcorn kernels to test the heat of the oil. Once they begin to pop, reduce the heat to medium and add about ⅓ cup/80ml of popcorn kernels. Cover the pan.

3 Put on a pair of oven mitts and shake the pan back and forth over the heat. Hold the lid slightly off the pan to allow steam to escape. Don't leave too big a space between the lid and the edge of the pan, or the corn will jump out of the pan as it pops.

4 Once the popping slows, remove the pan from the heat and pour the popped corn into a bowl. Add butter and salt to taste.

OTHER FLAVORINGS
Instead of the usual butter and salt, why not sprinkle some freshly grated Parmesan cheese over your popcorn? Or for a sweeter flavor, you could season it with sugar and butter.

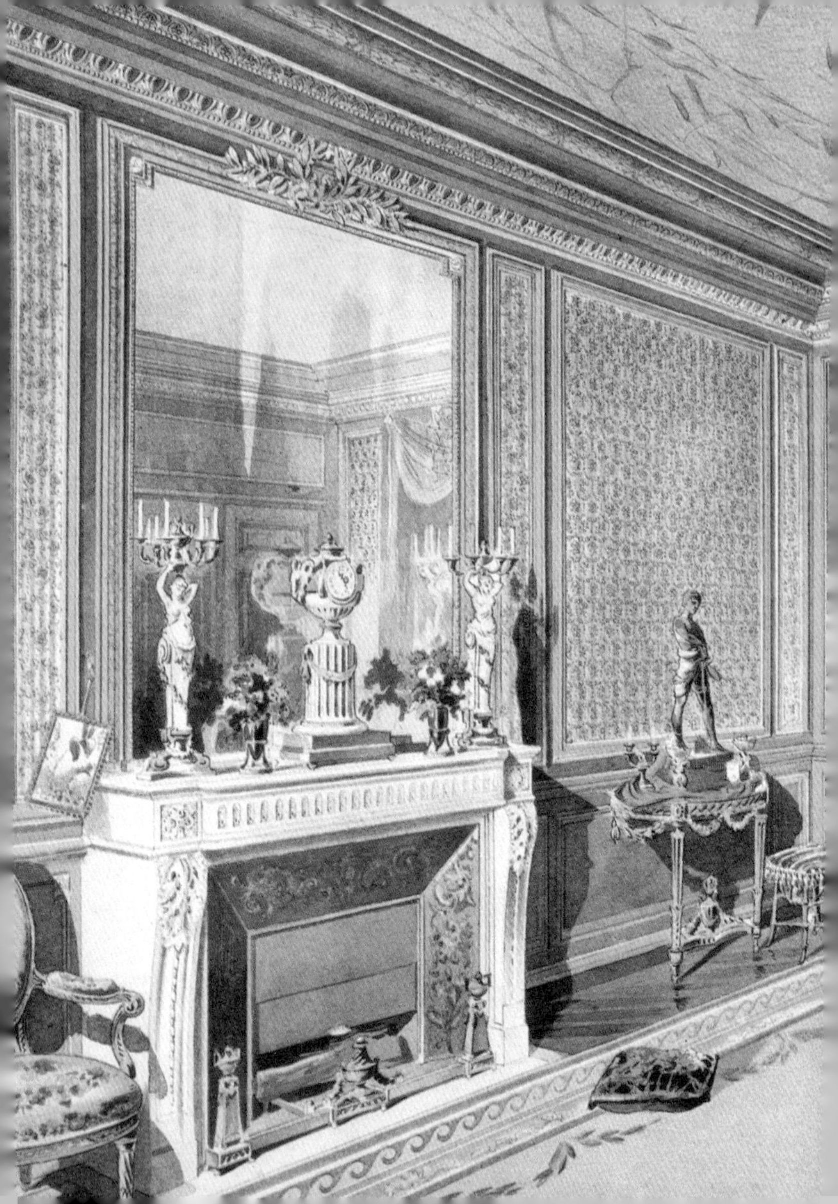

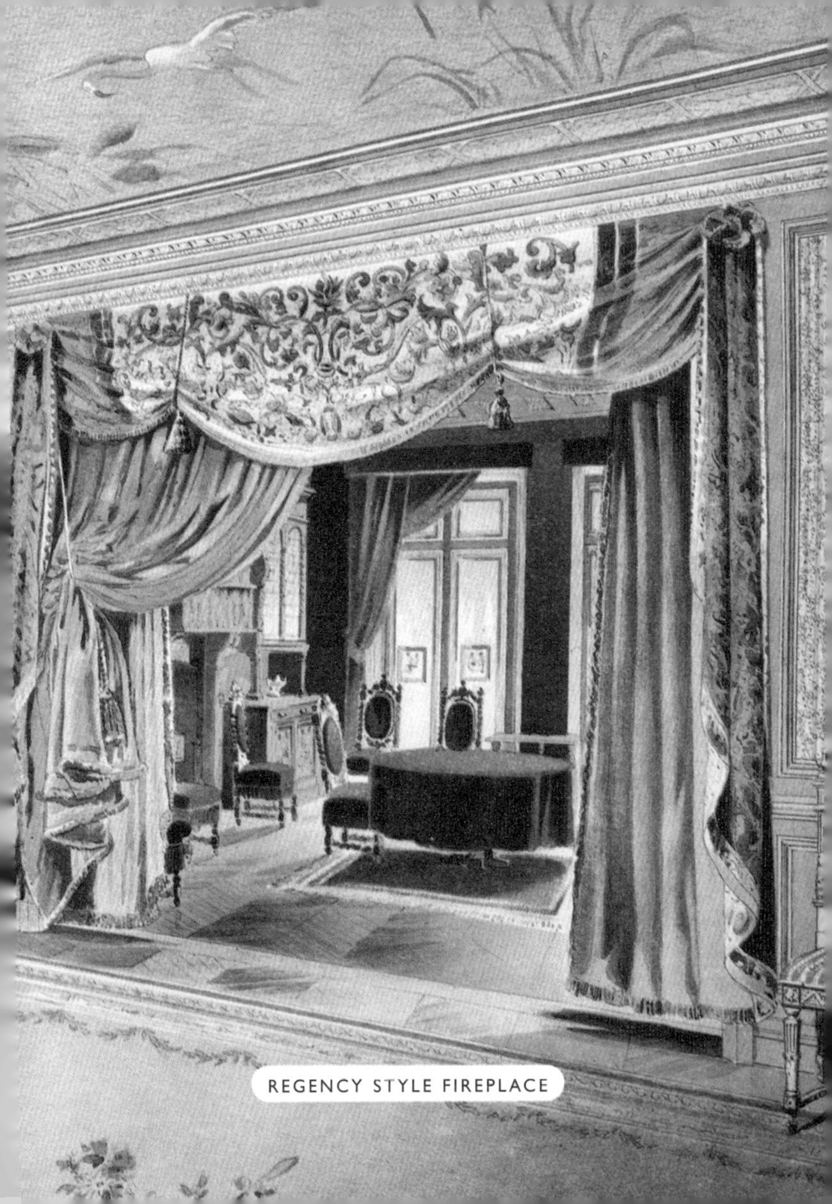
REGENCY STYLE FIREPLACE

Fireside Nursery Rhymes

The fireside is often the center of family life, so perhaps it is not surprising that it is also a prominent feature in many beloved children's stories, poems, and rhymes. Here are a few nursery rhymes that you might enjoy teaching to your children as you sit in front of the fire on a cold winter evening.

Pussy-cat by the Fire

PUSSY-CAT SITS BY THE FIRE;
HOW CAN SHE BE FAIR?
IN WALKS THE LITTLE DOG;
SAYS: "PUSSY, ARE YOU THERE?
HOW DO YOU DO, MISTRESS PUSSY?
MISTRESS PUSSY, HOW D'YE DO?"
"I THANK YOU KINDLY, LITTLE DOG,
I FARE AS WELL AS YOU!"

Dame Trot and Her Cat

DAME TROT CAME HOME ONE WINTRY NIGHT,
A SHIVERING, STARVING SOUL,
BUT PUSS HAD MADE A BLAZING FIRE,
AND NICELY TRUSSED A FOWL.

The Cat Sat Asleep

THE CAT SAT ASLEEP BY THE SIDE OF THE FIRE,
THE MISTRESS SNORED LOUD AS A PIG:
JACK TOOK UP HIS FIDDLE, BY JENNY'S DESIRE,
AND STRUCK UP A BIT OF A JIG.

Cross Patch

CROSS PATCH, DRAW THE LATCH,
SIT BY THE FIRE AND SPIN.
TAKE A CUP, AND PICK IT UP.
THEN CALL YOUR NEIGHBORS IN.

Fireside Charades

"They spoke of "playing charades," but I in my ignorance did not understand the term. The servants were called in, the dining-room tables wheeled away, the lights otherwise disposed, the chairs placed in a semi-circle opposite the arch. While Mr. Rochester and the other gentlemen directed these alterations, the ladies were running up and down stairs ringing for their maids. Mrs. Fairfax was summoned to give information respecting the resources of the house in shawls, dresses, draperies of any kind; and certain wardrobes of the third story were ransacked, and their contents, in the shape of brocaded and hooped petticoats, satin sacques, black modes, lace lappets, etc., were brought down in armfuls by the Abigails; then a selection was made, and such things as were chosen were carried to the boudoir within the drawing-room."

from *Jane Eyre*, Charlotte Brontë

In this extract from Charlotte Brontë's literary masterpiece, her heroine discovers the game of charades for the first time. Clearly, poor little Jane Eyre had not been brought up in a happy family that played charades, but the game has been an essential part of Christmas fireside fun for generations. The game was probably even popular in the quiet Brontë family.

Charades is a great dressing-up game for family members of all ages. It gives players a chance to open the dressing-up wardrobe or even that plastic bag full of old clothes intended for the charity shop. It is surprising how well a mother's old slip or nightdress can look when worn as an evening gown by her ten-year-old daughter!

Ideally, Charades is a team game. Teams of not more than five or six are best—although they can be as small as only two players. The game can be played either as an acting game, with the players speaking a script, or it can be mimed. A mimed charade is, obviously, more spontaneous because no script has to be written in advance.

To play the game, one team thinks up a word of at least two syllables, and then acts out short scenes that illustrate the syllables in the word and, finally, the whole word. Thus, for a two-syllable word the team must plan at least three separate scenes. When the word is guessed, the other team takes over and plays a charade of their own.

Words made up of just two simple words with only one pronunciation or spelling—horseshoe or drawbridge, for instance—are good for novice players to start with. After a bit of practice at the game, more complicated words could be chosen, such as manufacture (man, ewe, fact, err).

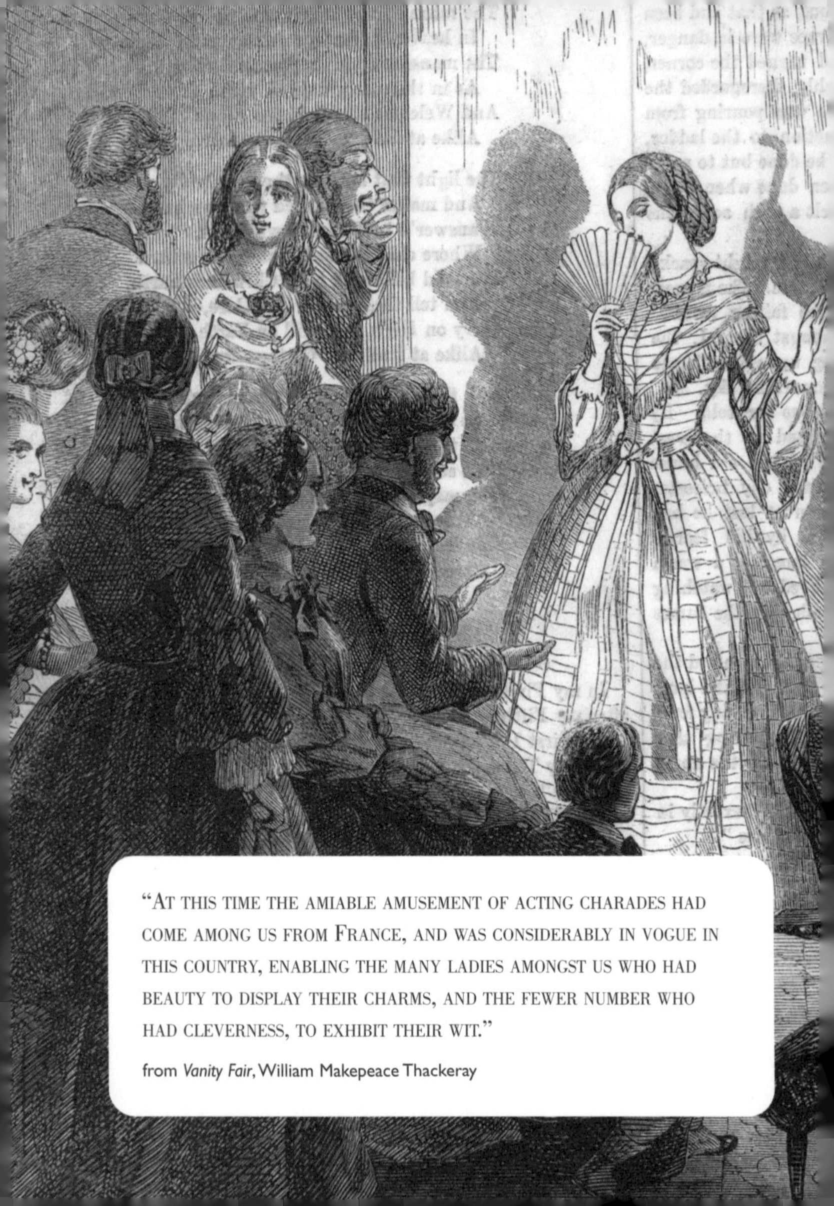

"AT THIS TIME THE AMIABLE AMUSEMENT OF ACTING CHARADES HAD COME AMONG US FROM FRANCE, AND WAS CONSIDERABLY IN VOGUE IN THIS COUNTRY, ENABLING THE MANY LADIES AMONGST US WHO HAD BEAUTY TO DISPLAY THEIR CHARMS, AND THE FEWER NUMBER WHO HAD CLEVERNESS, TO EXHIBIT THEIR WIT."

from *Vanity Fair*, William Makepeace Thackeray

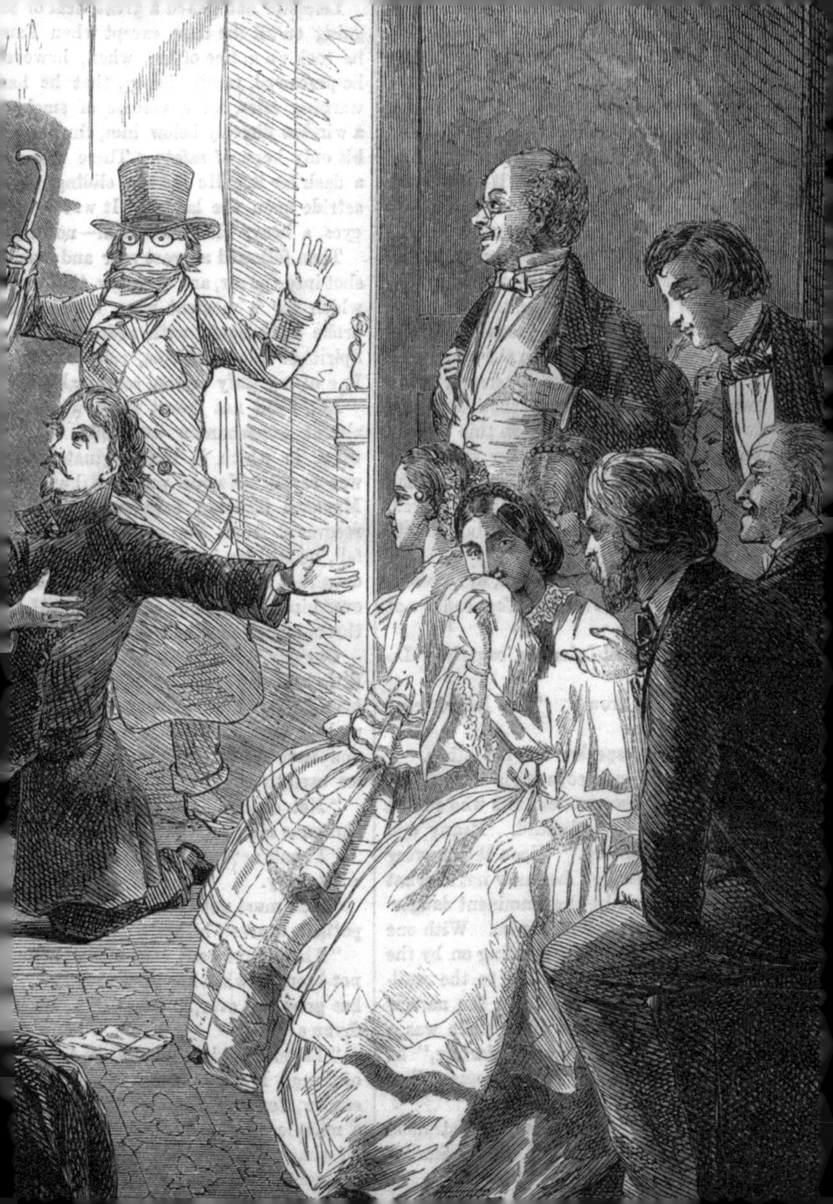

Give Us A Clue

This is a great miming game for playing round the fire on a rainy day, or on special occasions like Thanksgiving, Christmas, or birthdays. It is a game that requires everyone to have a reasonably good knowledge of books, plays, films, and television programs because it is played by miming the titles of them. It can be played either in teams or with everyone in the room having a solo turn.

If it is to be a team game, it is best played on the basis of the teams taking turns to draw a slip of paper from a bag or hat. The title of a book, play, film, or television program should be written on the slips of paper in advance. If the game is not being played in teams, solo players may think up their own title.

To begin the game, the player(s) must indicate what category their title falls into.

- **To indicate a book, the player puts both hands together, then lets them fall open, palms up, to suggest an open book.**

- **To indicate a film, the player uses both hands to suggest the film being wound in a movie camera.**

- **To indicate a play, both hands are used to suggest the stage curtains being swept open: hold the hands high, palms together, then separate them in two downward curving movements.**

- **To indicate a television program, the player draws a rectangle in the air with his forefingers.**

Next, the player holds up the relevant number of fingers to indicate the number of words in the title. If he is going to act the whole title in one mime, he draws a circle in the air.

The player also holds up the relevant number of fingers to show which word in the title he is miming. To indicate how many syllables there are in the word, he places the relevant number of fingers on the opposite forearm.

- **To indicate "the," the two index fingers are held up in a T-shape.**

- **To indicate "a" and "an," the index finger is held a short distance from the thumb.**

Warmy warmy totey wotes
Warmy warmy totey wotes
Warmy warmy totie-wotes
Warmy by the fire
Warmy warmy totie-wotes
The men have gone
    to plough
If you want to warm
    your toties
Warm your toties now...

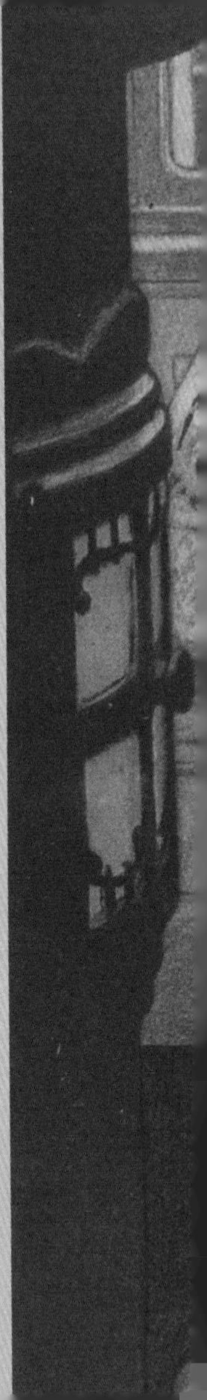

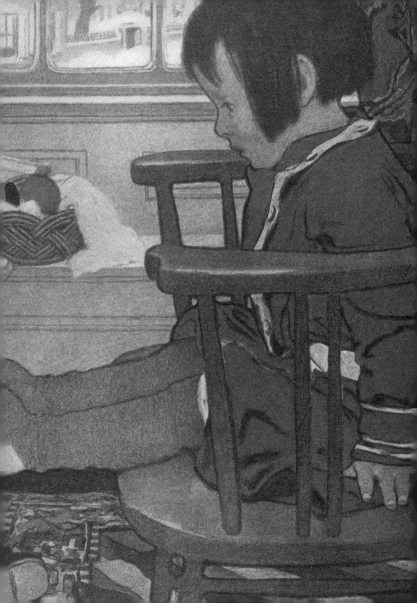

Fireside Foot Warmers

"After many serious discussions with Meg and Jo, the pattern was chosen, the materials bought, and the slippers begun. A cluster of grave yet cheerful pansies, on a deeper purple ground, was pronounced very appropriate and pretty; and Beth worked away early and late, with occasional lifts over the hard parts. She was a nimble little needlewoman, and they were finished before any one got tired of them. Then she wrote a very short, simple note and, with Laurie's help, got them smuggled on to the study-table one morning before the old gentleman was up."

from *Little Women*, Louisa May Alcott

In this extract from Louisa May Alcott's classic novel, Beth March sews a pair of slippers for her neighbor, Mr. Laurence. This is one of the many activities that Beth and her sisters Meg, Jo, and Amy carry out in front of the fire. The book opens with the young heroines gathered around the fireside, their faces brightened by the firelight, while Jo, in her typically tomboyish style, lies on the hearth rug. As their story progresses, the fireside becomes a focal point for their lives. Beside it, they knit, sew, read, sing, talk, daydream, and entertain their friends.

Slippers can be easy to make, and great fun as well, if you design your own decorative features. Why not follow Beth March's example and pick up a needle and thread next time you are relaxing at your fireside and try making your own? Slippers also make wonderful presents—although you are unlikely to get in return anything as splendid as the little cabinet piano that Mr. Laurence gave Beth March after he found the embroidered slippers she made for him on his study table.

Types of slippers that may be made at home include:

- **KNITTED SLIPPERS:** When made from coarse, oiled knitting wool, with a softer inner sole inserted, slippers are hard-wearing as well as warm. Knitted from soft angora wool, they are luxuriously soft and cuddly. Visit your local craft or department store or try the internet for knitting patterns.

- **SUEDE OR SHEEPSKIN SLIPPERS:** These are more hard-wearing than knitted slippers, but do require special equipment. The materials for them are available in kit form. Look for them on the leather and sheepskin stalls at craft fairs.

- **FELT SLIPPERS:** Felt is a wonderfully hard-wearing wool fabric, available in a bright array of colors and in various weights and thicknesses. The fabric is easy to embroider or decorate. You can cut shapes from several colors, then sew or glue them to the tops or sides of the slippers. Craft shops sell not only the felt, glue, tracing paper, and other materials but, often, the patterns for a wide range of felt "makes," including slippers, as well.

- **NEEDLEWORK (TAPESTRY) SLIPPERS:** These are often included in the catalogs of mail-order needlework designers. They can look very handsome, especially on a pair of male feet.

- **VELVET SLIPPERS:** Lined with silk, and perhaps embroidered with gold thread, these are the ultimate fireside luxury. Try wearing them with a long robe or a caftan! Patterns for these may be found in craft shops, or a pattern for felt slippers could be used.

Make Your Own Slippers

These super-easy slippers would bring a smile to anyone's face—they are designed for a child, but can easily be adapted for an adult if you wish. They are great fun and perfect to keep your children's little feet warm and comfortable as they sit in front of the fire after a hot bath. The template provided must be enlarged to the correct size.

MATERIALS

- Canvas for the soles
- Two contrasting strong cotton fabrics for the tops
- Piece of wadding for the tops and soles
- Terry toweling for lining the tops and soles
- Contrasting bias binding

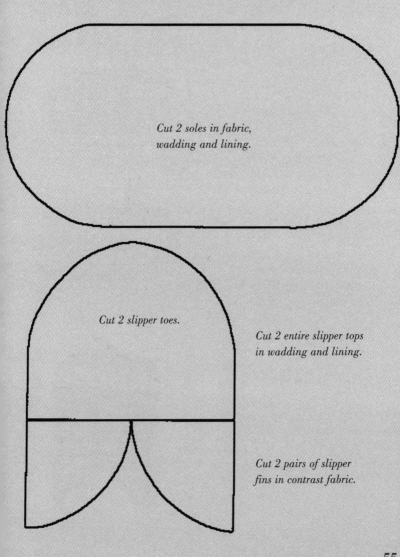

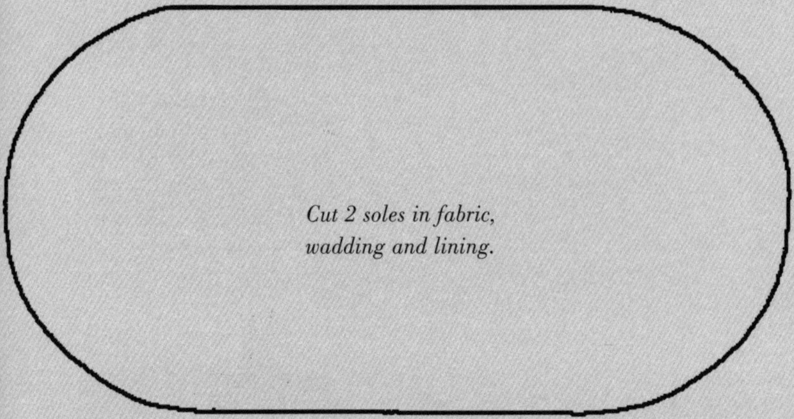
Cut 2 soles in fabric,
wadding and lining.

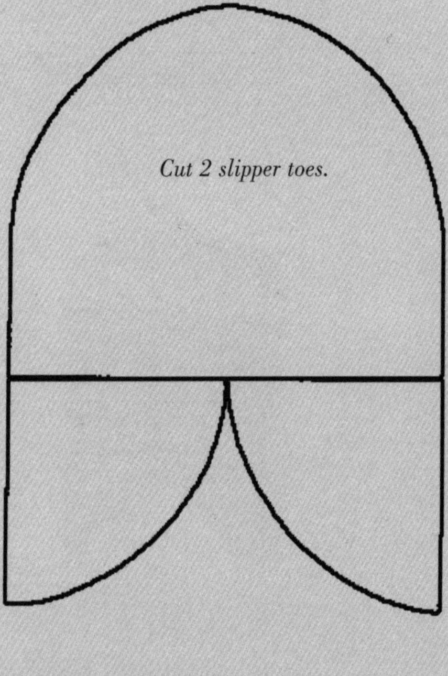
Cut 2 slipper toes.

Cut 2 entire slipper tops in wadding and lining.

Cut 2 pairs of slipper fins in contrast fabric.

1 Measure one of your child's feet from the heel to just in front of the toes. Enlarge the templates provided (page 55) to the correct size on a photocopier and cut them out. Cut out two fabric soles, two pieces of toweling lining, and two pieces of wadding. Cut contrasting fabric pieces for the slipper tops and two pieces of toweling and wadding. To make the soles, place the cotton fabric right side down, cover with a piece of wadding and overlay with the toweling right side up. Tack the three layers together.

2 Bind the heel half of the sole with bias binding by stitching the wrong side of the binding along the seam, then fold over and stitch again, or slip stitch in place. Continue sewing around the remainder of the sole and tidy the seams.

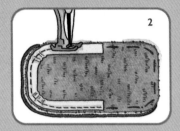

3 To make the slipper tops, with right sides together, and allowing a $\frac{1}{4}$ in/5mm seam, tack, then sew the slipper toe

to the slipper fin. Press the seam down toward the toe and tidy the seam edges.

4 Place the toweling lining for the slipper top right side down, cover with wadding, then place the top fabric right side up. Allowing a $\frac{1}{4}$in/5mm seam, tack, then sew the three layers together. Sew the bias binding, right sides together along the exposed edge of the V.

5 Stitch close to the seam or slip stitch the bias binding along the underside of the V-shaped edge, keeping a neat center of the V. Repeat this step on the underside of the V-shape.

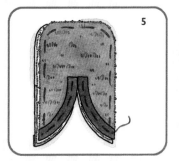

6 With fabric sides together and the toweling linings facing out, tack, then stitch the slipper top to the sole allowing a $\frac{1}{4}$in/5mm seam. Tidy the edges. Strengthen the starting and finishing points with additional stitching. Then turn right sides out, and at the point where the bindings meet, hand stitch for extra strength.

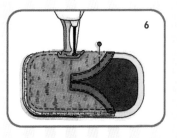

Don't you stay at home of evenings?
Don't you love a cushioned seat
In a corner, by the fireside, with
your slippers on your feet?

OLIVER WENDELL HOLMES

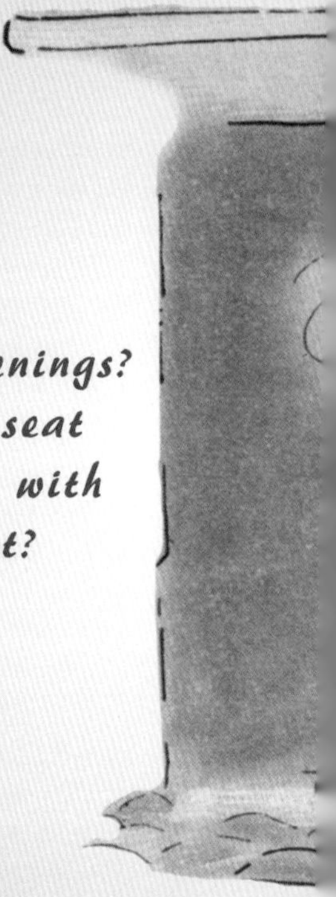

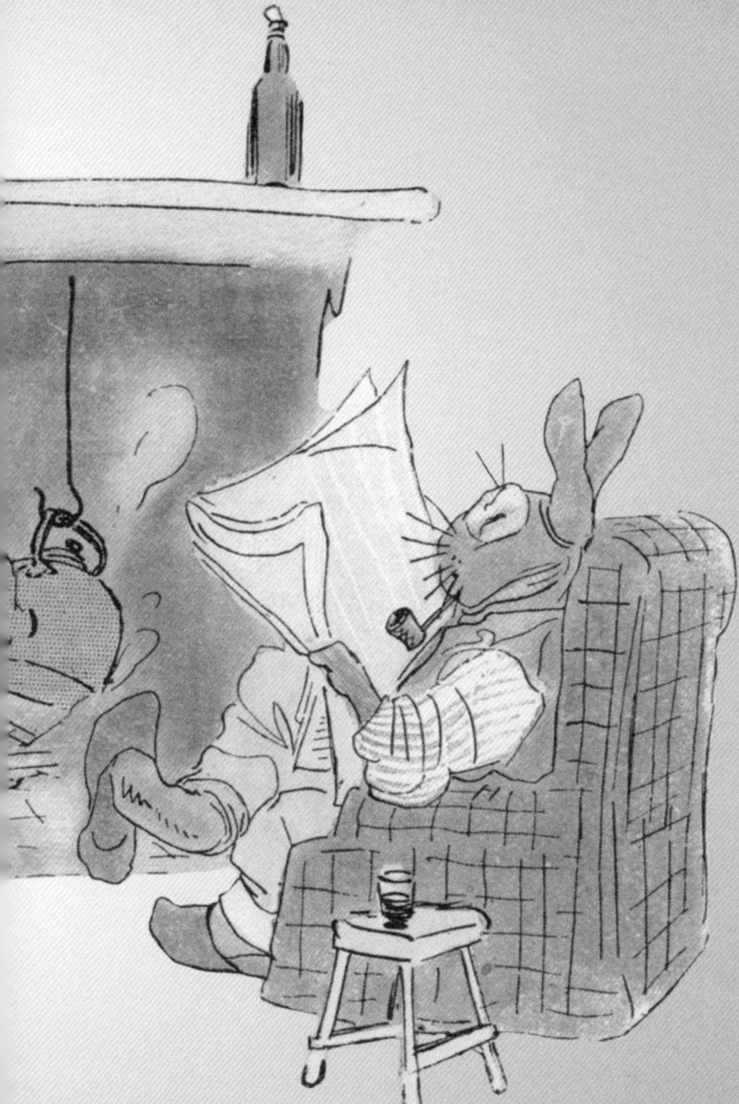

EXTRACT FROM

Silas Marner

by

GEORGE ELIOT

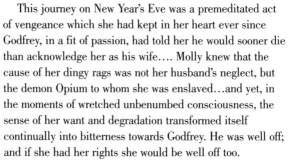

While Godfrey Cass was taking draughts of forgetfulness from the sweet presence of Nancy…Godfrey's wife was walking with slow uncertain steps through the snow-covered Raveloe lanes, carrying her child in her arms.

This journey on New Year's Eve was a premeditated act of vengeance which she had kept in her heart ever since Godfrey, in a fit of passion, had told her he would sooner die than acknowledge her as his wife…. Molly knew that the cause of her dingy rags was not her husband's neglect, but the demon Opium to whom she was enslaved…and yet, in the moments of wretched unbenumbed consciousness, the sense of her want and degradation transformed itself continually into bitterness towards Godfrey. He was well off; and if she had her rights she would be well off too.

She had set out at an early hour, but had lingered on the road, inclined by her indolence to believe that if she waited under a warm shed the snow would cease to fall. She had waited longer than she knew, and now that she found herself belated in the snow-hidden ruggedness of the long lanes, even the animation of a vindictive purpose could not keep her spirit from failing. It was seven o'clock, and by this time she was not very far from Raveloe, but she was not familiar

enough with those monotonous lanes to know how near
she was to her journey's end. She needed comfort, and
she knew but one comforter—the familiar demon in her
bosom...; In another moment Molly had flung something
away, but it was not the black remnant—it was an empty
phial. And she walked on again under the breaking cloud,
from which there came now and then the light of a quickly
veiled star, for a freezing wind had sprung up since the
snowing had ceased. But she walked always more and more
drowsily, and clutched more and more automatically the
sleeping child at her bosom.

Slowly the demon was working his will, and cold and
weariness were his helpers. Soon she felt nothing but a
supreme immediate longing that curtained off all futurity—
the longing to lie down and sleep. She had arrived at a spot
where her footsteps were no longer checked by a hedgerow,
and she had wandered vaguely, unable to distinguish any
objects, notwithstanding the wide whiteness around her,
and the growing starlight. She sank down against a
straggling furze bush, an easy pillow enough; and the bed
of snow, too, was soft. She did not feel that the bed was
cold, and did not heed whether the child would wake and
cry for her. But her arms had not yet relaxed their
instinctive clutch; and the little one slumbered on as gently
as if it had been rocked in a lace-trimmed cradle.

But the complete torpor came at last: the fingers lost
their tension, the arms unbent; then the little head fell

away from the bosom, and the blue eyes opened wide on the cold starlight. At first there was a little peevish cry of "mammy", and an effort to regain the pillowing arm and bosom; but mammy's ear was deaf, and the pillow seemed to be slipping away backward. Suddenly, as the child rolled downward on its mother's knees, all wet with snow, its eyes were caught by a bright glancing light on the white ground, and, with the ready transition of infancy, it was immediately absorbed in watching the bright living thing running towards it, yet never arriving. That bright living thing must be caught; and in an instant the child had slipped on all-fours, and held out one little hand to catch the gleam. But the gleam would not be caught in that way, and now the head was held up to see where the cunning gleam came from. It came from a very bright place; and the little one, rising on its legs, toddled through the snow, the old grimy shawl in which it was wrapped trailing behind it, and the queer little bonnet dangling at its back—toddled on to the open door of Silas Marner's cottage, and right up to the warm hearth, where there was a bright fire of logs and sticks, which had thoroughly warmed the old sack (Silas's greatcoat) spread out on the bricks to dry. The little one, accustomed to be left to itself for long hours without notice from its mother, squatted down on the sack, and spread its tiny hands towards the blaze, in perfect contentment, gurgling and making many inarticulate communications to the cheerful fire, like a new-hatched gosling beginning to find itself comfortable. But presently the warmth had a lulling effect, and the little golden head sank down on the old sack, and the blue eyes were veiled by their delicate half-transparent lids.

But where was Silas Marner while this strange visitor had come to his hearth? He was in the cottage, but he did not see the child. During the last few weeks, since he had lost his money, he had contracted the habit of opening his door and looking out from time to time, as if he thought that his money might be somehow coming back to him, or that some trace, some news of it, might be mysteriously on the road, and be caught by the listening ear or the straining eye. It was chiefly at night, when he was not occupied in his loom, that he fell into this repetition of an act for which he could have assigned no definite purpose, and which can hardly be understood except by those who have undergone a bewildering separation from a supremely loved object. In the evening twilight, and later whenever the night was not dark, Silas looked out on that narrow prospect round the Stone-pits, listening and gazing, not with hope, but with mere yearning and unrest.

This morning he had been told by some of his neighbours that it was New Year's Eve, and that he must sit up and hear the old year rung out and the new rung in, because that was good luck, and might bring his money back again. This was only a friendly Raveloe-way of jesting with the half-crazy oddities of a miser, but it had perhaps helped to throw Silas into a more than usually excited ☞

state. Since the on-coming of twilight he had opened his door again and again, though only to shut it immediately at seeing all distance veiled by the falling snow. But the last time he opened it the snow had ceased, and the clouds were parting here and there. He stood and listened, and gazed for a long while—there was really something on the road coming towards him then, but he caught no sign of it; and the stillness and the wide trackless snow seemed to narrow his solitude, and touched his yearning with the chill of despair. He went in again, and put his right hand on the latch of the door to close it—but he did not close it: he was arrested, as he had been already since his loss, by the invisible wand of catalepsy, and stood like a graven image, with wide but sightless eyes, holding open his door, powerless to resist either the good or the evil that might enter there.

When Marner's sensibility returned, he continued the action which had been arrested, and closed his door, unaware of the chasm in his consciousness, unaware of any intermediate change, except that the light had grown dim, and that he was chilled and faint. He thought he had been too long standing at the door and looking out. Turning towards the hearth, where the two logs had fallen apart, and sent forth only a red uncertain glimmer, he seated himself on his fireside chair, and was stooping to push his logs together, when, to his blurred vision, it seemed as if there were gold on the floor in front of the hearth. Gold!—his own gold—brought back to him as mysteriously as it had been taken away! He felt his heart begin to beat violently, and for a few moments he was unable to stretch out his hand and grasp the restored treasure. The heap of gold seemed to glow and get larger beneath his agitated gaze. He leaned forward at last, and stretched forth his hand; but instead of the hard coin with the familiar resisting outline, his fingers encountered soft warm curls. In utter amazement, Silas fell on his knees and bent his head low to examine the marvel: it was a sleeping child—a round, fair thing, with soft yellow rings all over its head. Could this be his little sister come back to him in a dream—his little sister whom he had carried about in his arms for a year before she died, when he was a small boy without shoes or stockings? That was the first thought that darted across Silas's blank wonderment. Was it a dream? He rose to his feet again, pushed his logs together, and, throwing on some dried leaves and sticks, raised a flame; but the flame did not disperse the vision—it only lit up more distinctly the little round form of the child, and its shabby clothing. It was very much like his little sister. Silas sank into his chair powerless, under the double presence of an inexplicable surprise and a hurrying influx of memories. How and when had the child come in without his knowledge? He had never been beyond the door. But along with that question, and almost thrusting it away, there was a vision of the old home and the old streets leading to Lantern Yard—and within that vision another, of the thoughts which had been present with him in those

 far-off scenes. The thoughts were strange to him now, like old friendships impossible to revive; and yet he had a dreamy feeling that this child was somehow a message come to him from that far-off life: it stirred fibres that had never been moved in Raveloe—old quiverings of tenderness— old impressions of awe at the presentiment of some Power presiding over his life; for his imagination had not yet extricated itself from the sense of mystery in the child's sudden presence, and had formed no conjectures of ordinary natural means by which the event could have been brought about.

But there was a cry on the hearth: the child had awaked, and Marner stooped to lift it on his knee. It clung round his neck, and burst louder and louder into that mingling of inarticulate cries with "mammy" by which little children express the bewilderment of waking. Silas pressed it to him, and almost unconsciously uttered sounds of hushing tenderness, while he bethought himself that some of his porridge, which had got cool by the dying fire, would do to feed the child with if it were only warmed up a little.

He had plenty to do through the next hour. The porridge, sweetened with some dry brown sugar from an old store which he had refrained from using for himself, stopped the cries of the little one, and made her lift her blue eyes with a wide quiet gaze at Silas, as he put the spoon into her mouth. Presently she slipped from his knee and began to toddle about, but with a pretty stagger that made Silas jump up and follow her lest she should fall against anything that would hurt her. But she only fell in a sitting posture on the ground, and began to pull at her boots, looking up at him with a crying face as if the boots hurt her. He took her on his knee again, but it was some time before it occurred to Silas's dull bachelor mind that the wet boots were the grievance, pressing on her warm ankles. He got them off with difficulty, and baby was at once happily occupied with the primary mystery of her own toes, inviting Silas, with much chuckling, to consider the mystery too. But the wet boots had at last suggested to Silas that the child had been walking on the snow, and this roused him from his entire oblivion of any ordinary means by which it could have entered or been brought into his house. Under the prompting of this new idea, and without waiting to form conjectures, he raised the child in his arms, and went to the door. As soon as he had opened it, there was the cry of "mammy" again, which Silas had not heard since the child's first hungry waking. Bending forward, he could just discern the marks made by the little feet on the virgin snow, and he followed their track to the furze bushes. "Mammy!" the little one cried again and again, stretching itself forward so as almost to escape from Silas's arms, before he himself was aware that there was something more than the bush before him—that there was a human body, with the head sunk low in the furze, and half-covered with the shaken snow.

Fireside Toasts

Toasting bread in front of the fire has long been popular at breakfast time and teatime. In some houses in the seventeenth and eighteenth centuries, when large quantities of toasted bread were wanted at once, wrought-iron toasters were put in front of the kitchen range or drawing-room fire and revolved. In most houses, however, simple toasting forks—albeit often very elegantly designed ones with pierced-metal handles—were common sights hanging by the fireplace in family kitchens and living rooms. Even today toasting forks are often brought out to use on wintry afternoons when the fire has been lit and is burning brightly.

Toasting bread in front of the fire is a fun alternative to using your normal electric toaster and, if you are careful, it can be enjoyed by the whole family. Once you have toasted your bread, there are many delicious ways to enjoy it. Why not try one of these favorite recipes the next time you are relaxing in front of a warm fire with your family or friends?

CINNAMON TOAST: Lightly toast slices of bread, remove the crusts, and spread liberally with butter. Then sprinkle over cinnamon and sugar. These are best served cut into fingers.

SARDINE TOAST: Mash the contents of a can of sardines with some tomato sauce, a squeeze of lemon juice, and a few drops of Worcestershire sauce. Spread on lightly toasted bread, then garnish with slices of pickle.

SAVORY TOAST: Mix a tub of cream cheese with a small jar of sweet brown vegetable relish (Branston pickle) until well-blended. Serve on toasted bread, garnish with slices of green onion, and cut into small rounds or squares for bite-size snacks.

Teatime Treats

Favorite English teatime treats toasted at the fireside include muffins, crumpets, and bread slices. Halved day-old scones also toast well. Although Mrs. Beeton, in *The Book of Household Management*, gave recipes for making English muffins and crumpets at home, even she agreed that they were not easy to make and suggested it was best to simply buy them. Despite the many years that have passed since Mrs. Beeton wrote her book, the various points she made about toasting teatime snacks in front of the fire still hold true:

- **First and most important of all, the fire must be very bright and burning clearly.**

- **Never hold the foods being toasted too close to the fire, as they will burn on the outside before they are properly warmed in the middle.**

- **Do not use fresh bread for toast as it eats "heavy," and "besides," said Mrs. Beeton austerely, "it is extravagant." The best bread for toasting is a standard two-day-old loaf. Cut it into slices about ½in/1cm thick and toast the slices on both sides until they are a good color, but not** too dark. When each slice is toasted, put it on a plate and put small dabs of butter on the toast and set it before the fire. When the butter is beginning to melt, spread it over the toast. If you are planning to put a pile of toast on the plate, trim the crusts off, and cut each slice in two before putting it on the pile. Waiting to cut the toast until you have completed the pile will only cause the melted butter to be pressed down through it so that the bottom slice is left swimming in butter.

- To toast English muffins successfully, their edges should be pulled apart before they are put on the toasting fork. They should not be toasted too quickly, or they will burn. Once each muffin is toasted to a good color on both sides, butter it lightly on the inner sides (and on the outer sides, if you like), and put it together again. Put the muffin on a very hot plate or in a covered muffin dish while you finish toasting the others.

- Sorry, but butter is the only topping for these fireside treats. Low-fat spreads or margarine will not do—they turn a treat into a penance.

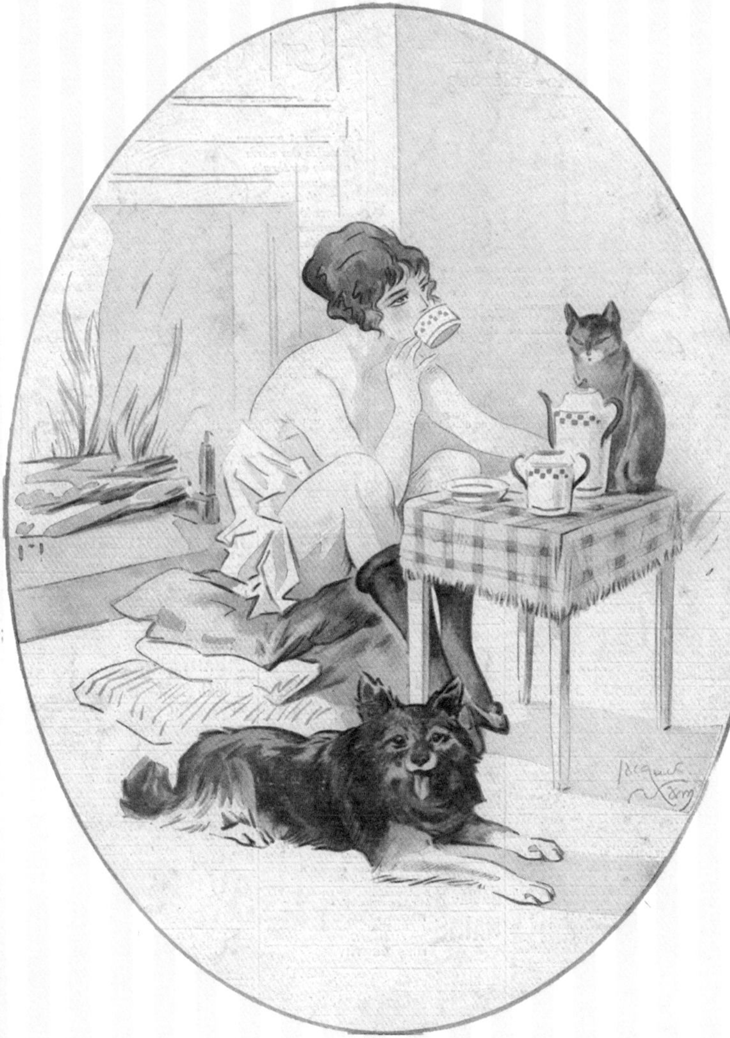

The Cup That Cheers

Transcending vistas of time and place, a cup of tea beside the fire has become a metaphor for perfect domestic peace and tranquillity. It provided morning refreshment for a pert mademoiselle of the French *demi-monde,* or a welcome pick-me-up for the characters of English author Flora Thompson's *Lark Rise to Candleford.* The hearth was where the women of Candleford village could enjoy "their precious half-hour's peace with a cup of tea before the fire in the afternoon."

The poet William Cowper, in "The Winter Evening," part of his long poem *The Task,* expressed the same view in phrases that have become part of our cultural language:

Now stir the fire, and close the shutters fast,
Let fall the curtains, wheel the sofa round,
And, while the bubbling and loud-hissing urn
Throws up a steamy column, and the cups,
That cheer but not inebriate, wait on each,
So let us welcome peaceful evening in.

Tea, Glorious Tea!

Tea reached Europe from China early in the seventeenth century and found its way into England soon afterward. Samuel Pepys had his first "cup of tee" in 1661, and within five or six years his wife was drinking the hugely expensive new drink because the apothecary had told her it was "good for her cold and defluxions."

Whatever it was good for, tea became so popular with the English that within a century it had become a national drink. The hours of meals changed and teatime, an occasion in the later afternoon spent by the drawing room or living room fire, became an established custom for all social classes.

The new beverage created a vast new industry for the provision of what the anti-tea drinking social commentator William Cobbett contemptuously called "the tea tackle." Silversmiths, porcelain and pottery manufacturers, and cabinet-makers all turned their attention to servicing this new, enormously popular social occasion.

Silversmiths produced handsome tea-making sets that included teapots, jugs, and bowls, as well as the teakettle. In time, the teakettle became a very handsome item indeed. Rather than being set on the hob of the drawing room fire, the teakettle, made of silver plate or polished and lacquered brass, came to be set on a stand over a spirit lamp (an alcohol or other liquid fuel burning lamp) on its own small tea table. Some tea kettles were designed to hang on a stand, allowing them to be tipped over for pouring water into the teapot without having to be lifted up.

From the established porcelain manufacturers—Bow, Chelsea, Worcester, and Derby—came stylishly designed and delicately decorated tea sets that included cups, saucers, and plates as well as the teapots, jugs, and bowls of the silversmith. The earliest teacups were made in the Chinese style, that is, without handles, but by the mid-eighteenth century, they had been given handles.

Cabinetmakers and furniture-makers, including the great Chippendale and Sheraton and many other smaller companies, also got in on the tea "tackle" business. They produced the small galleried tea tables, china tables, and tea trays that became essential items in every drawing room. They also made the tea caddies and small tea chests, most of which could be locked, in which the still expensive tea was kept. The lady of the house was always in charge of the tea chest, keeping its key on her belt, and opening it only to measure out the spoonfuls of tea leaves into the teapot.

A Canadian Folk-Song

BY WILLIAM WILFRED CAMPBELL

The doors are shut, the windows fast,
Outside the gust is driving past,
Outside the shivering ivy clings,
While on the hob the kettle sings.
Margery, Margery, make the tea
Singeth the kettle merrily.

The streams are hushed up where they flowed,
The ponds are frozen along the road,
The cattle are housed in shed and byre
While singeth the kettle on the fire.
Margery, Margery, make the tea
Singeth the kettle merrily.

The fisherman on the bay in his boat
Shivers and buttons up his coat;
The traveller stops at the tavern door,
And the kettle answers the chimney's roar.
Margery, Margery, make the tea
Singeth the kettle merrily.

The firelight dances upon the wall,
Footsteps are heard in the outer hall,
And a kiss and a welcome that fill the room,
And the kettle sings in the glimmer and gloom.
Margery, Margery, make the tea
Singeth the kettle merrily.

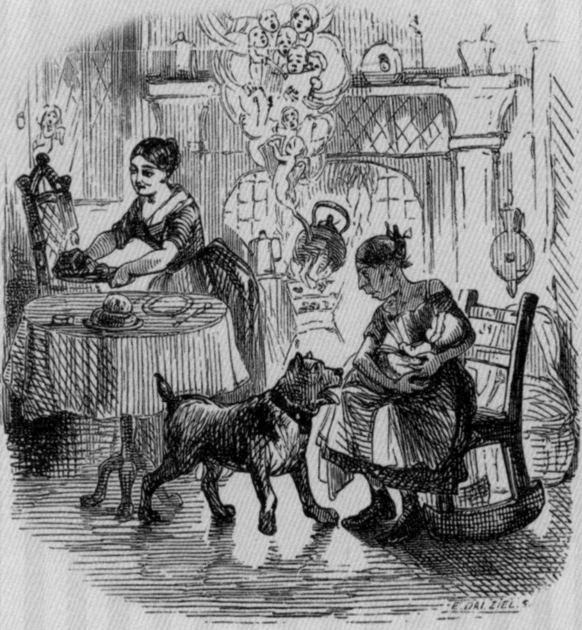
E. DALZIEL. S.

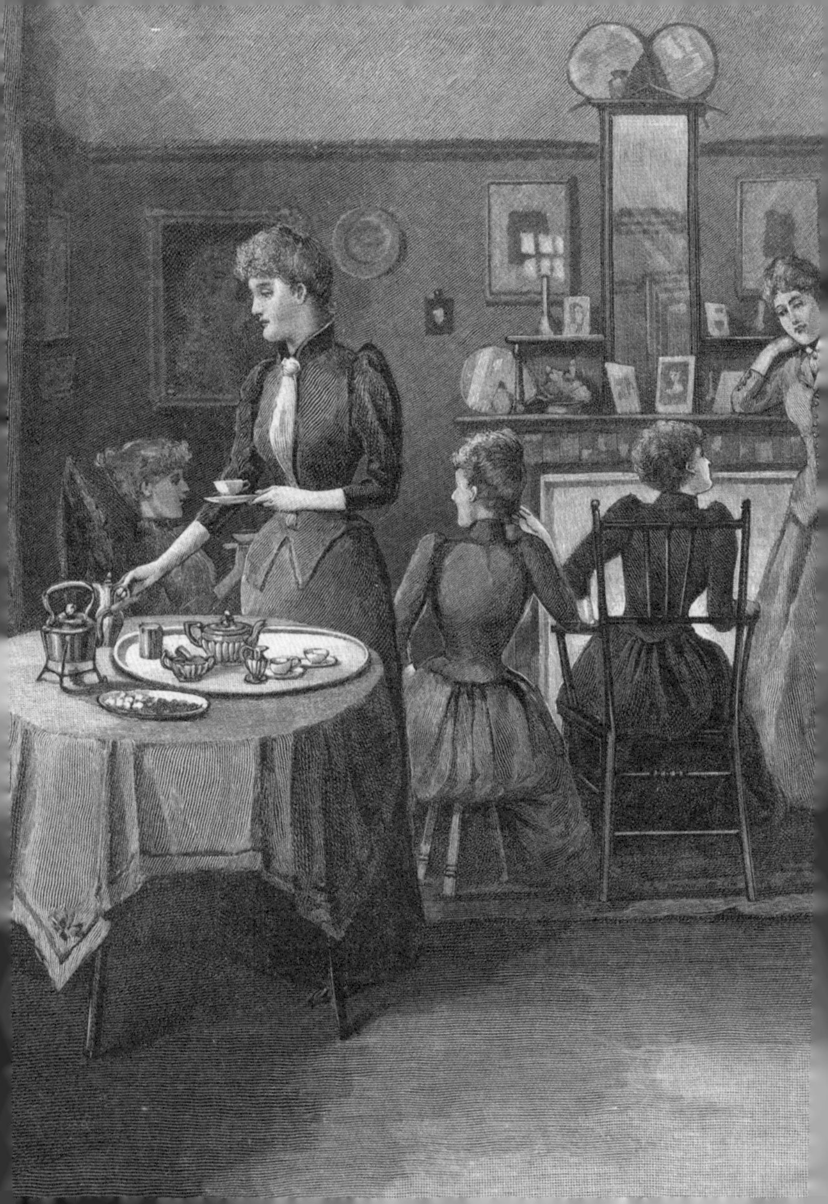

Fireside Scones

Ingredients:

1⅔ cup/250g plain flour	3–4 tbsp/40g butter
pinch of salt	4 tbsp milk
½ tsp baking soda	4 tbsp water
1 tsp cream of tartar	milk, for glazing

1 Move an oven rack to near the top of the oven, and preheat the oven to 450°F/230°C/Gas mark 8.

2 Sift together into a bowl the flour, salt, baking soda, and cream of tartar. Cut the butter into pieces and rub it into the flour with your fingertips until the mixture resembles fine breadcrumbs.

3 Mix the milk and water together and use a round-bladed knife to stir the mixture gradually into the flour to a soft but workable dough. If the dough seems a little dry, add just a little more milk and water.

4 Pull the dough into a ball and turn it out onto a lightly floured surface. Knead it quickly to remove all cracks. Roll it out to a thickness of about ½ in/1cm. Use a 2-in/5-cm pastry cutter to cut out 8–10 scones.

5 Put the scones on a heated, ungreased baking sheet and brush them with milk. Bake near the top of the oven for about 10 minutes, or until golden brown and well risen.

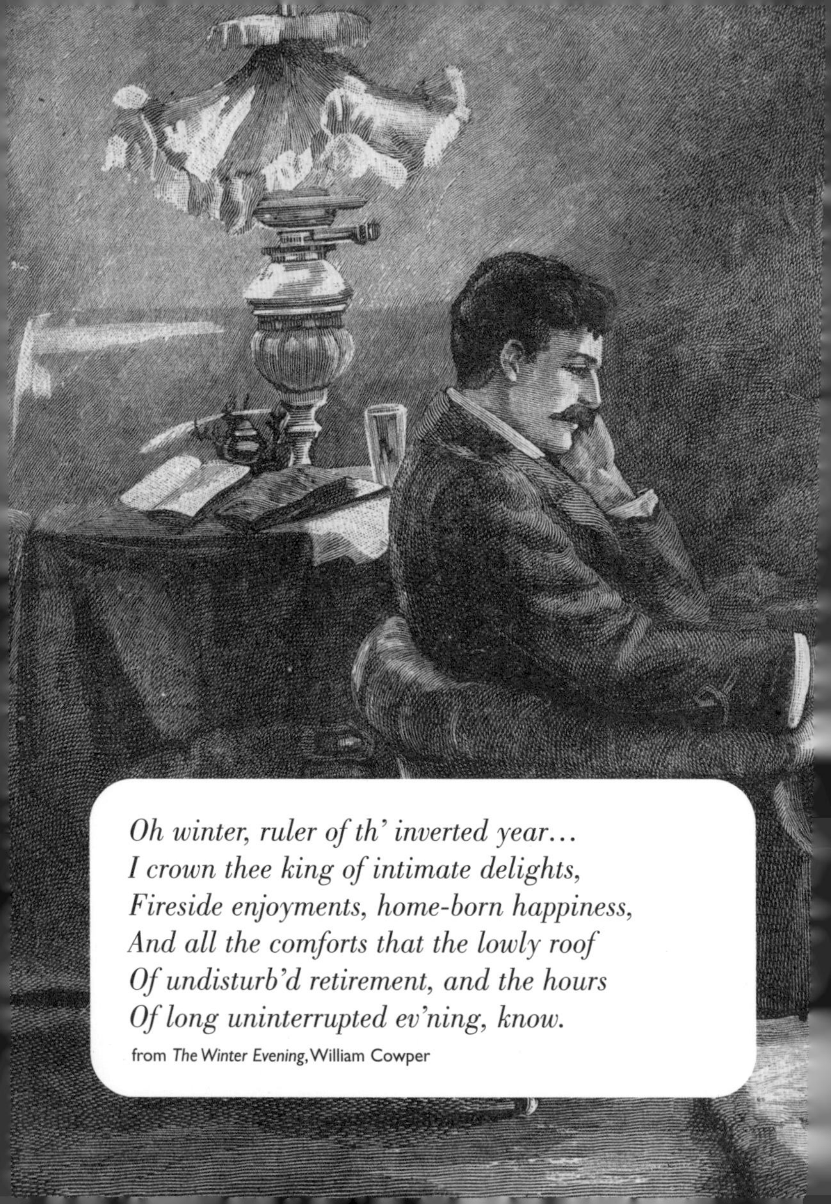

Oh winter, ruler of th' inverted year…
I crown thee king of intimate delights,
Fireside enjoyments, home-born happiness,
And all the comforts that the lowly roof
Of undisturb'd retirement, and the hours
Of long uninterrupted ev'ning, know.

from *The Winter Evening*, William Cowper

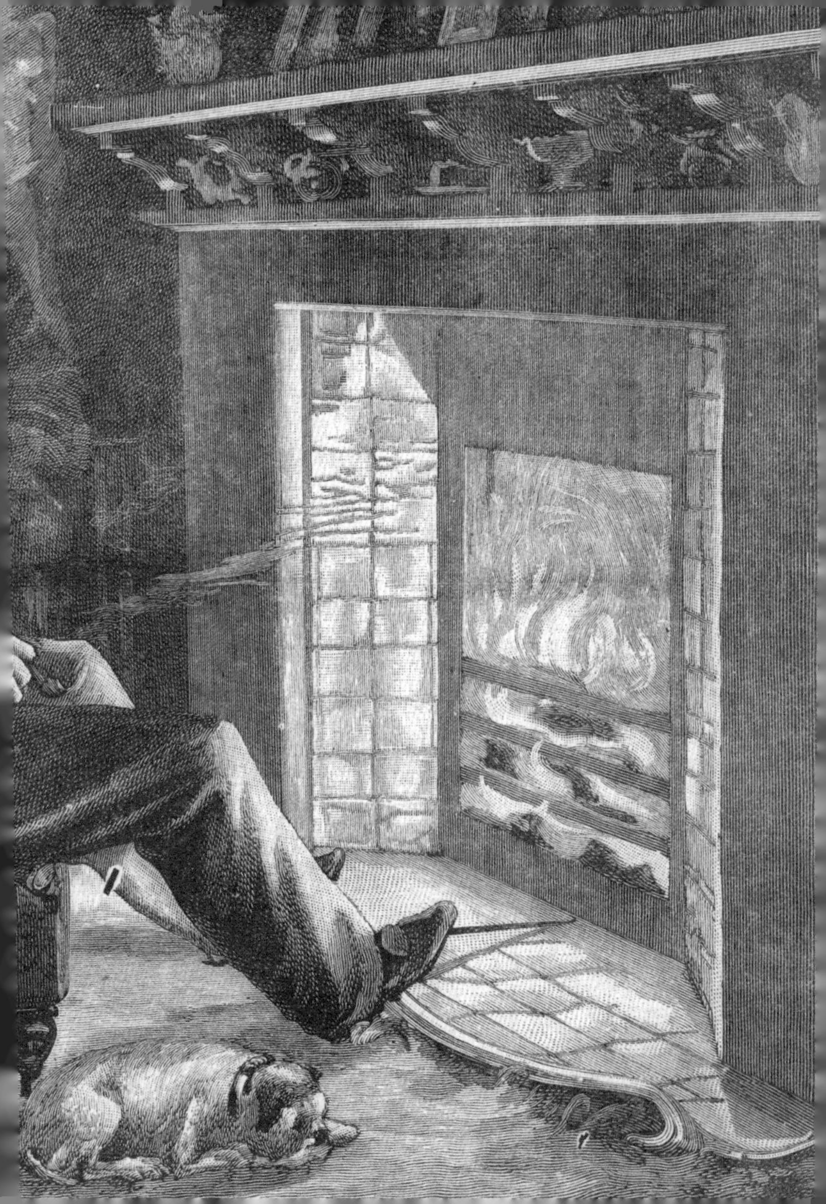

Chocolate Chip Muffins

Ingredients:

3 cups/350g self-rising flour
6 tbsp sugar
$\frac{2}{3}$ cup/125g good-quality
semisweet chocolate chips
4 tbsp/55g butter

6oz/175g good-quality semisweet
chocolate, broken into pieces
2 eggs, beaten
$1\frac{1}{4}$ cups/300ml buttermilk
$\frac{1}{2}$ cup/120ml milk

1 Preheat the oven to 425°F/200°C/Gas 7. Place 15 paper muffin cups into a muffin pan.

2 Mix together the flour, salt, sugar, and chocolate chips in a large bowl.

3 Melt the butter and chocolate together in a bowl set over a pan of simmering water, then let cool. Whisk in the eggs, buttermilk, and milk.

4 Combine the wet and dry ingredients and stir briskly until the flour is moistened. The mixture should appear rough and lumpy.

5 Fill the paper muffin cups about two-thirds full. Bake 20 minutes, until risen. To serve, drizzle with melted chocolate.

The Muffin Man

YOU'VE heard about the muffin man,
the muffin man, the muffin man,
You've heard about the muffin man
who lives in Drury Lane?
Well, here you see that muffin man—
that celebrated muffin man,
And if you try his muffins, you'll be sure to buy again.

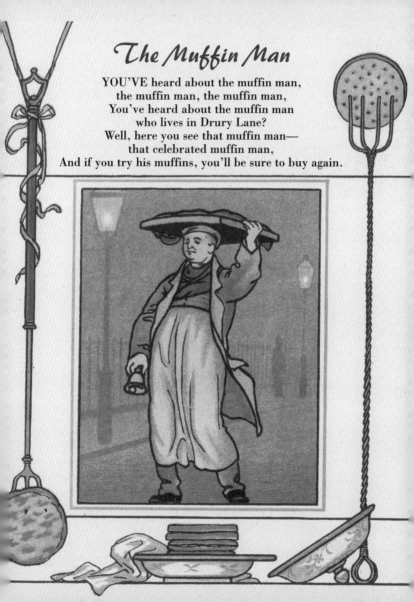

The Hearth Goddess

Every family in ancient Greece and Rome worshipped the goddess of the hearth. In Greece, she was named Hestia, and was a sister of Zeus, King of the gods. In Rome, the hearth goddess was named Vesta. Because fire was such a precious commodity in the earliest days of Rome, one of the round huts in the primitive village on the Palatine Hill would have been set aside for keeping alive the communal fire. Even when Rome had become a great city, the tradition of keeping the sacred fire in a round building continued.

Vesta was worshipped in every Roman house and also officially at a circular temple in the Forum. At the heart of the Temple of Vesta was a sacred fire. Romans believed that this fire had been brought to Rome by Aeneas, the Trojan hero whom they regarded as their great ancestor. Vesta was the custodian of this sacred fire, which, if it had ever gone out, would have been a national calamity. The goddess was served in her temple by priestesses, who were maidens of spotless chastity, called Vestal Virgins. Never more than seven in number, the Vestal Virgins were chosen at a very early age and they served for 30 years. Their main duty was to ensure that the fire in the temple was always burning, day and night. They also assisted in the state ceremonies. Any Vestal Virgin who lost her chastity was buried alive.

The cult of Vesta remained a Roman practice and did not spread outside Italy, but Vesta's sacred fire continued to be tended by Vestal Virgins in Rome right up to the fourth century AD. The Temple and Atrium of the Vestal Virgins, which stand in the Forum today are reconstructions made in 1930. However, it is still possible, walking among the ruins and looking at the statues of the Vestal Virgins in their house, to feel something of the atmosphere of those centuries in Rome when fire was so important in the home and in national life.

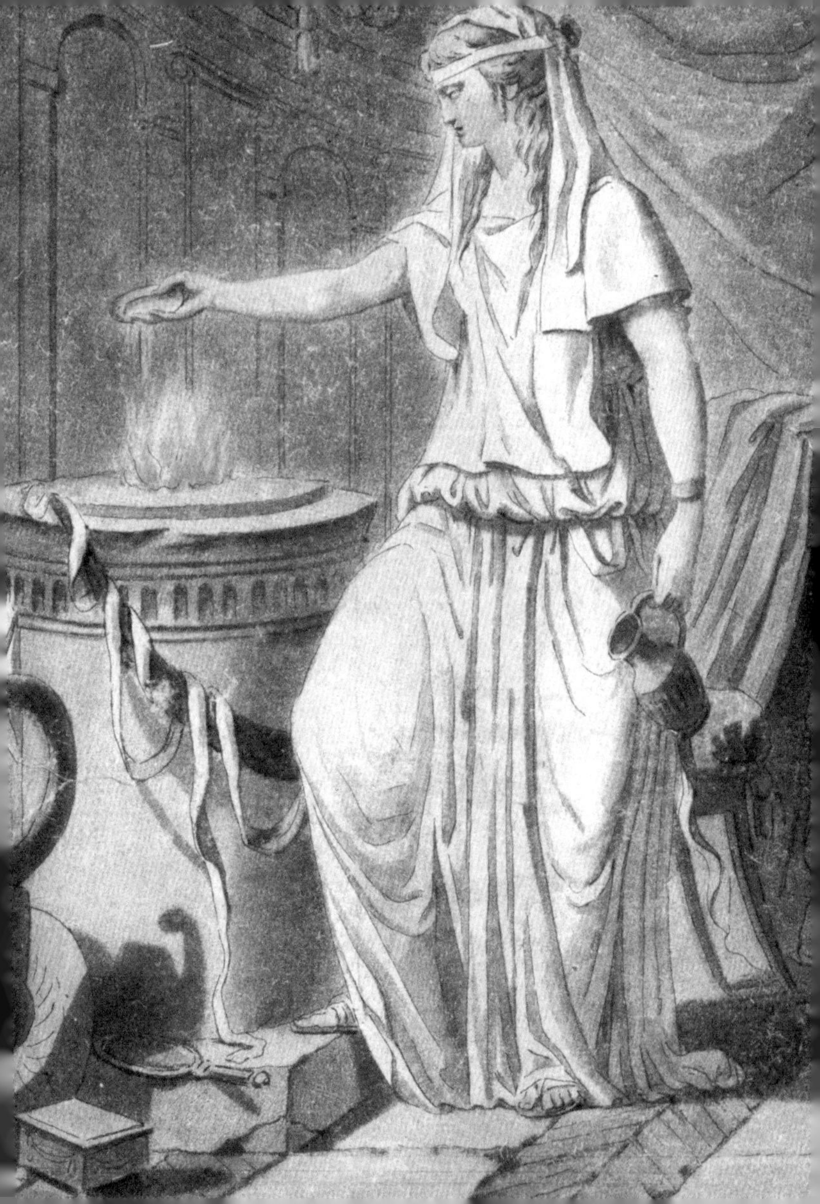

Hearthrugs

A rug on the floor in front of the fire was perhaps the most comforting embellishment in living rooms when the fireside was the center of family life. As William Winthrop Kent, an American architect and historian of domestic life, wrote in his authoritative *The Hooked Rug* (published in New York in 1937), "Many dwellings, especially cottages where no other rug or carpet was used, had the hearthrug.…The Englishman, whatever his lot in life, has always loved his fireside and valued all that…added to its comfortable aspect. Hence, among rugs, the hearthrug…has in England long held a place."

The same may be said of North America. From the early east coast settlements, through the pioneering years and in the present, the hearthrug, hooked, braided, woven, sheepskin, pelt, or even burlap sack, has held pride of place among floor coverings.

The hearthrug's considerable significance in the home is confirmed in literature. Two examples make the point:

Just before World War I, in England, D. H. Lawrence could describe in *Sons and Lovers* how his hero, Paul Morel, unable to get into his home late at night, wrapped himself in one of his mother's old hearthrugs, thrown out with the trash, to keep warm. Perhaps it was the same rug that had figured in this moment from Paul's childhood:

"…he opened his eyes to see his mother standing on the hearth rug with the hot iron near her cheek, listening, as it were, to the heat…She spat on the iron, and a little ball of spit bounded, raced off the dark, glossy surface. Then, kneeling, she rubbed the iron on the sack lining of the hearthrug vigorously."

Paul Morel's family could afford a few basic home comforts. However, as Flora Thompson noted in *From Lark Rise to Candleford*, the rural poor in England could often only afford "superannuated potato sacks" thrown down on the floor in front of the fire as their hearthrugs!

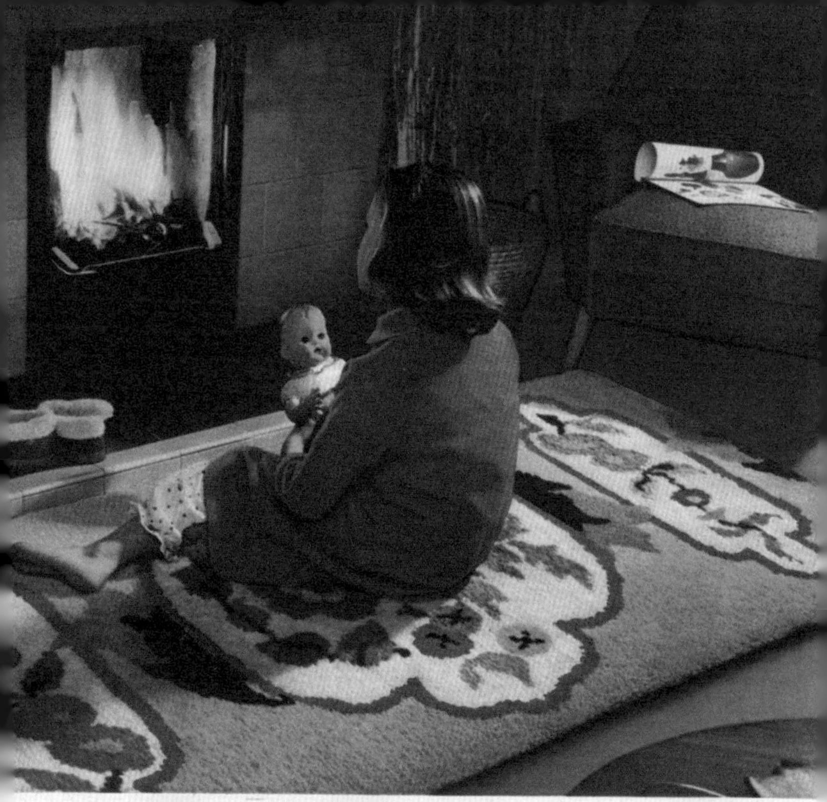

the Readicut way!

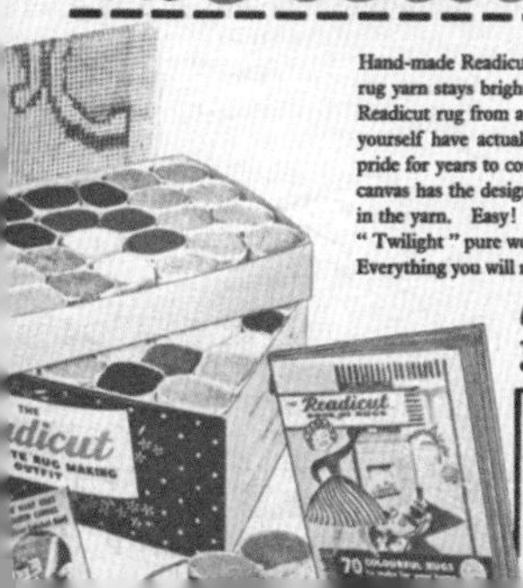
THE
dicut
TE RUG MAKING
OUTFIT
Readicut
70

Hand-made Readicut rugs are really luxurious, and the rich, super-soft rug yarn stays bright and lovely for years! *Everyone* enjoys making a Readicut rug from a complete Readicut outfit, and the fact that you yourself have actually made the loveliest rug in your home will give you pride for years to come! You don't need skill or experience—Readicut canvas has the design stencilled on it in colour, so all *you* do is match in the yarn. Easy! And there are rug yarns in two qualities: "Twilight" pure wool, or "Terry" rayon and wool blend at a lower price. Everything you will need comes in the outfit, *and you can buy it on easy terms!*

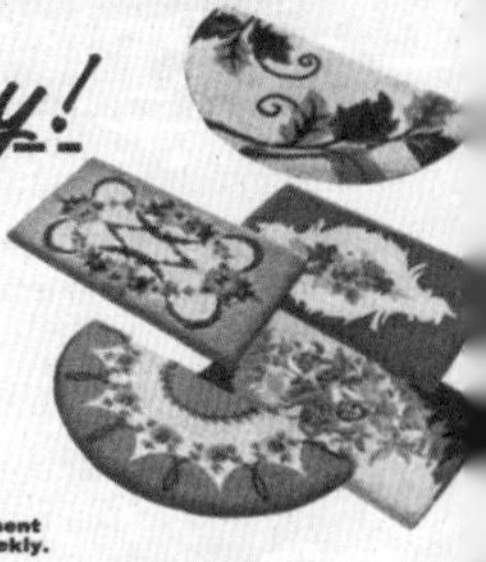

OUTFITS from 35/- cash.

TERMS - Complete outfits delivered on 1st payment of 10/-: balance payable at the rate of 5/- weekly.

Send today for the superb Readicut BOOK OF RUGS

This year's Readicut Book of Rugs is better than anything even Readicut have prepared before! 70 marvellous rug designs by

To THE READICUT WOOL CO. LTD. · Dept. 25K · OSSETT · YORKSHIRE

Please send a FREE copy of the Readicut Book of rugs.

NAME ....

ADDRESS..

....

Hooked Rugs

Making rugs from strips of rags is a very old craft that, although it originated in Britain, found its finest expression in North America. In America, hooked rugs, called "hookies" and "clippies," are still widely made, collected, and treasured. However, in Britain old hooked rugs are not so easily found. They were not generally considered to be of any value and, therefore, have not been handed down as heirlooms. They were discarded when worn and dirty. In Britain, where the craft was a social activity involving the whole family, for centuries, it is now slowly being revived.

In both North America and Britain, rag rugs were simple, humble objects made by ordinary, thrifty folk out of whatever materials were available to them. In pioneering America and rural Britain, where there were few luxuries, nothing was wasted that could be put to a good second use. The best use for old woolen clothes and other materials was on the floor at the fireside in the form of a hooked rug. The strips of fabric were hooked through a backing that, in many cases, had first seen life as a hessian sack holding grain or animal food.

Hooked rugs were not something for the very poor because making them required some basic equipment, including fabric of some kind and the means to cut it into strips, which the poor simply did not have. To make these hooked rugs, the most important equipment is: long-bladed scissors (in our own more sophisticated time a machine cutter is usually used), a frame to keep the work taut, and the correct hooks. British makers of hooked rugs often make do with just one hook, or a crochet hook given a handle, but American rug-makers can now choose from a wide array of hooks in a range of sizes, shapes, and handle styles.

Rug styles are different on either side of the Atlantic, too. It is in the United States that the most stylish and sophisticated designs are found, often incorporating the major aspects of country and small town life, especially crops, animals, plants, and flowers.

Today, minimalism style has had an effect on rug design. Now hooked rugs sold for spreading on the floors of elegant loft apartments use high-quality fabrics to grab attention. Their construction often depends on using expensive strips of high-quality fabrics, such as suede or leather, or alternatively, finely graded shades of the same color of different materials, rather than sophisticated design elements.

Make Your Own Hooked Rug

It is a true pleasure to sit in front of a roaring fire on a frosty winter evening with your feet resting on your own homemade rug. Why not try making your own version of this beautiful Shaker-style hooked rug?

The Shaker community had a profound influence on modern design through their creation of simple and functional, yet highly beautiful furnishings. Although their furniture and surroundings appeared austere, the Shakers lived in relative comfort, and they had specially designed cast-iron stoves to heat their homes. The Shaker laws, which covered most aspects of community life, were essentially practical and, among other things, advocated the use of rugs and floor coverings to cover the wooden floors. Each Brother and Sister had a small hooked, braided, or knitted rug beside their bed, and longer woven carpets were used in other parts of the building.

The rugs were often made from the fabric of old clothes, cut into strips. The strips were either pushed through heavy burlap to produce a pile, or plaited into long braids that were coiled and stitched into place. The Shaker laws banned figurative design but made no other restrictions, with the result that the rugs are the most colorful of the Shaker textiles.

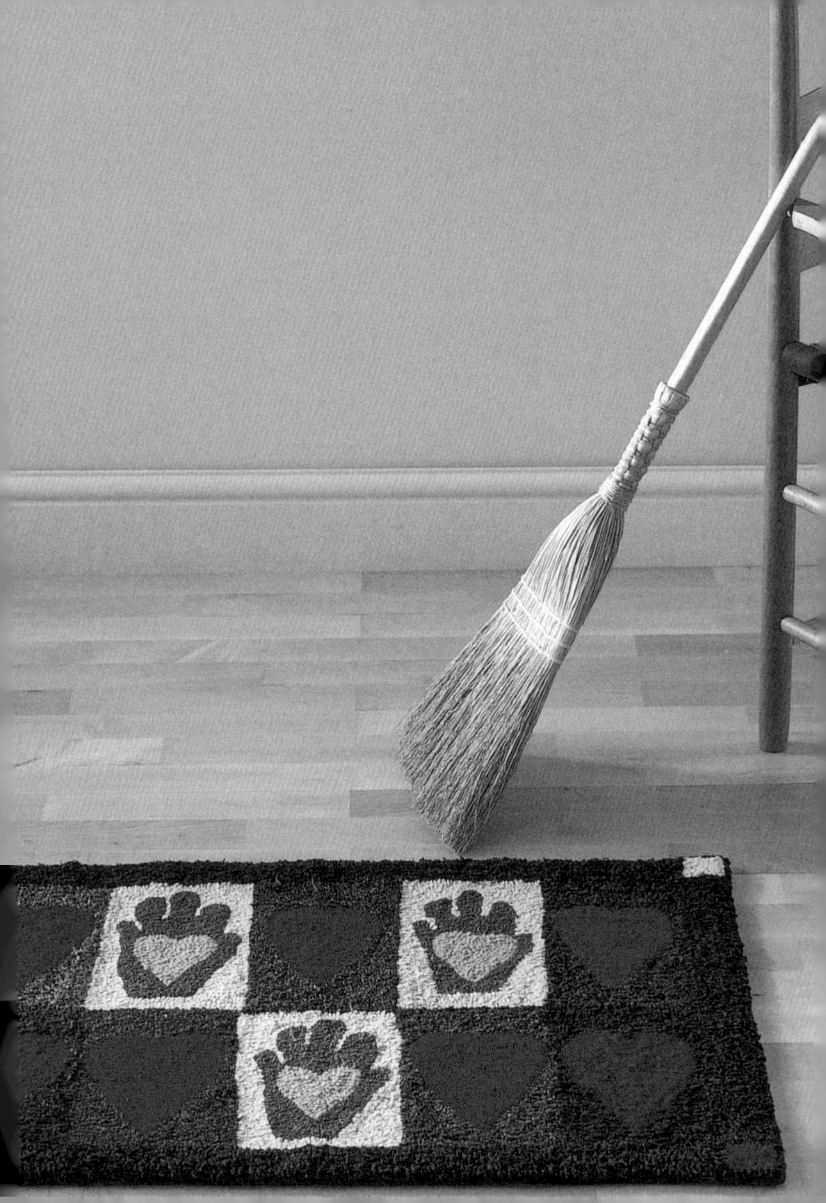

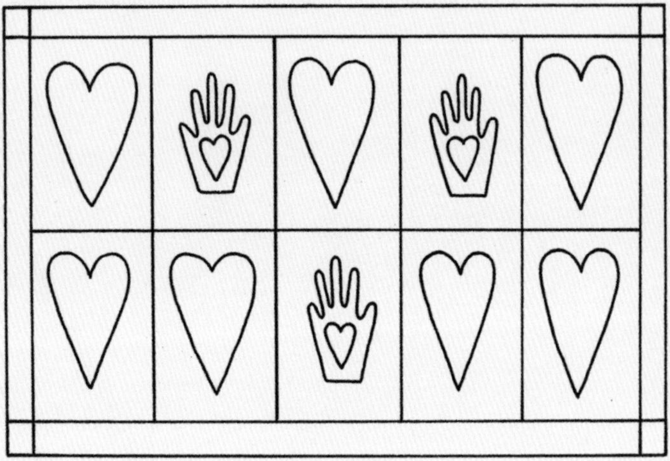

Plan the color scheme of your rug carefully before you begin, and, for maximum effect, make sure the motif is in clear contrast to the background color. Collect wool fabric for this hooked rug by searching for old blankets and suitable garments in charity shops. Here the same tweed fabric has been dyed in several different shades to make the backgrounds for the hearts.

MATERIALS:

- $\frac{3}{4}$ yd x 1yd/0.75 x 1m burlap
- Assorted wool fabric cut into $\frac{1}{4}$ in/5mm strips
- Wide twill tape, pre-washed and dyed to match border fabric
- Wood frame and rug hook
- Staple gun and staples
- Black permanent felt pen
- Damp cloth and iron

Finished size: about 22 x 32$\frac{1}{2}$in/56 x 82.5cm

1 Stretch the burlap onto the wood frame with the straight grain parallel to the long sides. Start at one corner and staple along one long side, then work around the frame, stapling each side in turn.

2 Enlarge the template (page 92) to the required size and transfer to the burlap, leaving a 2–4in/5–10cm border all around. To mark straight lines, draw the pen nib between two threads.

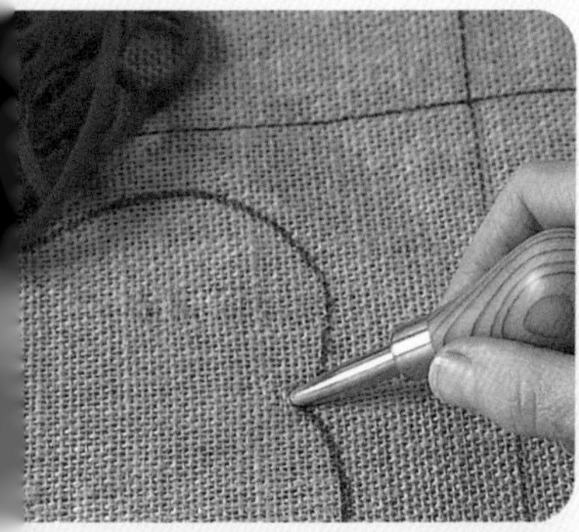

3 Select the wool fabric you need and cut it into $\frac{1}{4}$in/5mm strips. As a guide, you need to cut strips from a piece of fabric about four times the motif size to have enough strips to cover it.

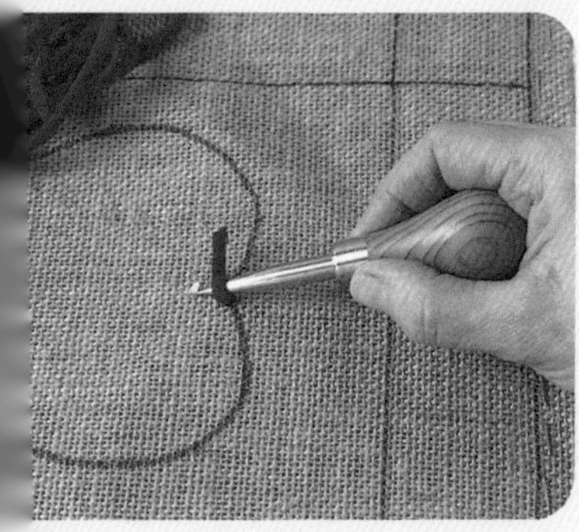

4 Hold the hook as if you are holding a pen. Hold a strip of fabric between your finger and thumb on the underside of the burlap. Push the hook firmly through the weave on the line at the corner of a motif and bring the end of the strip through to the right side.

5 Leaving the end on the top side, push the hook through the weave two threads away on the marked line and pull a small loop through to the top. The loop should be about $\frac{1}{4}$in/5mm high.

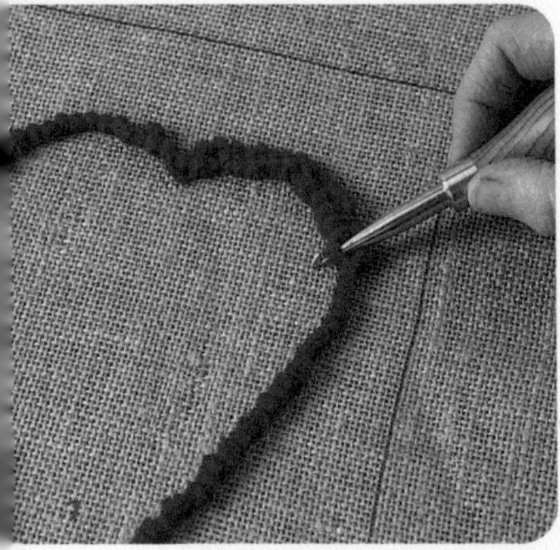

6 Continue around the edge of the motif, making loops of the same size every two threads. The wool strips should be close enough to cover the burlap, but not so close that it bunches up.

7 Leave the end of each strip of wool on the top before starting a new strip as before. Work in lines echoing the outside shape and work in toward the center to fill the shape completely.

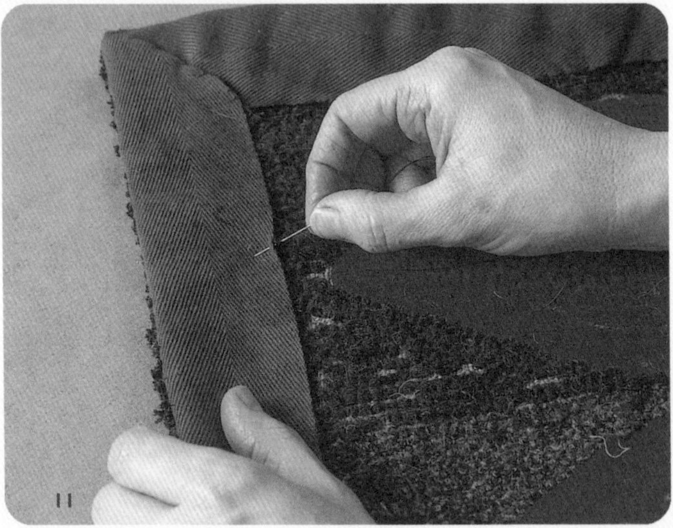

8 Work the rest of the design in the same way. Once complete, carefully take the rug off the frame and press on the wrong side with a damp cloth and a hot iron.

9 Cut strips of twill tape to fit down each side. With right sides together, sew the twill tape to the burlap, close to the last row of hooking.

10 Trim the burlap to 1in/2.5cm and turn the tape over onto the wrong side. Miter the corners neatly and slip stitch in place.

11 Hem the twill tape to the wrong side of the rug.

American Braided Rugs

While woven and hooked rugs are found all over the world, braided rugs are uniquely American. The tradition for making fabric rugs in braided form began in New England, also the same region where America's textile industry began. The techniques involved could be easily learned—after all, girls all had long hair in those days and began very early in life learning how to braid it. Unlike other forms of rugs, braided rugs needed almost no special equipment and were not so fine a form of work that the rug maker needed a well-lit environment. Braided rugs, like hooked rugs, brought color, softness, and warmth into the otherwise plain and austere homes of pioneering New Englanders.

After a great revival of interest in braided rug-making in the mid-twentieth century, saw mills all over northeastern America sold rug making fabric by the pound. Today there are many synthetic and blended fibers available to the rug maker that both repel dirt and outlast natural materials. Rugs intended for outdoor use, perhaps on a patio or in a barbecue area, can be made with polypropylene fabrics that will survive in all weathers and can even be hosed down when they get dirty.

Braided rugs are very sturdy and last for years. They are comfortable to walk on and easy to care for. But shaking them roughly or hanging them over a line to beat them is not a good idea because it puts a great strain on the lacing and stitching. It is much better to run a vacuum cleaner regularly over both sides. Since they are reversible, regular turning over greatly extends their life. Sponge stains away with soapy water or have them professionally dry-cleaned.

The techniques used in making braided rugs have changed little over the centuries. Most rugs are constructed from pre-braided fabric. Three strips of fabric are braided or plaited together, then the completed braids are all braided together, forming the rug. Thick bundles of a yarn such as wool also can be braided together. The braids, which may be of varying thicknesses within one rug, are formed into round, oval, rectangular, or heart-shaped rugs.

When buying a braided rug, you should look for tight braiding and tight stitching. The tighter the braids are assembled and sewn together, the better the quality of the rug. A tightly braided rug is thick and soft to walk on. It also picks up less dirt than a loosely braided and sewn rug. If you want to make your own braided rug, as a beginner it is best to start by trying to braid something smaller, such as chair pads, a stair runner, or a simple tote bag, before moving on to a larger, more difficult rug.

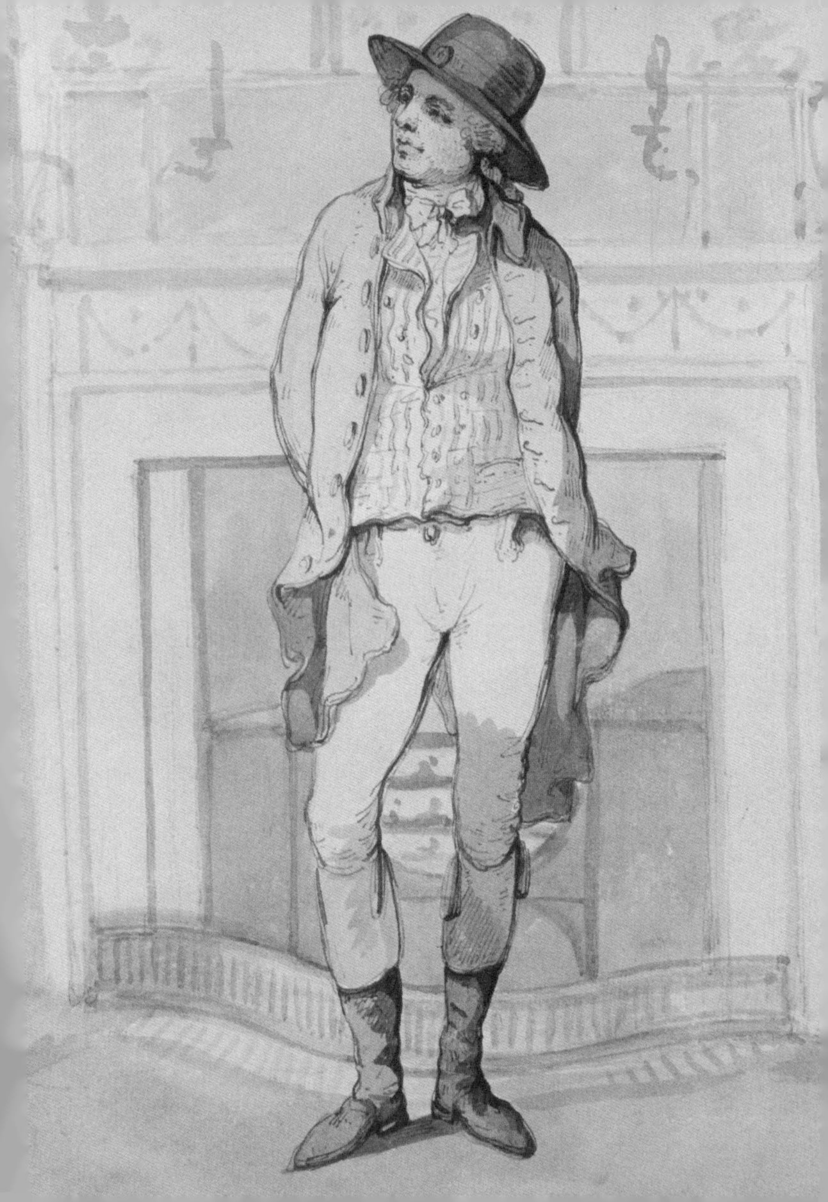

Men on the Hearthrug

Nineteenth-century novels always seem to have at least one scene in which a prominent male figure dominates the room from his place by the fireside. Think of David Copperfield's first sight of his new father, Mr. Murdstone. Think of Jane Eyre, encountering for the first time Mr. Brocklehurst of Lowood school: "a black pillar!—such, at least, appeared to me, at first sight, the straight, narrow, sable-clad shape standing erect on the rug." Then there is Anthony Trollope's much more warm and genial Archdeacon Grantly, dominating the climax of *The Last Chronicle of Barset* from his position by the hearth in his library.

A couple of generations ago, when the fireside was still commonplace in most houses, there was a schoolboy joke for why men warmed their coat tails in front of the fire. It all had to do with Noah and his Ark. One day, while still floating on the waters that flooded the Earth, the Ark sprang a leak. The dog was the first to try to stop the leak, with his nose, but he failed, achieving only a cold nose in the process. Then Mrs. Noah put her foot against the leak. The only result was that ever since, women have had cold feet. Then Noah set his backside against the leak. The result was much the same, except Noah got a cold bottom! And that is why men stand on the hearthrug with their backs to the fire.

"They both of them sit by my fire every Evening and wait my return with Impatience; and, at my entrance, never fail of running up to me, and bidding me Welcome, each of them in its proper Language. As they have been bred up together from Infancy, and have seen no other Company, they have acquired each other's Manners: so that the Dog gives himself the Airs of Cat, and the Cat, in several of her Motions and Gestures, affects the Behavior of the little Dog."

from *The Tatler*, Richard Steele

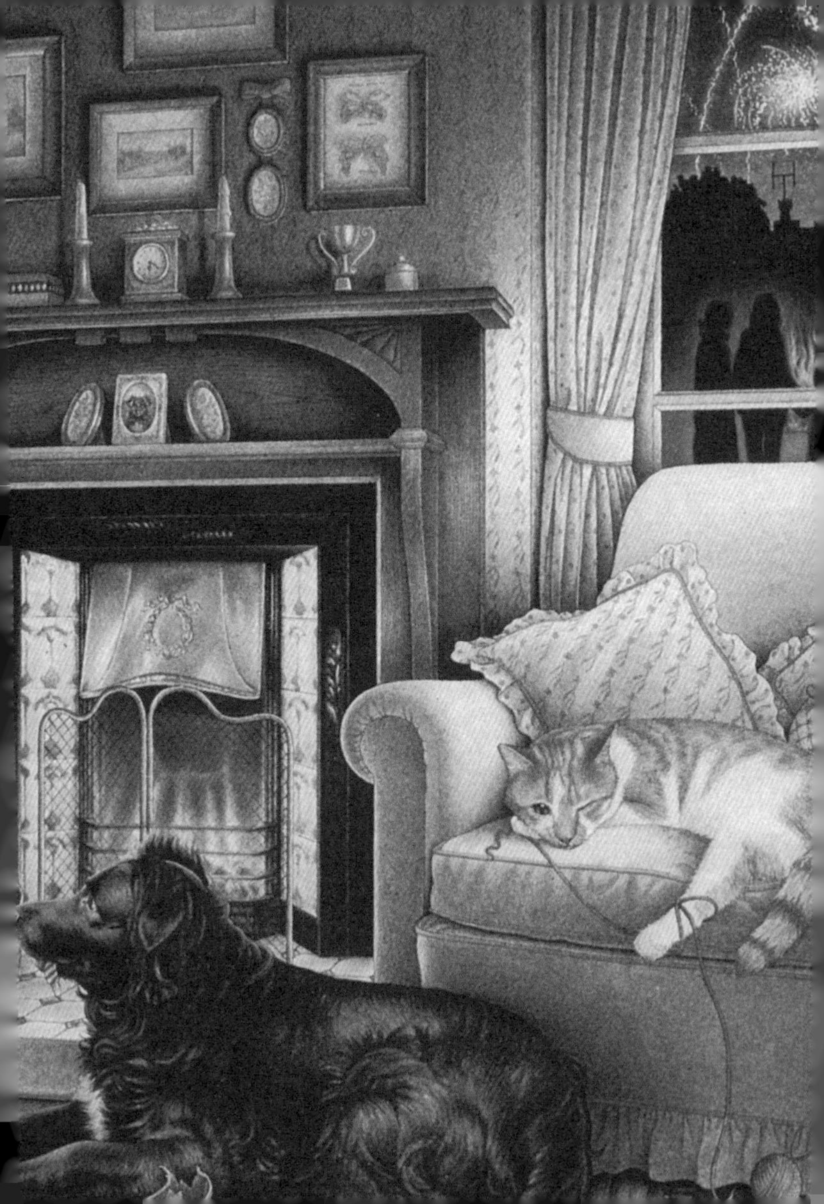

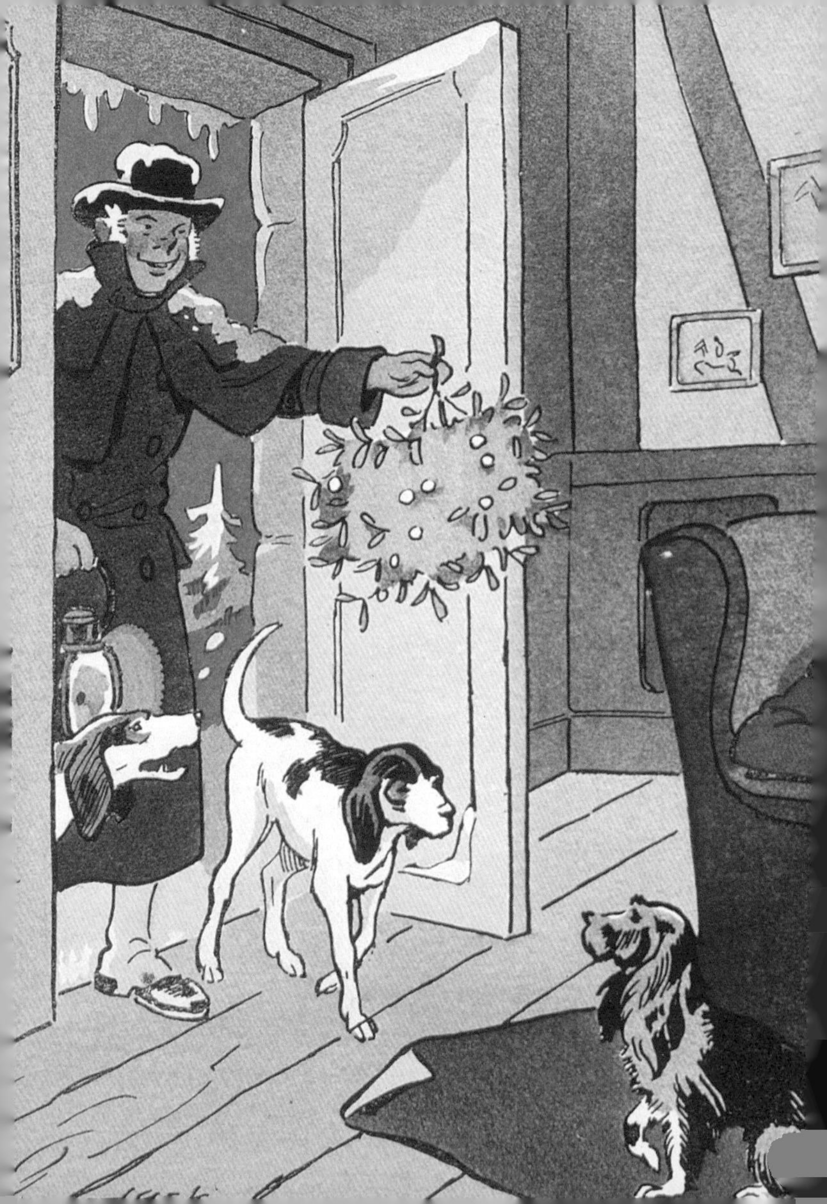

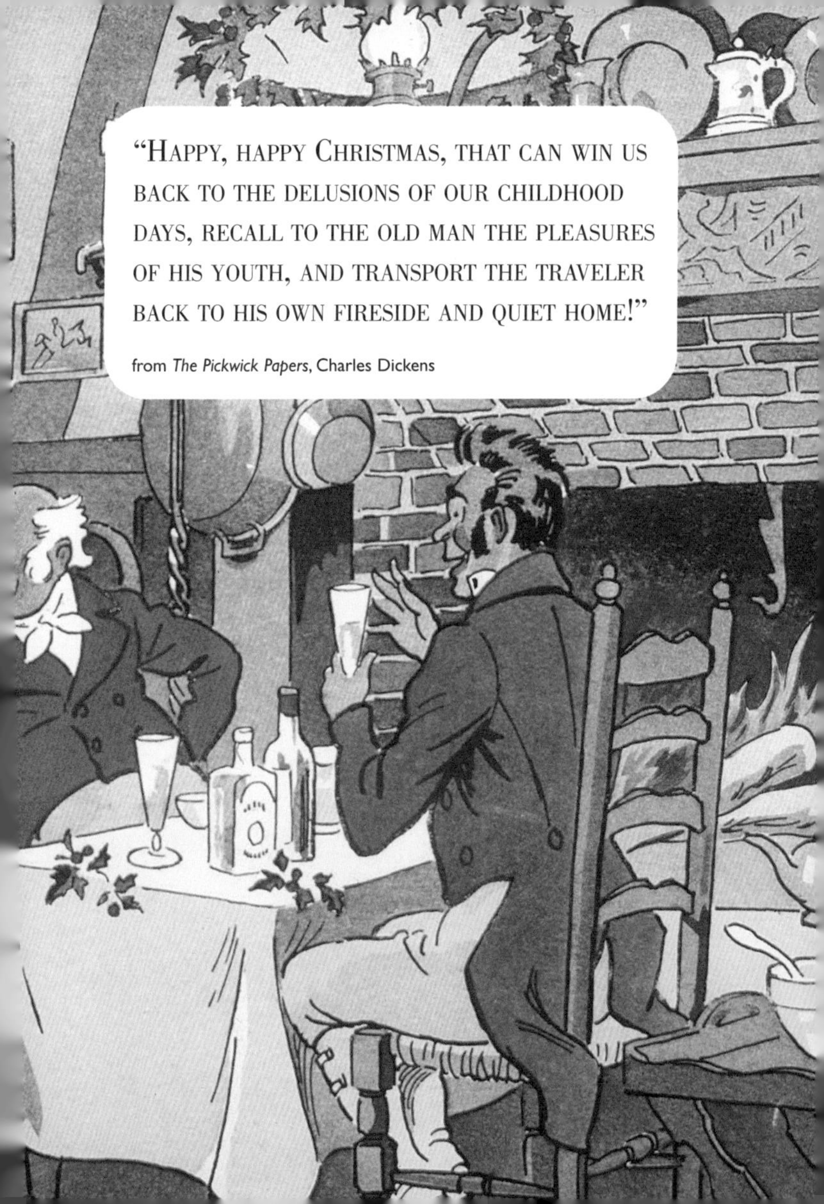

"HAPPY, HAPPY CHRISTMAS, THAT CAN WIN US BACK TO THE DELUSIONS OF OUR CHILDHOOD DAYS, RECALL TO THE OLD MAN THE PLEASURES OF HIS YOUTH, AND TRANSPORT THE TRAVELER BACK TO HIS OWN FIRESIDE AND QUIET HOME!"

from *The Pickwick Papers*, Charles Dickens

Warming Christmas Drinks

"At last the dinner was all done, the cloth was cleared, the hearth swept, and the fire made up. The compound in the jug being tasted and considered perfect, apples and oranges were put upon the table, and a shovel-full of chestnuts on the fire. Then all the Cratchit family drew round the hearth.... Then Bob proposed: 'A Merry Christmas to us all, my dears. God bless us!'"

from *A Christmas Carol*, Charles Dickens

Charles Dickens certainly knew how to describe the perfect Christmas Day. In this short extract he immortalized the Christmas of the poor but cheerful Cratchit family as they treated themselves to a warm, delicious, and satisfying Christmas drink in front of their glowing fire.

As family and friends come together in front of the hearth at Christmastime, what could be better than a comforting and traditional eggnog, posset, punch, or mulled drink (pages 106–107)? There are as many different recipes for Christmas drinks as there are spices and other flavorings in the kitchen cupboard, but special occasions do demand special recipes.

Festive Ale Posset

Ingredients:

$\frac{1}{2}$ pint/300ml sherry	I tbsp sugar
$\frac{1}{2}$ pint/300ml ale	nutmeg, for sprinkling
2 pints/1.2 liters milk	

1 Put the sherry and ale into a warmed jug. Bring the milk to a boil and pour it over the sherry and ale.

2 Stir in the sugar. Pour the posset into glasses or beer mugs and sprinkle nutmeg over the top.

Mulled Fireside Drinks

"Mulling" an alcoholic drink involves sweetening it and flavoring it with spices, then heating it. Ale and red wine are the most commonly mulled drinks. Ale was often heated at the fireside, where it was usually drunk, and many hearths had special heating vessels for the purpose. These were filled with the spiced brew and thrust into the fire to heat up.

A Christmastime Mull

Ingredients:

2 bottles heavy red wine (such as burgundy)	8 cloves
	1 tsp cardamom seeds (optional)
6fl oz/175ml gin	2-in/5-cm piece cinnamon stick
3oz/75g seedless raisins	thinly pared zest of 2 lemons
4oz/115g sugar	

1 Put the wine, half the gin, and all the remaining ingredients into a large saucepan. Heat gently, stirring regularly, until the sugar has completely dissolved, then bring to a boil.

2 Turn the heat down as low as possible and simmer gently for 30 minutes. Stir in the remaining gin, reheat, and strain into a warmed jug. Serve at once.

Mulled Wine

Ingredients:

2 oranges	1 pint/600ml boiling water
2 pints/1.2 liters red wine	1½ tbsp curaçao
4–5 tbsp sugar	1½ tbsp brandy
12 cloves	grated nutmeg, for spinkling
½ tsp ground cinnamon	
(or ½ cinnamon stick)	

1 Slice one of the oranges thinly, and pare the zest off the other one as thinly as possible, being careful not to cut into the pith.

2 Pour the wine into a large saucepan and add the orange slices and zest. Add the sugar, cloves, and cinnamon, and heat slowly.

3 When hot, add the water, curaçao, and brandy.

4 Strain the mulled wine into a jug and pour from there into warm glasses. Sprinkle nutmeg over each glass before serving.

VARIATION: To make a St. Clements Mulled Wine, replace the two oranges with the thinly peeled zest of one orange and one lemon. Add half a whole nutmeg to the wine as it heats as an alternative to sprinkling grated nutmeg over the glasses.

Down the Chimney

On Christmas Eve all over the world children go reluctantly to their beds and dream that Santa Claus, who is also known as St. Nicholas, will slide down the chimney and leave special gifts in the stockings they have left hanging on the mantelpiece above the fire. Clement C. Moore beautifully described this wonderful tradition and Santa Claus' magical journey in his famous nineteenth-century poem *The Night Before Christmas*.

The Night Before Christmas

'Twas the night before Christmas, when all through the house
Not a creature was stirring, not even a mouse;
The stockings were hung by the chimney with care,
In hopes that St. Nicholas soon would be there;

The children were nestled all snug in their beds,
While visions of sugarplums danced in their heads;
And Mamma in her 'kerchief, and I in my cap,
Had just settled our brains for a long winter's nap;

When out on the lawn there arose such a clatter,
I sprang from the bed to see what was the matter.
Away to the window I flew like a flash,
Tore open the shutters and threw up the sash.

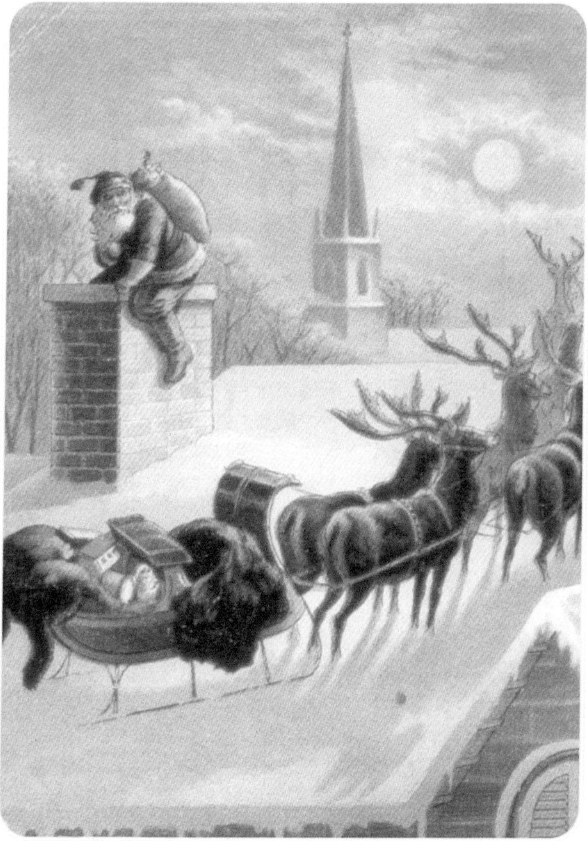

The moon on the breast of the new-fallen snow,
Gave the lustre of midday to objects below,
When, what to my wondering eyes should appear,
But a miniature sleigh, and eight tiny reindeer,

With a little old driver, so lively and quick,
I knew in a moment it must be St. Nick.
More rapid than eagles his coursers they came,
And he whistled, and shouted, and called them by name;

"Now, *Dasher*! Now, *Dancer*! Now, *Prancer* and *Vixen*!
On, *Comet*! On, *Cupid*! On, *Donner* and *Blitzen*!
To the top of the porch! To the top of the wall!
Now dash away! Dash away! Dash away all!"

As dry leaves that before the wild hurricane fly,
When they meet with an obstacle, mount to the sky;
So up to the housetop the coursers they flew,
With the sleigh full of toys, and St. Nicholas too.

And then in a twinkling, I heard on the roof,
The prancing and pawing of each little hoof—
As I drew in my head, and was turning around,
Down the chimney St. Nicholas came with a bound.

He was dressed all in fur, from his head to his foot,
And his clothes were all tarnished with ashes and soot;

A bundle of toys he had flung on his back,
And he looked like a pedlar just opening his pack.

His eyes-how they twinkled! His dimples, how merry!
His cheeks were like his roses, his nose like a cherry!
His droll little mouth was drawn up like a bow,
And the beard of his chin was as white as the snow;

The stump of his pipe he held tight in his teeth,
And the smoke it encircled his head like a wreath;
He had a broad little face and a little round belly,
That shook when he laughed, like a bowlful of jelly.

He was chubby and plump, a right jolly old elf,
And I laughed when I saw him, in spite of myself,
A wink of his eye and a twist of his head,
Soon gave me to know I had nothing to dread;

He spoke not a word, but went straight to his work,
And filled all the stockings; then turned with a jerk,
And laying his finger aside of his nose,
And giving a nod, up the chimney he rose;

He sprang to his sleigh, to his team gave a whistle,
And away they all flew like the down of a thistle.
But I heard him exclaim, ere he drove out of sight,
"Happy Christmas to all. And to all a good night."

Christmas Stockings

As a symbol of bounty and giving, a stocking hanging by the hearth adds the finishing touch to your Christmas decorations. Children and adults alike enjoy the fun of hanging up socks or stockings at Christmas in the hope that Santa Claus will fill them with special gifts.

The easiest way to make your own Christmas stockings is simply to buy extra-large socks and give them a touch of individuality with some clever decorating. Use craft fur or cotton balls to suggest snow or Santa's beard (sewing on other things such as buttons or felt shapes for the rest of his face); use Christmas-tree baubles or decorative tassels; or embroider each person's name on the stockings in brightly colored wool.

You could also try knitting Christmas stockings. Standard sock patterns, knitted in the largest size, are ideal. You can add a special festive touch by knitting them in colorful stripes. Use traditional Christmas colors, such as as red, white, and green.

If sewing is your forte, the simple, step-by-step project instructions on the following pages will show you how to make your own fun, brightly colored Christmas stockings. Kids will love these big, bold felt stockings—especially when they're packed full of Santa's surprises!

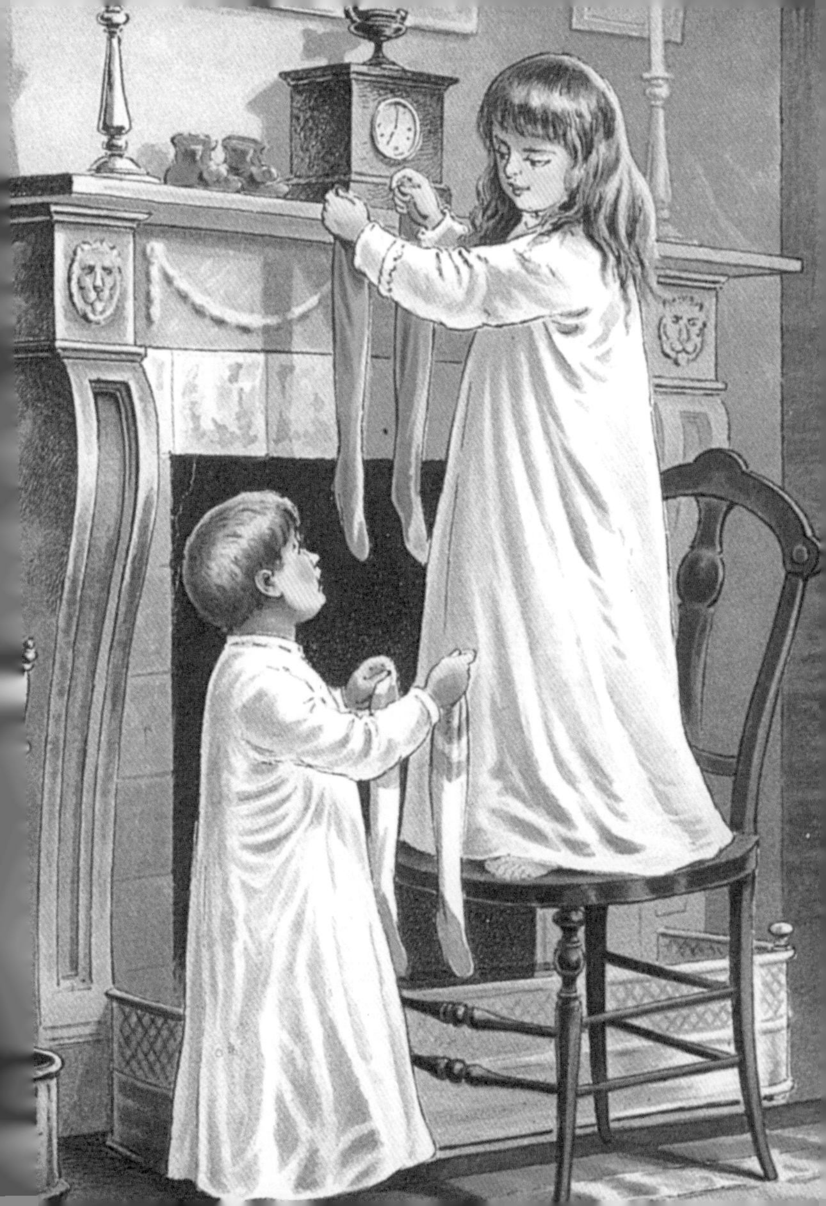

Make Your Own Stockings

These instructions are for the red stocking pictured, but they can be personalized with any number of decorative features, including hand-embroidered snowflakes, punched holes, or any festive decoration, including stars, angels, bells, or leaves, made of felt.

MATERIALS:

- 20 x 36in/50 x 90cm main color felt for stocking
- 20 x 8in/50 x 20cm contrast color felt for cuff
- 12in/30cm square contrast color felt for the decoration
- Sewing kit

- Craft glue
- Scissors
- Heavy paper for templates
- Hand and machine embroidery thread to match all three colors of felt

1 Draw the outline of a simple stocking shape on heavy paper to measure approximately $17\frac{1}{2}$in/44.5cm in height from the top to the bottom of the heel. Then draw a simple shape for the cuff the same width as the stocking. Cut out both to use as templates.

2 Draw around both the cuff and the stocking templates on the correct color of felt. Cut out two of each shape.

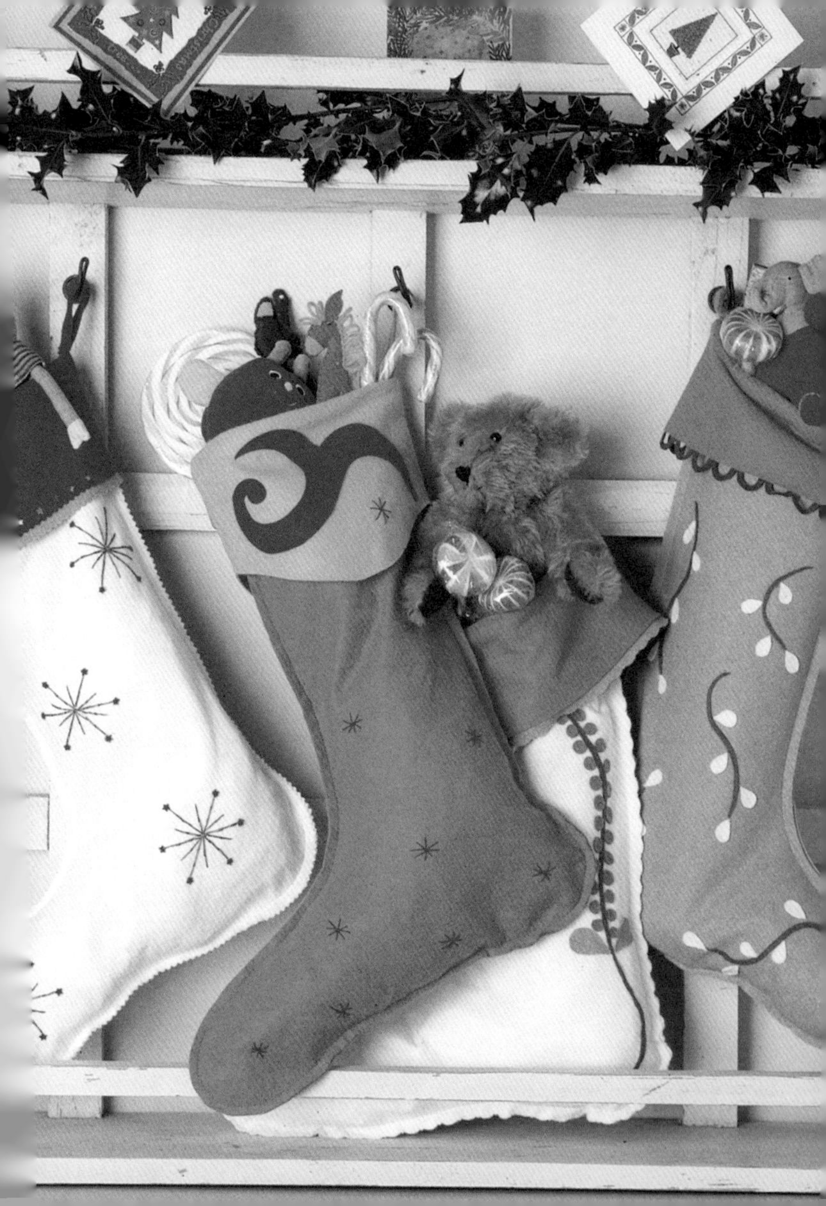

3 From scraps of felt cuff, cut a strip $\frac{1}{3}$ x 8in/1 x 20cm. Use this to make a strong hanging loop.

4 Embroider the small six-point stars in a random pattern on the front and back of the stocking with three strands of hand embroidery thread.

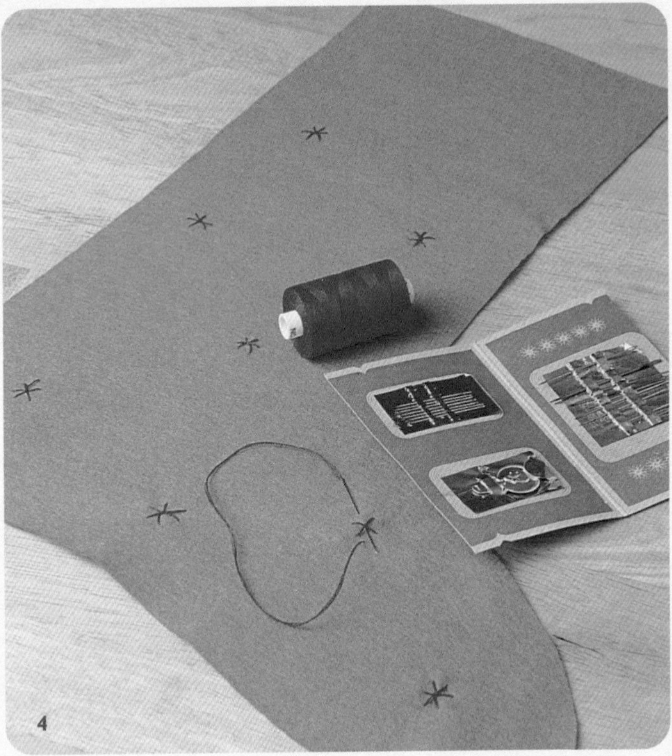
4

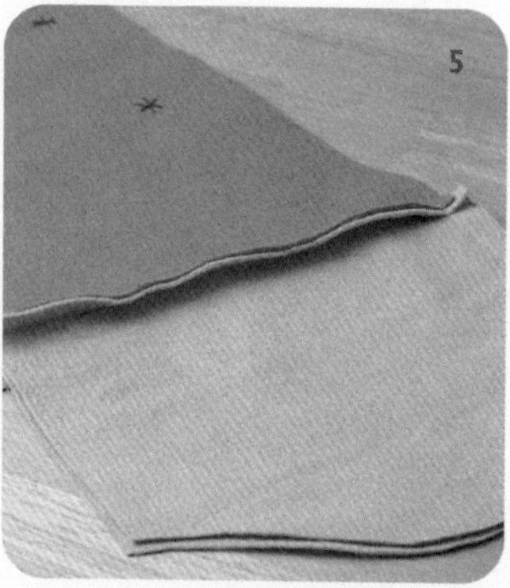
5

5 With the right sides together, stitch the top of each cuff to the top of each stocking. Sew the cuff side seams together, pressing the seam allowance in the same direction on both sides.

6 Stitch the two halves of the stocking together using a $\frac{1}{4}$ in/ 5mm seam. Fold the cuff down.

7 Cut out a decoration of your choice from the third contrasting color of felt and stick onto the cuff with craft glue.

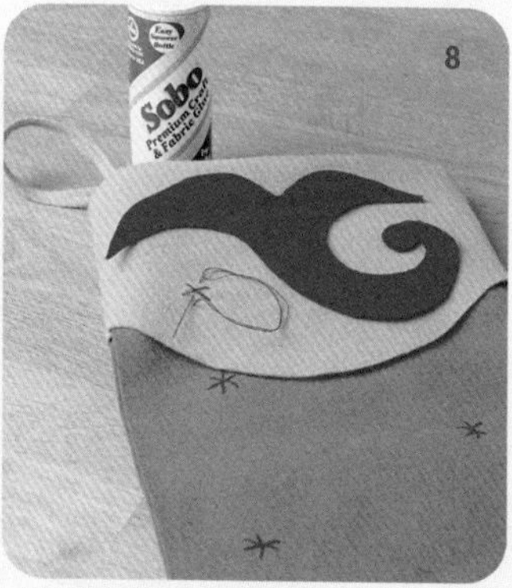
8
Sobo

8 Fold the hanging loop in half lengthwise. Sew through both layers, from end to end, using matching thread. Fold the loop in half and baste the two ends together. Sew in place inside the back of the cuff. Embroider a six-point star on the cuff.

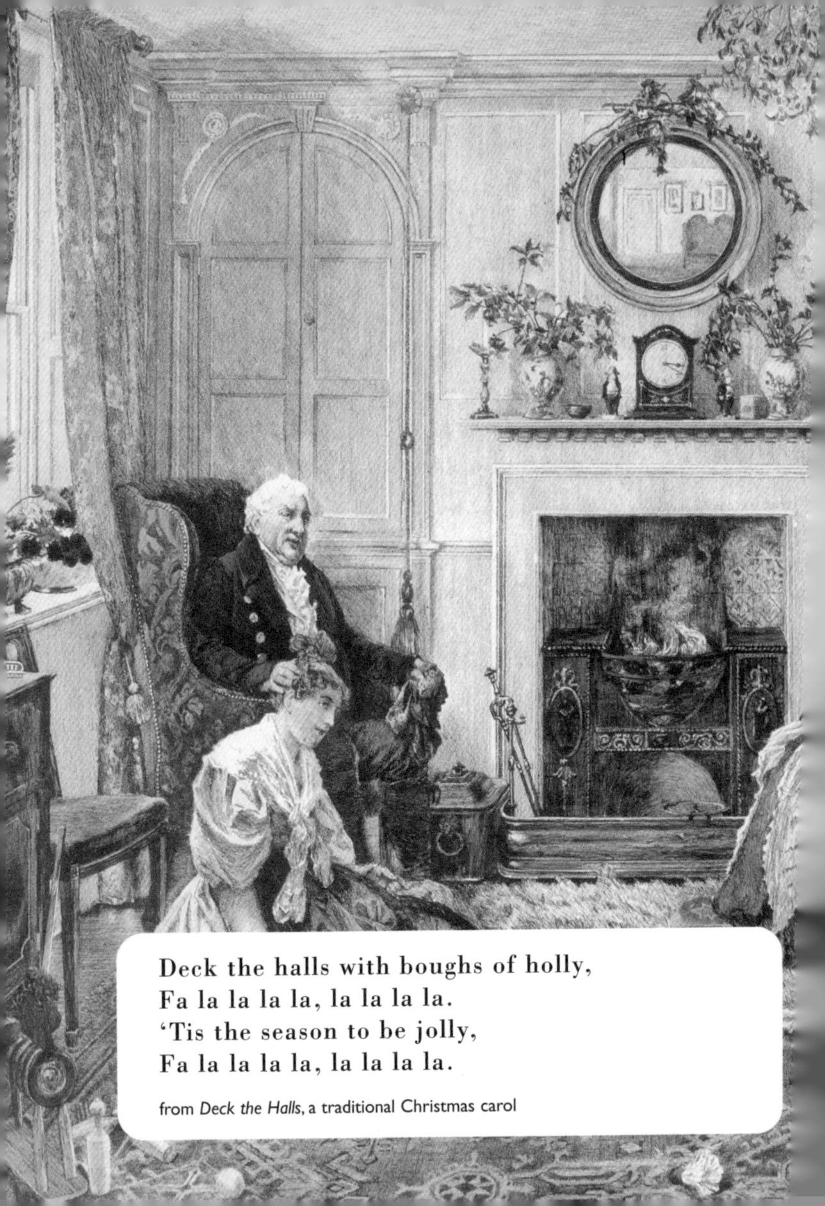

Deck the halls with boughs of holly,
Fa la la la la, la la la la.
'Tis the season to be jolly,
Fa la la la la, la la la la.

from *Deck the Halls*, a traditional Christmas carol

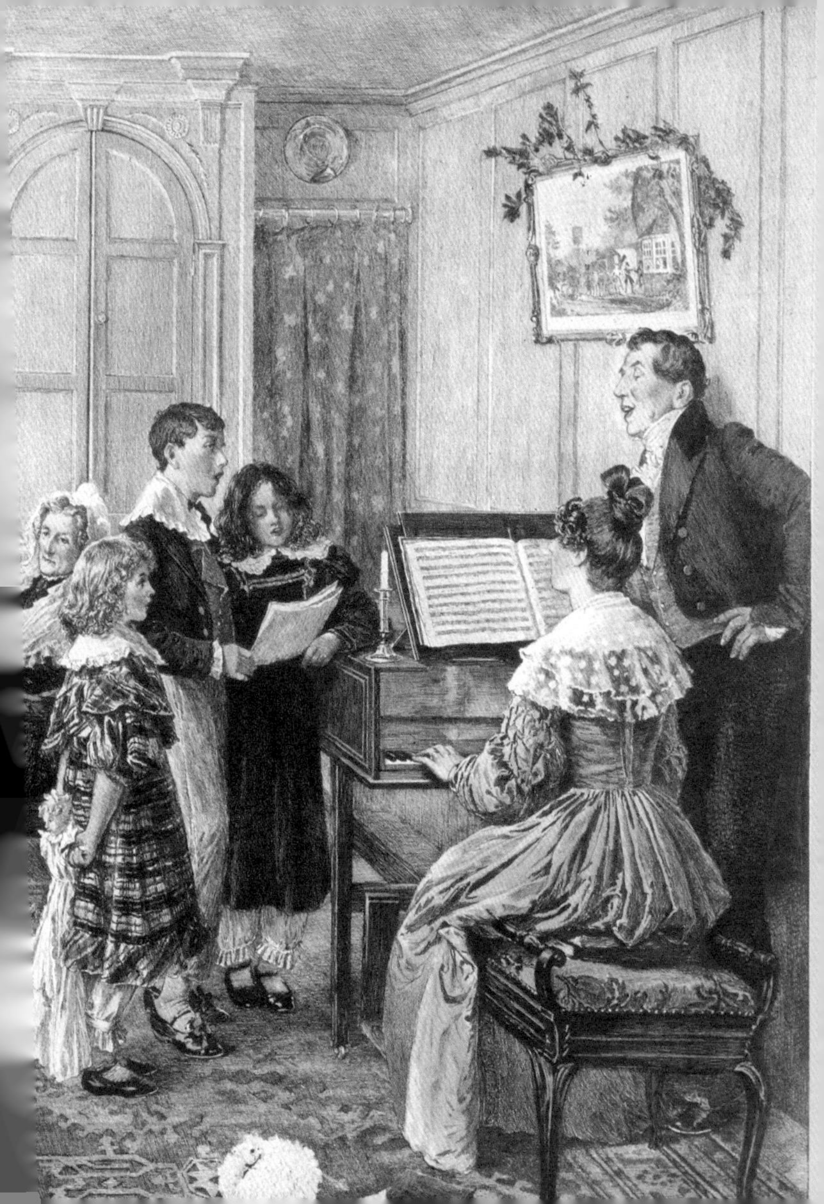

Roasting Chestnuts

Don't waste the hot coals of your open fire. Use them to make the simplest and most delicious treat of all—roast chestnuts. This is one of the oldest wintertime and Christmas traditions, and it's very easy to do.

The Victorians used a special roasting box on a long handle to roast their chestnuts. Today it is possible to buy a modern chestnut-roasting pan, but if you can't find one, you can improvise using an old aluminum frying pan with a lid. Simply modify the pan by carefully drilling holes into the base. This allows the chestnuts to roast properly. For a 12-in/30-cm pan, there should be about 25–30 holes in the pan, each being $\frac{1}{2}$ in in diameter. Try to space the holes evenly apart. Wash the pan carefully before you use it to roast your chestnuts.

1 To prepare your chestnuts for roasting, wash them in cold water and allow them to dry. When the chestnuts are dry, sort them by size for cooking.

2 Take chestnuts of a similar size and make a cut into the skin of each one using a small, sharp, pointed knife. Carefully slice into the chestnut's skin from left to right, making sure not to cut into the chestnut's meat. The cut should be no longer than $\frac{1}{2}$ in/1 cm. This cut lets the chestnut release steam while cooking so that it does not explode.

3 Place the chestnuts in the pan, making sure that they lie on the bottom of the pan in a single layer.

4 Make an even bed of hot coals and put the covered pan on it. Roast the chestnuts for a few minutes. After a while, remove the lid and stir the chestnuts so that they do not roast only on one side.

5 This process of covering, roasting, stirring, and re-covering must be repeated frequently throughout the roasting process. Alternatively, you could simply gently shake the covered pan frequently while cooking. For an average-size chestnut, about the size of a large walnut, the roasting time is approximately 20–25 minutes. You will know that the chestnuts are cooked when, if you remove one chestnut from the pan, its skin breaks easily, making a crackling sound.

6 When the chestnuts are roasted, place them in a large bowl lined with paper towels and cover them with a cloth. The chestnuts should be left to sit in their own heat for approximately 2–4 minutes, since this makes them easier to peel.

7 Chestnuts are best served hot, accompanied by apple cider or fruit juice.

Fireside Fun

Not so long ago, most people made their own Christmas decorations—and every home had sweetly simple paper garlands draped carefully around the rooms or over the mantel or Christmas tree. If you want to bring back these happy memories, let your children have bushels of fun making these long, linked, paper chains to decorate your home.

They're very easy to make and you can even buy pre-glued packs of garland strips from craft and gift shops. But it's much more fun to start from scratch and choose your own colors and designs.

1 Gather a nice selection of colored paper from craft, gift, or stationery stores—the more varied the colors, the more fun and attractive the paper chains will be.

2 Cut the sheets of paper into narrow strips—these should be approximately 1in/2.5cm wide and 6in/15cm long. Arrange the strips in piles according to color.

3 Take a tube of solid stick glue, put a small amount on one end of a strip, then loop the piece back to form a ring. Press the end firmly onto the glued surface.

4 Insert another piece of paper through the ring, then put glue on one end and loop around to make the second link. Continue until all of the paper is used up.

5 Allow the glue to dry before hanging the garlands. For extra glamour, you can decorate some of the paper links with glitter, or stick-on stars.

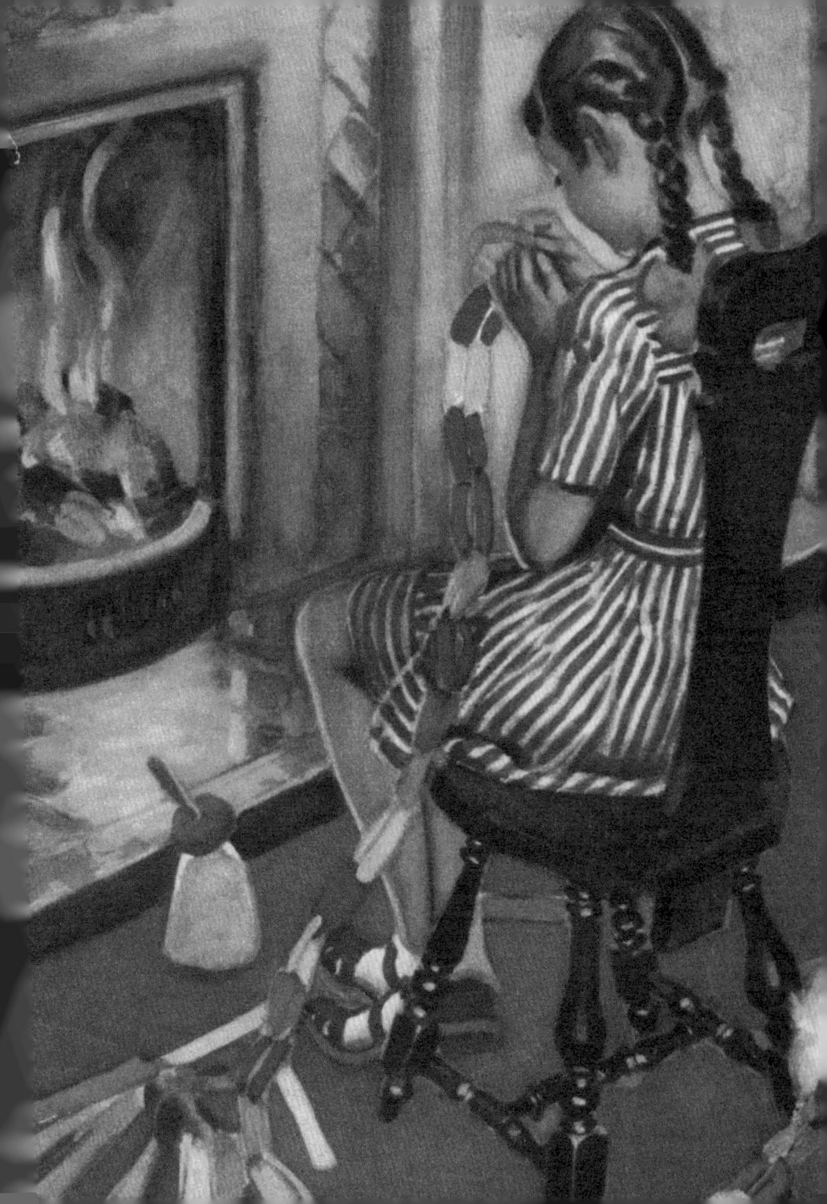

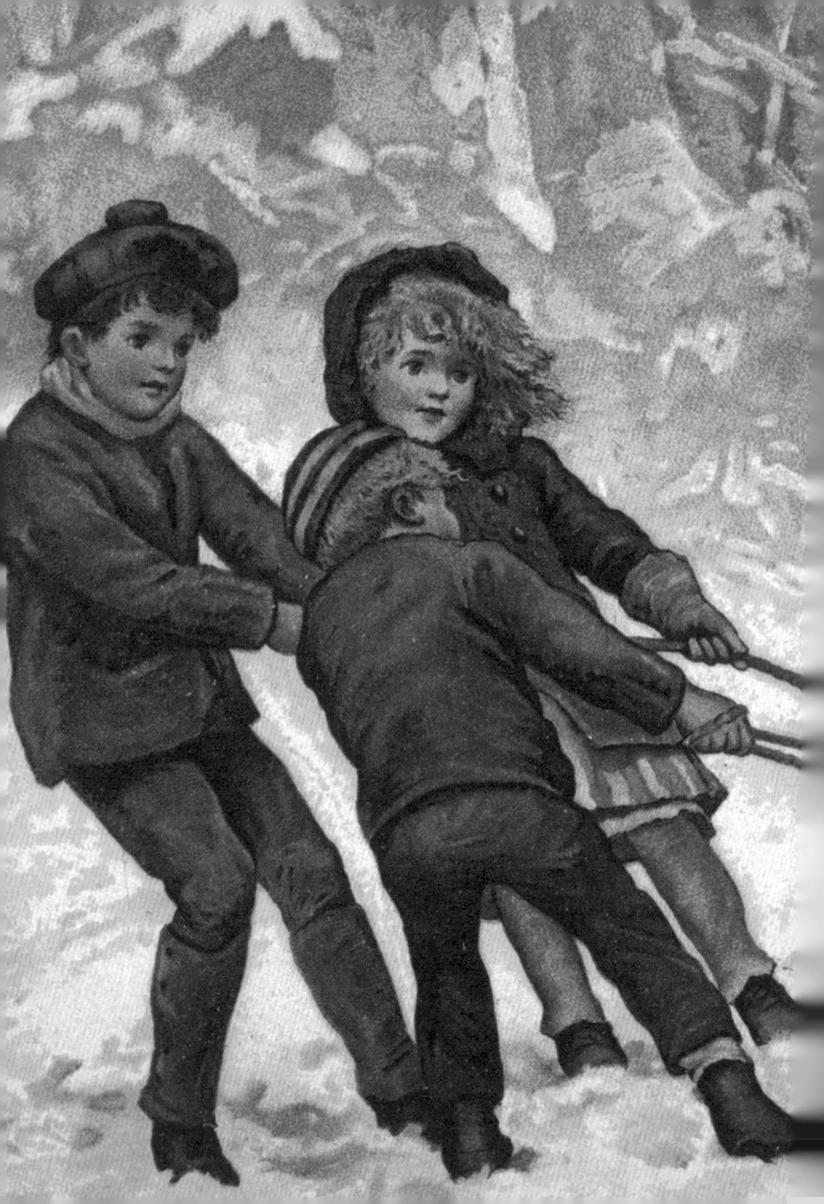

Come, bring with a noise,
My merry, merry boys,
The Christmas log to the firing.

from *Ceremonies for Christmas*, Robert Herrick

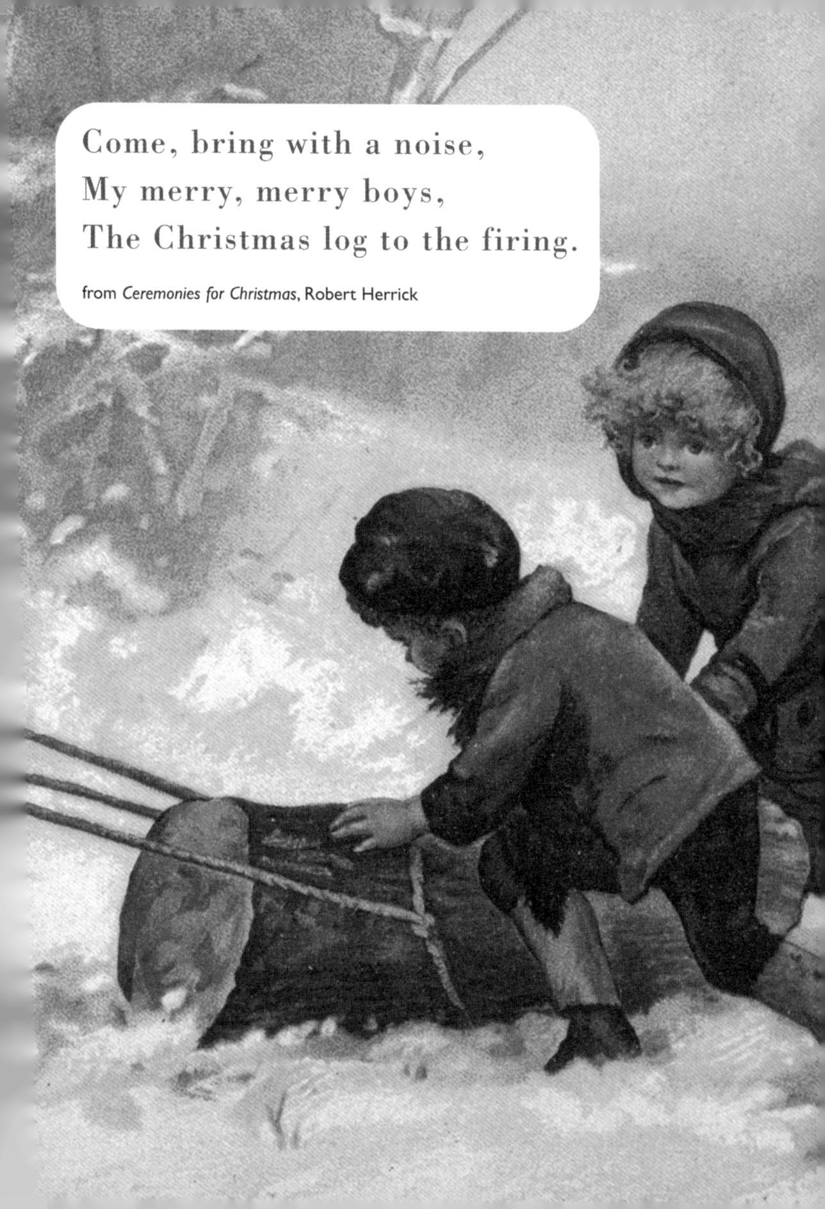

Buying and Storing Wood

An increasing number of people, many of whom live in centrally-heated houses in cities, are installing wood-burning, glass-doored stoves in their living rooms. A "real fire" is simply more friendly than a central-heating radiator.

Suddenly, these people are finding they need to buy and store large quantities of wood. But buying it in sackfuls from a local supplier on Saturday mornings is often expensive and inconvenient. It also can be counter-productive, because the wood may be so green and sap-wet that either it will not burn at all or it will produce very little heat.

Here are a few useful tips for buying and storing wood, which should help you to achieve a delightful, warm fire:

- **Find a local supplier who is reliable, both in the quality of his wood and, if your property is small, in his ability to deliver it all year round. Remember your wood should cost you considerably less than the equivalent amount of coal: there will be a great many air gaps in the load of wood delivered to you, and weight for weight, it produces much less heat than coal.**

- **If you have space in the backyard or garden to store it, it is a good idea to have your coming year's supply** ☞

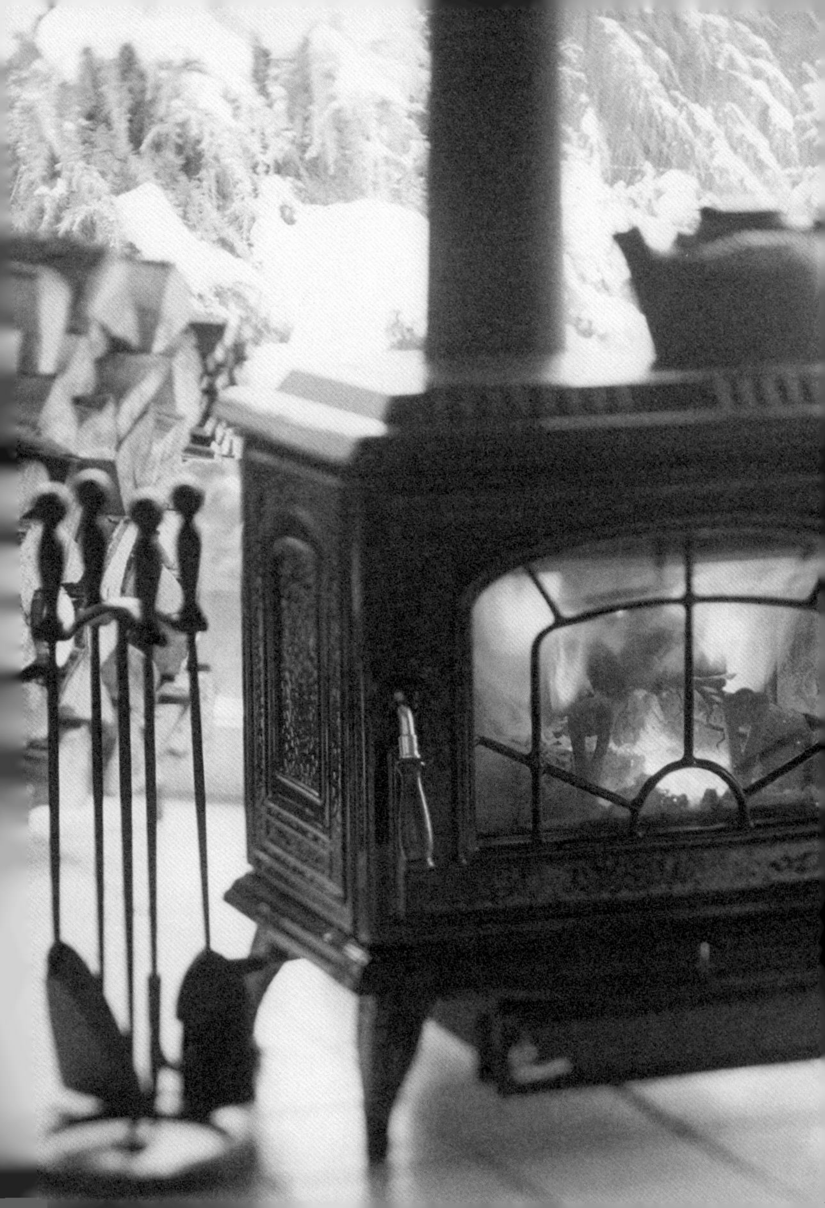

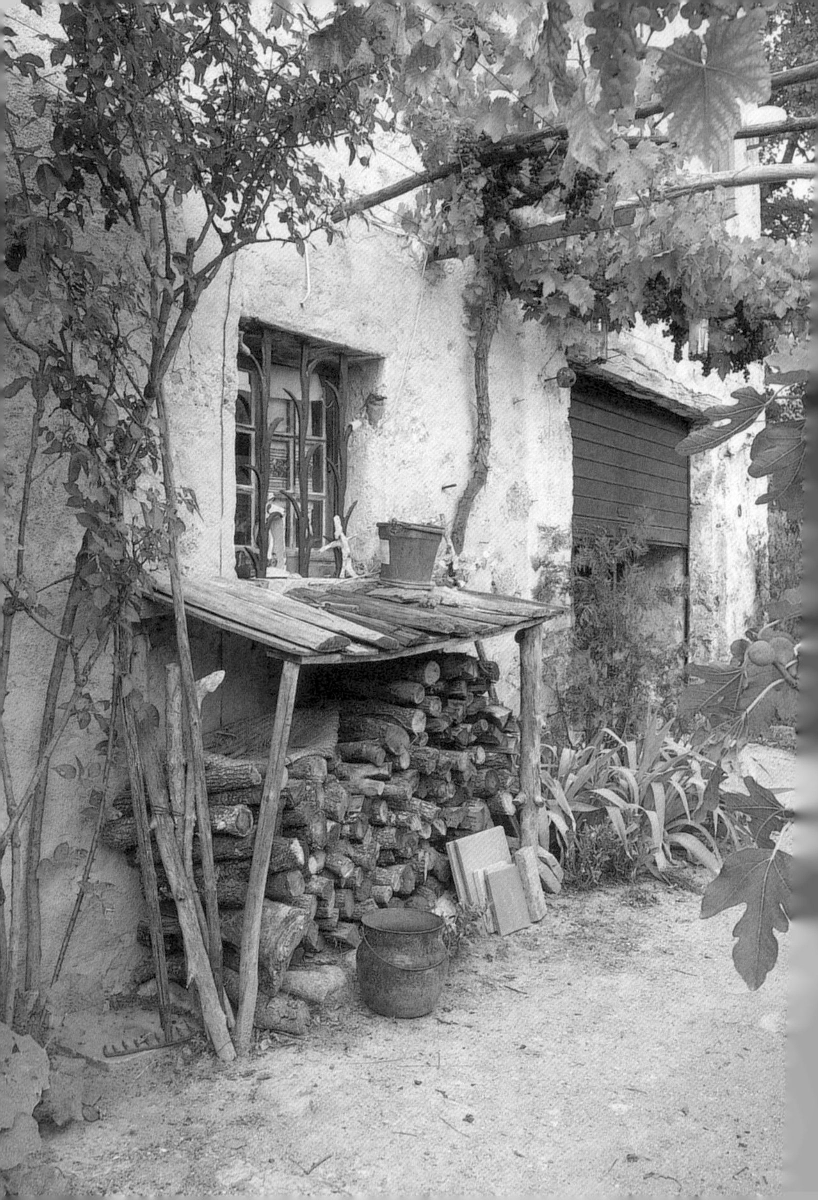

delivered in the spring. This will give it several months to dry out, if it is not air-dried when delivered, before you start using it.

- Try not to burn sap-wet wood on its own since it burns at a low temperature, causing the wood tar not to burn off. Instead, the tar deposits in a layer on the inner wall of the chimney flue. Over time, this reduces the size of the flue, reduces the fire's performance, and may even trap enough heat in the flue to set the tar alight. The consequent chimney fire could be very serious indeed.

- When they are delivered, chop or saw the logs into grate- or stove-friendly sizes and store them in a dry place outside. The wood should not be in an enclosed space, but rather stacked under a simple roof cover. Set them so the wind can blow under the cover and dry off any sap wetness still in the wood. You do not have to worry about the rain, because the wood's natural resin will prevent it from penetrating, and the wind will soon dry off any surface wetness.

- Have a good-size log basket or a built-in log store beside the fire, and keep it filled with enough dried logs from the stack outside for a whole evening's burning.

Recollections of a Tour Made in Scotland

by

DOROTHY WORDSWORTH

We entered by the cow-house, the house-door being within, at right angles to the other door. The woman was distressed that she had a bad fire, but she heaped up some dry peats and heather, and, blowing it with her breath, in a short time raised a blaze that scorched us into comfortable feelings. A small part of the smoke found its way out of the hole of the chimney, the rest through the open window-panes, one of which was in the recess of the fireplace, and made a frame to the little picture of the restless lake and the opposite shore, seen when the outer door was open....

On our return from Trosachs the evening had begun to darken, and it rained so heavily that we were completely wet before we had come two miles, and it was dark when we landed with our boatman, at his hut upon the banks of Loch Katrine. I was faint with cold: the good woman had provided, according to her promise, a better fire than we had found in the morning; and indeed when I sat down in the chimney corner of her smoky biggin' I thought I had never been more comfortable in my life. Coleridge had been there long enough to put a pan of coffee boiling for us, and having put our clothes in the way of drying, we all sat down, thankful for a shelter. We could not prevail on the man of the house to draw near the fire, though he was cold and wet, or to suffer his wife to get him dry clothes till she had served us, which she did, though most willingly, not very expeditiously....

He did not, however, refuse to let his wife bring out the whiskey-bottle for his refreshment at our request: "She keeps a dram," as the saying is; indeed, I believe there is scarcely a lonely house by the wayside in Scotland where travellers may not be accommodated with a dram. We asked for sugar, butter, barley-hand, and milk: and, with a smile and a stare more of kindness than wonder, she replied, "Ye'll get that," bringing each article separately.

We caroused our cups of coffee, laughing like children at the strange atmosphere in which we were; the smoke came in gusts, and spread along the walls and above our heads in the chimney, where the hens were roosting like light clouds in the sky. We laughed and laughed again, in spite of the smarting of our eyes, yet had quieter pleasure in observing the beauty of the beams and rafters gleaming between the clouds of smoke. They had been crusted over and varnished by many winters, till, where the firelight fell upon them, they were as glossy as black rocks on a sunny day cased in ice. When we had eaten our supper we sat about half an hour, and I think I had never felt so deeply the blessing of a hospitable welcome and a warm fire.

Safety Tips: Wood Stoves

- Check that your wood-burning stove is installed according to up-to-date building codes and manufacturer's instructions.

- Ensure the chimney and stovepipe are cleaned regularly by a professional chimney sweep. During the heating season check regularly for creosote buildup. Creosote is a normal by product of wood-burning stoves; it builds up in chimney flues and may cause a chimney fire. To lessen creosote buildup, avoid smoldering fires.

- The stove must be set on a non-combustible floor surface or on top of a code-specified or listed floor protector. This should extend 18in/45cm beyond the stove on all sides and will reduce the possibility of setting the floor alight.

- Position the stove at a safe distance from combustible walls. Also, follow the instructions on the stove label for the correct location.

- Any combustible items such as curtains, chairs, and firewood must be kept at least 3ft/1m away from the stove.

- Only use recommended fuel in the stove. Don't burn any trash in the stove, or use gasoline and other flammable liquids to start wood-stove fires. Gasoline will ignite and explode. If you do use coal, make sure it is approved by the manufacturer.

- Choose a metal container with a tight-fitting lid for removing ashes from the stove.

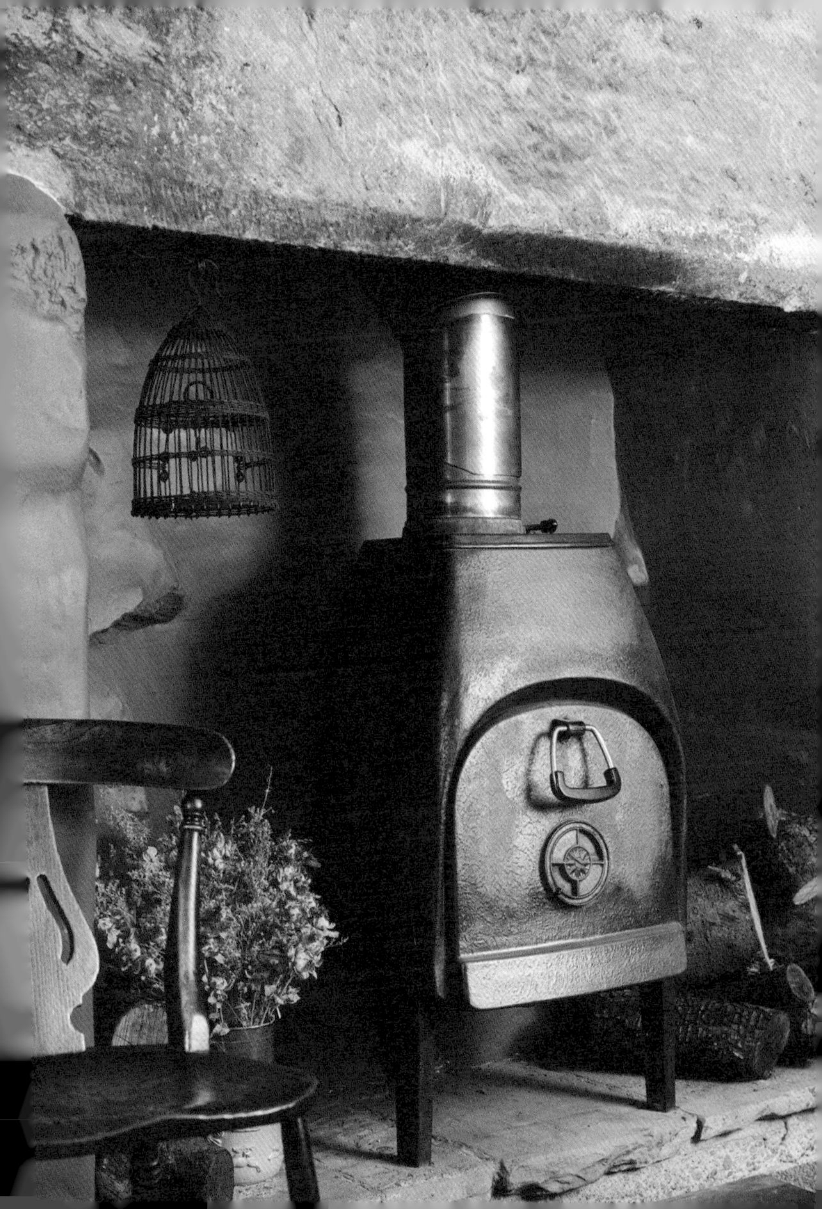

Sorting Your Firewood

Catharine E. Beecher and Harriet Beecher Stowe expected a lot from the women who read their 1869 book on household management, *The American Woman's Home*. As the following extract makes clear, they felt that every woman should know at a glance if the pile of wood delivered to her was the amount she ordered, so she wouldn't be cheated.

"Use green wood for logs, and mix green and dry wood for the fire; and then the wood-pile will last much longer. Walnut, maple, hickory, and oak wood are best; chestnut or hemlock is bad, because it snaps. Do not buy a load in which there are many crooked sticks. Learn how to measure and calculate the solid contents of a load, so as not to be cheated. A cord of wood should be equivalent to a pile eight feet long, four feet wide and four feet high; that is, it contains ($8 \times 4 \times 4 = 128$) one hundred and twenty-eight cubic or solid feet. A city 'load' is usually one third of a cord. Have all your wood split and piled under cover for winter. Have the green wood logs in one pile, dry wood in another, oven wood in another, kindlings and chips in another, and a supply of charcoal to use for broiling and ironing in another place. Have a brick bin for ashes, and never allow them to be put in wood."

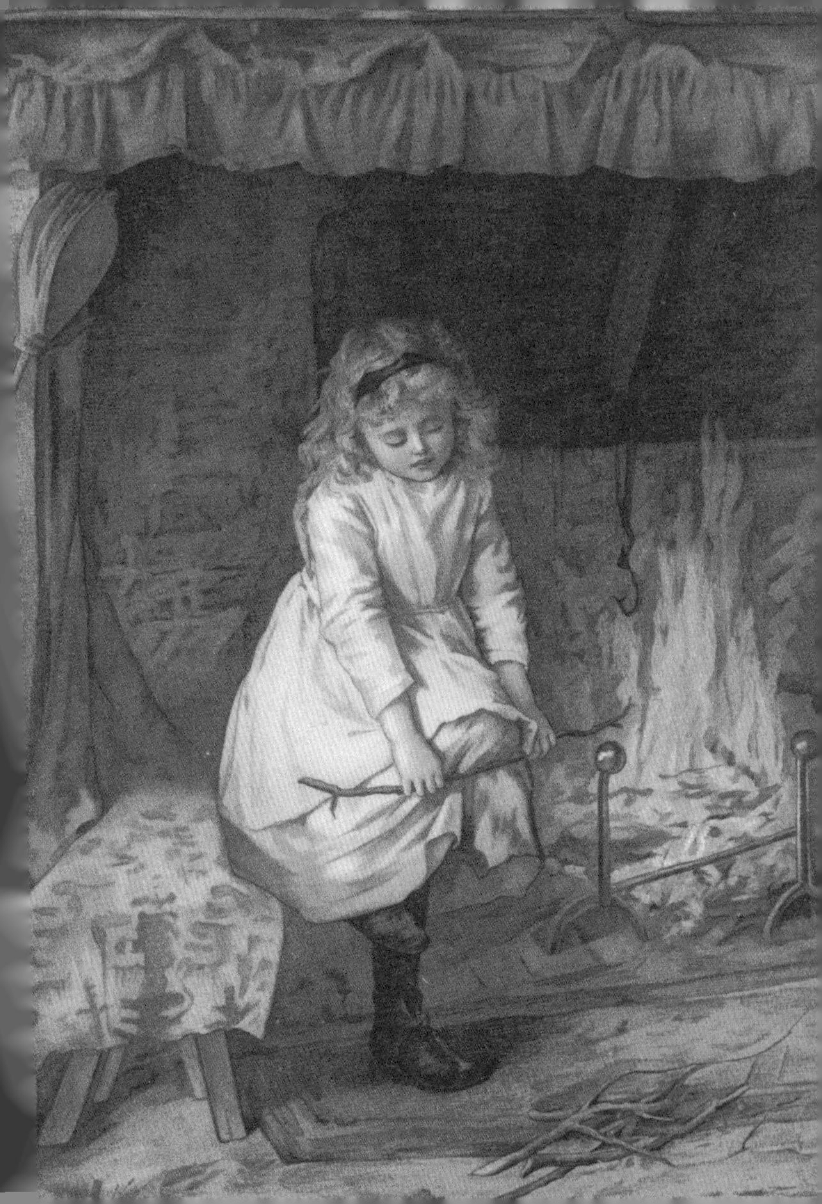

Choosing Firewood

Hickory makes the hottest coals in stoves when winter's bleak,
Apple wood like incense burning through the hall both
> *fragrance seek,*
Elm wood fires have little smoke and warm both serf and lord,
Oak logs split and dried this year make good next winter's hoard,
Beech burns bright and fills a room with warmth
> *and dancing light,*
Maple sweet, not white or red will burn throughout the night,
Birch logs cut, need ne'er be stored—they blaze, then heat the pot,
Ash, straight grain and easy split—the kettle sings,
> *and stove is hot,*
Poplar logs must need be dried lest smoke both then ensue,
Pine and fir midst showers of sparks burn fast and line the
> *blackened flue.*

Traditional English Song

It has been said that a long straight row of firewood standing in the yard in springtime is like money in the bank. It is indeed. As it dries in the summer sunshine, you're collecting interest. There are so many choices when it comes to selecting the best firewood, and everyone has a favorite. However, practicality suggests you use whichever type of wood is most plentiful in your area, is easy to split, and doesn't cover your hands and clothes with sticky sap.

There are many types of wood used for burning, and, technically, it is possible to burn any kind. Pound for pound, all varieties have almost the same heat content, but hardwoods such as oak, beech, hornbeam, ash, and maple have greater densities than softwoods. They tend to burn longer, produce longer-lasting coals, and give off a good heat. Although they are greatly prized as firewoods, ecological considerations mean that hardwoods, which are very valuable and not always plentiful enough just to throw on the fire, are not always the most practical choice.

It is usually more cost effective to burn softer woods that are available in good quantities locally, such as birch, pine, or poplar, than to order up hardwoods from long distances away. In truth, there is not much difference between the heating capacities of hardwoods and softwoods. However, if you are burning softwoods, you will need to replenish the fire more often. Ultimately, it is more important to cut and split your wood to the right size and to properly dry it before you use it on your fire than to get the hardest wood available.

"Joss stick" Woods

Some woods and plants give off such delicious scents as they burn on the fire that it is as if you have thrown giant-size joss sticks onto it.

Woods to burn for wonderful scents turning your living room into an aromatic paradise include:

- **Apple wood**
- **Pearwood**
- **Olivewood**
- **Grape vine stems and branches cut back after harvest; these are a popular barbecue wood in the south of France.**

Shrubs, bushes, and plants that give off fragrant scents when burned include:

- **Lavender, burned in bundles of the dried plant**
- **Juniper**
- **Fennel (especially cuttings of the mature herb)**
- **Thyme (bundles of the bush cut back in fall and dried).**

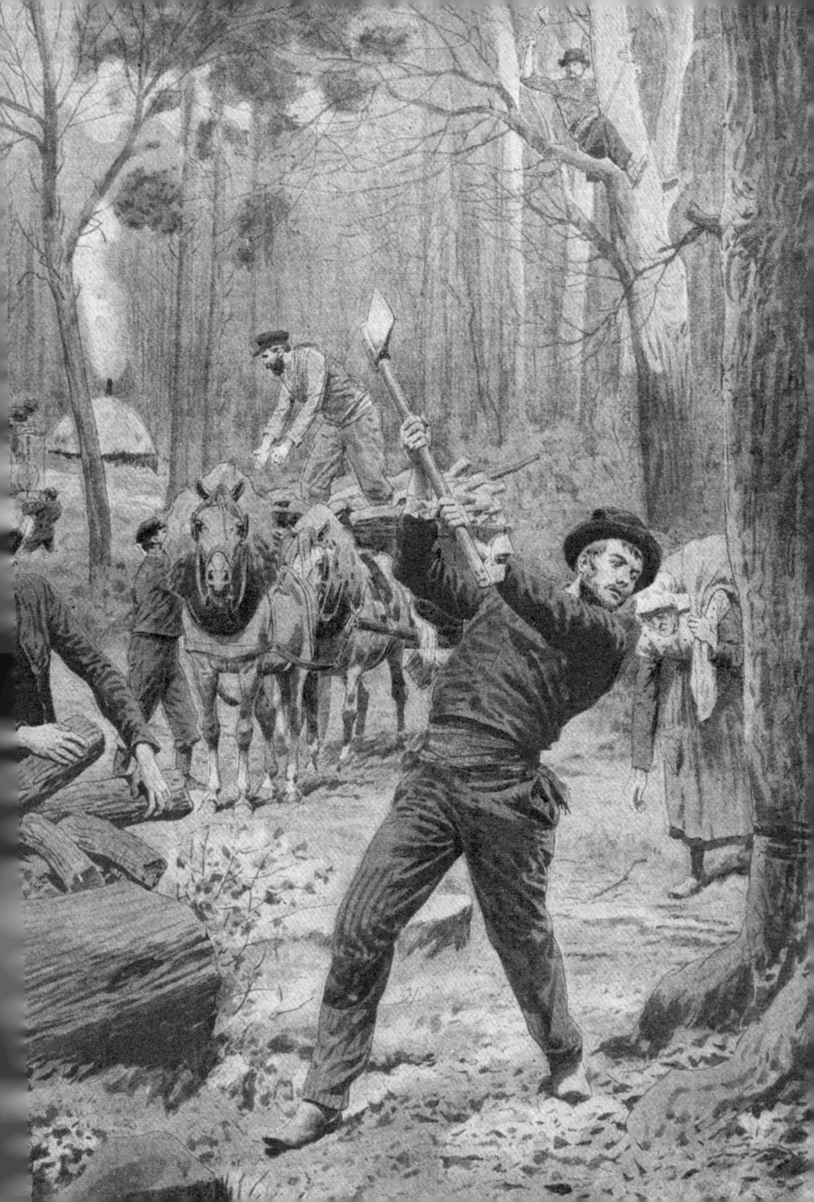

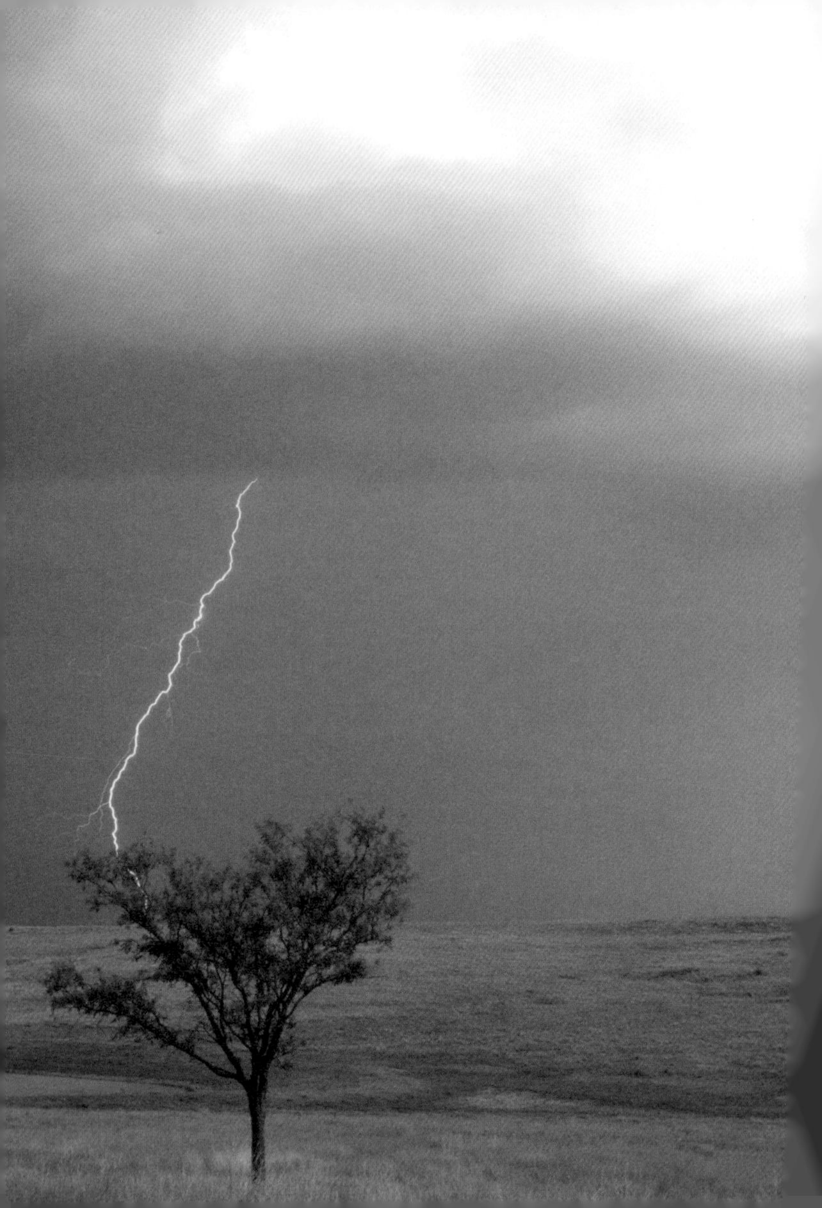

Woody Superstitions

TREES STRUCK BY LIGHTNING: In America, it is said that wood taken from a tree that has been struck by a bolt of lightning should never be burned on a domestic hearth as this will draw lightning toward the house itself.

Apparently, any fires started by lightning can be extinguished by pouring cow's milk over the flames!

ASH: In Scandinavian mythology the ash tree, or *Yggdrasil*, has roots that run in three directions, one to the Asa gods in heaven, a second to the Frost giants, and a third to the underworld. A fountain of wonderful virtues sits under each root, and an eagle, a squirrel, and four stags are said to live inside the tree, which also drips honey.

From this ancient mythology sprang many beliefs about the ash tree, most of them to do with the benign effects of the wood. It should not all be burned on the fire, but pieces should be kept because chips are very good for stopping nose bleeds and curing fevers, while an ash stick, burned at one end, will cure sores when the charred end is drawn in a circle round the sore.

WILLOW: It is believed that this wood should not be burned on the domestic hearth. This is partly because willow has long been associated with sorrow and lost love: think of Desdemona's sad song in Shakespeare's *Othello*, with its last lines:

"Sing willow, willow, willow:
Sing all a green willow must be my garland.
Let nobody blame him, his scorn I approve...."

Hansel and Gretel

by

THE BROTHERS GRIMM

Early in the morning, Gretel had to go out and hang up the cauldron with the water, and light the fire. "We will bake first," said the old woman, "I have already heated the oven, and kneaded the dough." She pushed poor Gretel out to the oven, from which flames of fire were already darting. "Creep in," said the witch, "and see if it is properly heated, so that we can put the bread in." And once Gretel was inside, she intended to shut the oven and let her bake in it, and then she would eat her, too. But Gretel saw what she had in mind, and said: "I do not know how I am to do it; how do I get in?" "Silly goose," said the old woman. "The door is big enough; just look, I can get in myself!" and she crept up and thrust her head into the oven. Then Gretel gave her a push that drove her far into it, and shut the iron door, and fastened the bolt. Oh! then she began to howl quite horribly, but Gretel ran away and the godless witch was miserably burnt to death.

Gretel, however, ran like lightning to Hansel, opened his little stable, and cried: "Hansel, we are saved! The old witch is dead!" Then Hansel sprang like a bird from its cage when the door is opened. How they did rejoice and embrace each other, and dance about and kiss each other!

143

Safety Tips: Open Fires

Countless people all over the world use fireplaces, wood stoves, and other fuel appliances to heat their homes, but many are unaware of the risks. Remember that fire safety is an important part of responsible enjoyment. You should be extremely careful with your open fire, whatever fuel you use, and consult a qualified professional if you need any help or advice.

- **Whatever fuel you use, coal or logs, have the chimney inspected annually and cleaned by a professional sweep if necessary, especially if it has not been used for some time. This prevents the buildup of soot or ash.**

- **Ensure proper ventilation and empty the ash in the bottom of the grate every day. A buildup reduces the ventilation under the fire and makes it less effective.**

- **Never use flammable liquids such as kerosene, gasoline, or oil, to start or accelerate any fire. Also, do not burn charcoal indoors—it can give off lethal amounts of carbon monoxide.**

- **Avoid using excessive amounts of paper to light roaring fires—the leaping flames can easily ignite deposits of creosote in the chimney.**

- **Hot ashes can be dangerous: never discard them inside or near the home. Put them in a metal container outside and well away from the home.**

- If you are using synthetic logs, follow the directions on the package. Avoid breaking one apart to quicken the fire and don't use more than one log at a time. They often burn unevenly, releasing higher levels of carbon monoxide.

- Place a securely fitted glass or metal fireguard screen in front of the fireplace to prevent embers or sparks from jumping out.

- Keep combustible materials well away from the fireplace. Stacks of old newspapers or magazines near the hearth, for example, could easily catch on fire.

- Don't throw household trash on an open fire—it might give off potentially toxic fumes.

- Never leave your fire unattended. Before you go to sleep, be sure your fire is out.

- Never close your damper while there are hot ashes in the fireplace. A closed damper will help the fire to heat up again and will force toxic carbon monoxide into the house.

- Place smoke detectors in appropriate places throughout your home, in case an accident does occur, and remember to check and replace the batteries regularly. Always follow the health and safety advice of the Fire Department.

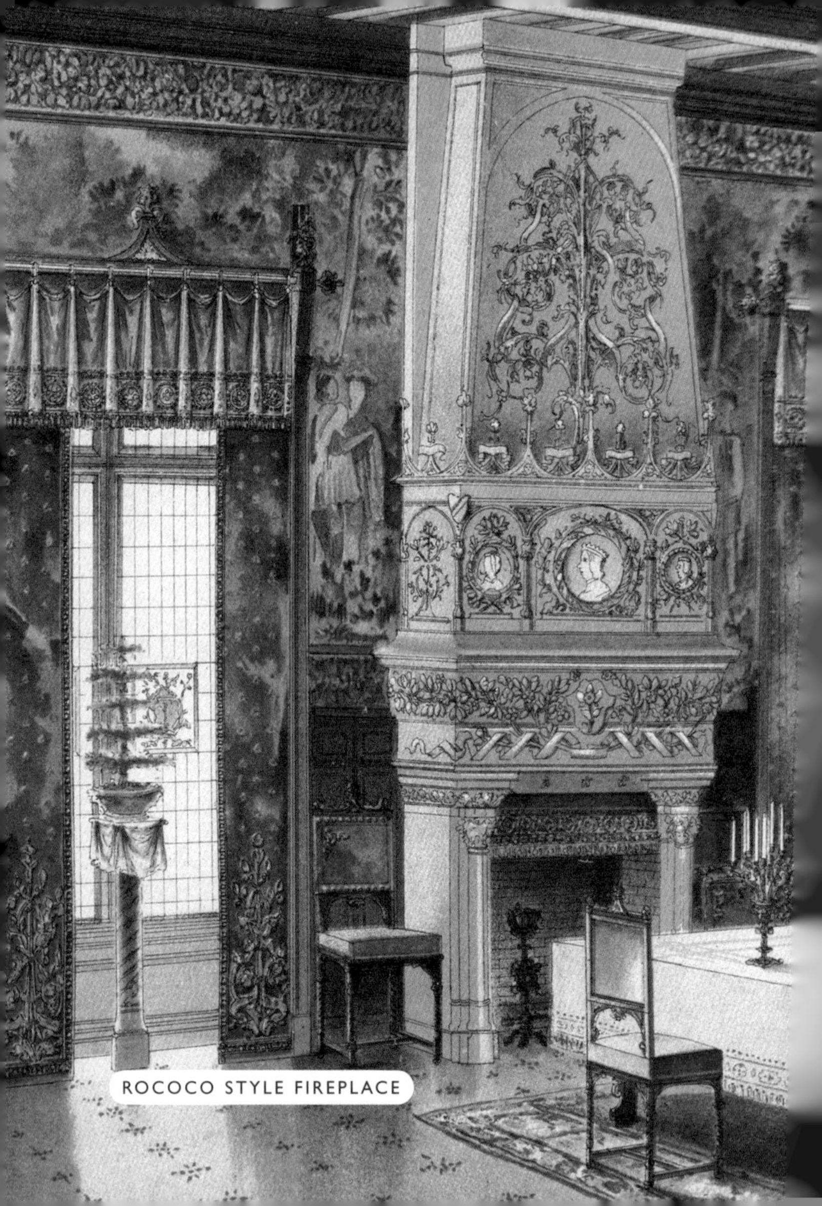

ROCOCO STYLE FIREPLACE

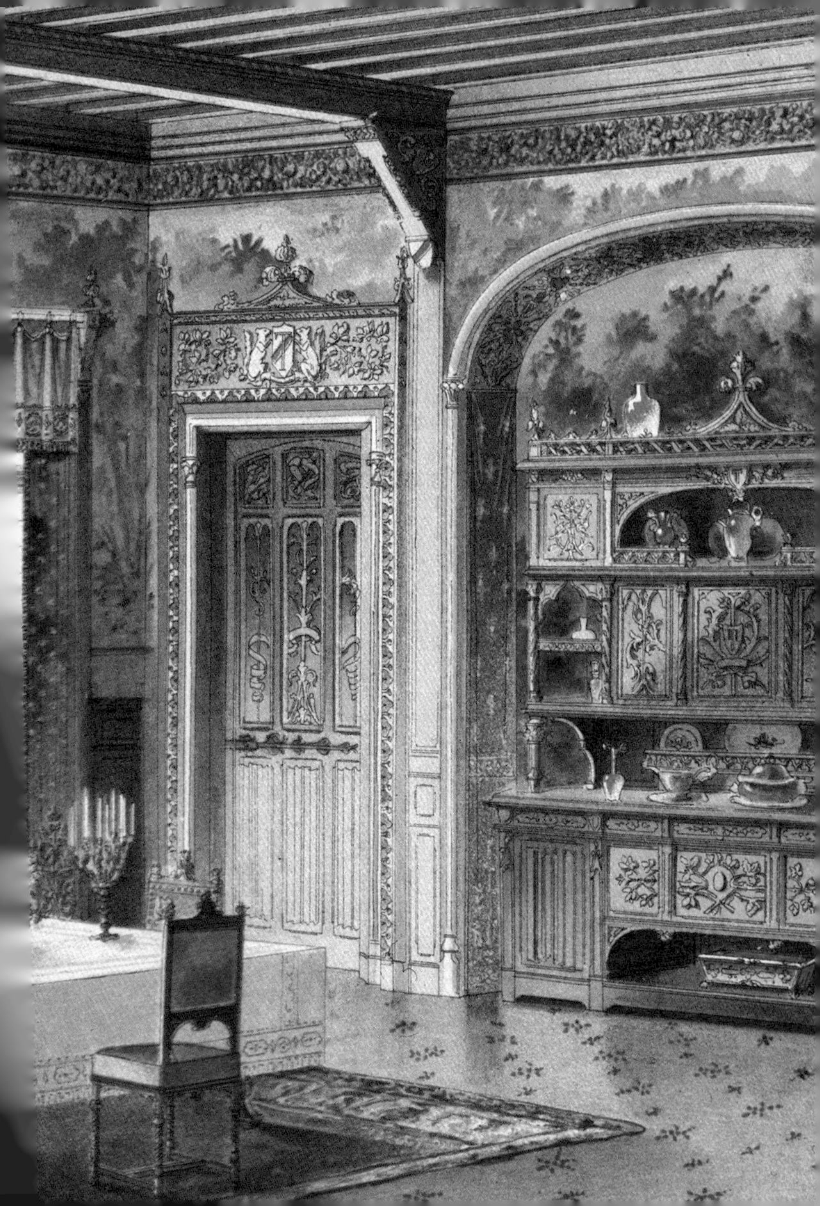

Fire Irons and Other Essentials

Advice to a chambermaid: "Oil the Tongs, Poker and Fire-shovel up to the Top not only to keep them from rusting, but likewise to prevent meddling people from wasting your master's coal with stirring the fire."

from *Directions to Servants*, Jonathan Swift

Fire Irons

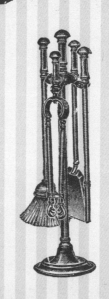

Three fireside tools—tongs, a poker, and a shovel—were essential metal items on every hearth. They were first made in matching sets in the late seventeenth century, and are still manufactured in the same style today. Old fire irons, particularly if they are well designed and decorated, are sought-after antiques. Sets of fire irons on a specially-built stand are usually called fireside companions.

The shovels are usually the most attractive items of the set, because their flat bases allowed metalworkers to elaborately decorate them.

Fenders

Fenders first appeared around hearths in English houses in the seventeenth century. Designed primarily to hold embers and ashes within the hearth, they became increasingly ornate in the eighteenth century. The finest were pierced and engraved iron, steel, and brass masterpieces displaying the metalworker's art. Later, in the Victorian period, fenders grew in height, and some were large enough to have leather-padded rails as casual fireside seating.

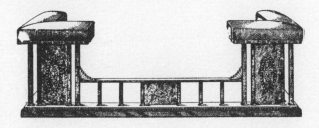

Coal Scuttles

Usually made of brass, iron, or wood, the coal scuttle, box, or hod was another essential fireside item. It kept the coal within reach but with its dust and dirt under cover. Most had removable interior containers and a small shovel hooked on the back for putting the coal on the fire. Some large and ornate fenders of the Victorian age included what looked like leather-covered box seats at either end; the leather tops lifted up to reveal coal stored in metal boxes inside. ☞

☞ Coal scuttles set by the drawing-room fire were often elegantly made and decorated. There are even historical examples of some nobles in the nineteenth century having their coronets, crests, or other badges of honor painted on their coal scuttles.

Trivets

"Right as a trivet!" This familiar phrase has nothing to do with things having three legs. Instead it acknowledges that something is perfectly right, and it refers to the fact that the trivet's three legs give it stability.

In the kitchen, trivets tended to be plain, flat metal plates on three short legs for use under a hot dish. Those intended for the drawing room hearth were often elegantly designed pierced brass stands that were placed underneath kettles. Occasionally, these trivets actually had four legs, in which case, they were called "footmen."

Another form of trivet was a bracket designed with three hooks or projections so that it could be hung from the bars of the grate, or from the fender, where it could hold a plate of hot toast or other foods.

Bellows

Bellows are instruments for producing a current of air to blow a low fire back to life. The best-known types of bellows are basically accordions of either leather or heavy paper with two handles for pulling them open and shut to produce air. Some grander drawing and living rooms had stylish brass rotary-fan bellows sitting in the hearth. They had a wheel to turn a fan with several blades inside the machine.

Perhaps because of their link with the mystical power of the fire, bellows feature in a number of superstitious beliefs. Giving bellows as a wedding present or lending them out to others is considered to be very bad luck by some superstitious people. Others believe that leaving a pair of bellows on a table will lead to a domestic argument or even a death in the household. On the positive side, one ancient English belief is that leaning against a pair of bellows will benefit anyone suffering with rheumatism.

Fireside Superstitions

Perhaps because it has been so essential for people to keep their home fires burning across the centuries, quite a few superstitions have developed concerning fireside etiquette, sustaining the fire, and using the fire irons.

The most common group of superstitions involved placing the poker in the fireplace at a particular angle to help the fire to burn well. Some superstitious English people also placed their poker perpendicularly up at a right angle to the grate so the bars formed a cross. It was believed that this would drive witches away from the home.

Others set the poker and tongs across one another in the hearth to make the fire burn. This was supposed to bless the fire by the sign of the cross and induce it to burn.

This practice lasted in some places in England well into the twentieth century. As late as the 1980s, an eighty-year-old woman was reported as putting "a poker up against the fire to draw it up. I done it hundreds of times—and a bit of paper over the poker."

Another myth claimed that holding a poker could also help ward off witchcraft: When a person had a poker in his or her hand, a witch could not harm them.

The act of poking the fire also drew numerous superstitions. Some said the nature of a girl's future husband could be divined from the way the fire acted when she poked it. If the fire burned bright when she stirred it, it was a sign she would have a brisk husband—or, in other parts of the country, a good-humored one. To some girls, the fire burning brightly after being poked was a sign their sweetheart was on the way.

Whatever their beliefs, most girls knew to be careful when poking the fire. Turning a coal right over while poking the fire was generally believed to bring bad luck.

Another group of beliefs revolved around the acceptability of stirring another person's fire—although this was as much about etiquette as superstition. Many people believed you had to be a friend of the household for at least seven years before you dared stir the fire. Or that you should never poke your neighbor's fire until you've known him for seven years or been drunk with him at least three times.

There was probably also a practical reason underlying this superstition. Coal was very expensive, and there were few things more annoying to a householder than seeing his carefully built fire being ruined by an inconsiderate outsider!

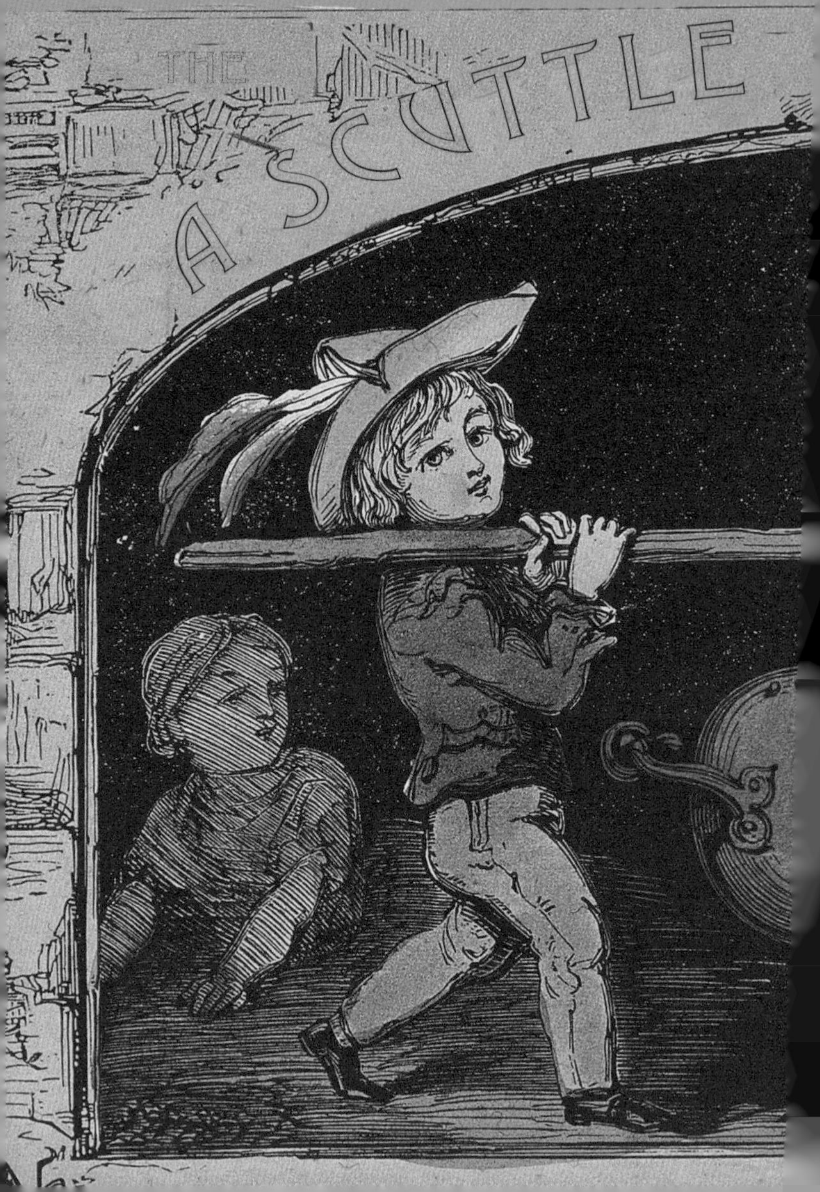
THE
A SCUTTLE

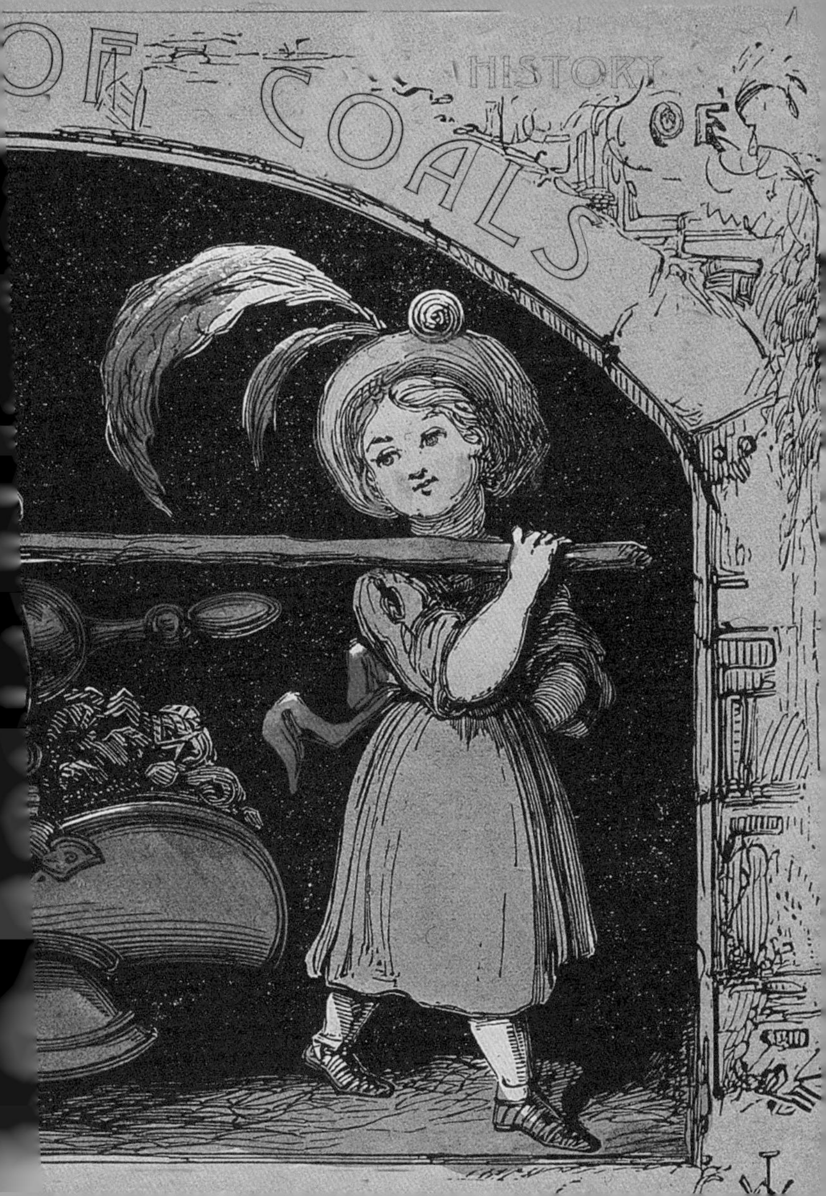
HISTORY
OF
COALS

Artistic Stoves

In the years when Paris was the center of the art world, several districts were virtually given over to artists' studios. Whether the men and women who rented them were successful enough to afford the luxuries of the good life or were so poor they lived on beans and what they could beg from their friends, their studios had one thing in common: a wood-burning stove, with a very long pipe issuing from it.

The stove was *almost* as important to the artists as their paints and canvases. When the young and very poor Claude Monet and Pierre-Auguste Renoir were sharing a studio in Paris in the early 1860s, fuel for their stove was essential because it kept their models warm. If they could not afford to keep their stove alight, many of their models would have refused to come and sit for them. For months, the two artists lived on only beans and lentils, which they cooked on top of their stove.

The standard artist's studio stove was a straight-sided, cast-iron cylinder, set on three feet and with a door in the front and a large pipe issuing from the back, near the top. This pipe would rise up toward the ceiling and then bend across the wall, sometimes going around two or three walls of the studio before reaching its vent out into the air. Another, cheaper type of stove, common in the mid-twentieth century, was made of tin and was shaped like a petrol can set on its side.

Both types of stove were very efficient. One relatively small stove with a long, hot pipe could warm a fairly large studio. A kettle of water was always kept on top of the stove, and the pipes were often used for drying clothes and bedding. Wood was the the least expensive fuel, though wealthier artists might have had a scuttle of coal beside their stove. Unlike the poet hero of Puccini's opera, *La Bohème*, who burned his manuscripts for warmth, an artist would have to be desperate to burn any of his paintings or drawings—they might find a buyer or at least someone willing to take a picture as payment for food or rent one day. Unsatisfactory paintings could always be painted over and the canvas used again.

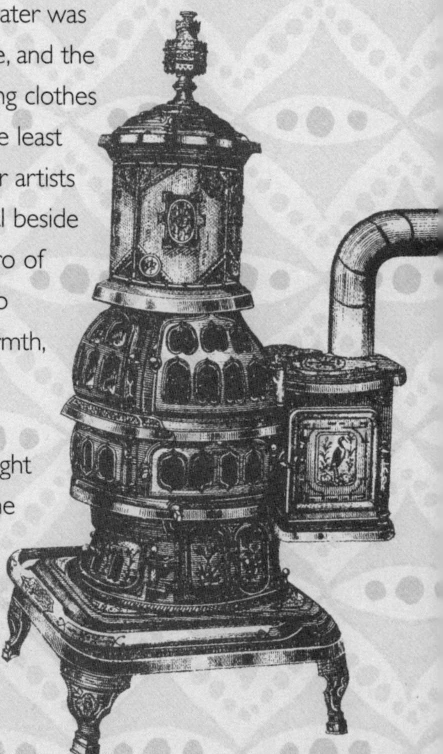

Burning Coal in the Fire

Coal is a relatively recent fuel for fireplaces and cooking stoves. The Romans knew nothing of it, instead using wood for their fires and oil for their lamps. In Britain, wood and, in some parts of the country, peat were plentiful and easy to get, so coal was rarely used.

Coal first gained importance in Britain through a charter granted by King Henry III to the city of Newcastle in 1272. This charter gave the citizens of Newcastle the right to dig for coal. Although coal was then distributed across the country, it was seen as little more than an item for the well-off to boast about before the Industrial Revolution.

By the reign of Charles I, in 1625, coal was in common use in towns and

cities across Britain. Within a few years of his son, Charles II, becoming King, London alone was burning about 200,000 chaldrons (an ancient measure for coal) every year. In the following century, coal would fire the Industrial Revolution that made Britain one of the world's wealthiest countries.

Mrs. Beeton, writing in the mid-nineteenth century, was able to name numerous types of coal available for use in the Victorian home, including pit, culm, slate, cannel, Kilkenny, sulphurous, bovey, and jet, all of them with "their specific differences," but all used as fuel.

At about the time when Mrs. Beeton was writing, many middle-size town houses burned a ton of coal a month—less in the summer, when only the kitchen range, which supplied the household with hot water as well as cooking facilities, was kept going all day. The coal was stored in a cellar, often built out under the pavement in the street, so the coalman did not have to heave his dirty sacks of coal into the house: he had only to lift a heavy metal coalhole cover set in the pavement and empty his sack down it.

Coals for the Fire

"And I have reason to believe there are good Coals also, for Observ'd, the Runs of Water have the same color as that which proceeds from the Coal-Mines in Wales."

Gabriel Thomas, Pennsylvania, 1698

Gabriel Thomas was right. There turned out to be bigger coal reserves in North America than anywhere else in the world, except Siberian Russia. Wood, being plentiful, was at first the most important fuel in the early days of colonial America. It was not until the end of the eighteenth century that grates and stoves began replacing wood-burning hearths in American house

By the time Harriet Beecher Stowe and her sister Catharine E. Beecher were writing their enormously influential book *The American Woman's Home*, first published in 1869, the use of coal was widespread enough to write about it in some detail:

"For those who use anthracite coal, that which is broken or screened is best for grates, and the nut-coal for small stoves. Three tons are sufficient in the Middle States, and four tons in the Northern, to keep one fire through the winter. That which is bright, hard, and clean is best; and that which is soft, porous, and covered with damp dust is poor. It will be well to provide two barrels of charcoal for kindling to every ton of anthracite coal. Grates for bituminous coal should have a flue nearly as deep as the grate; and the bars should be round and not close together. The better draught there is, the less coal-dust is made. Every grate should be furnished with a poker, shovel, tongs, blower, coal-scuttle, and holder for the blower. The latter may be made of woolen, covered with old silk; and hung near the fire…Coal-stoves should be carefully put up, as cracks in the pipe, especially in sleeping rooms, are dangerous."

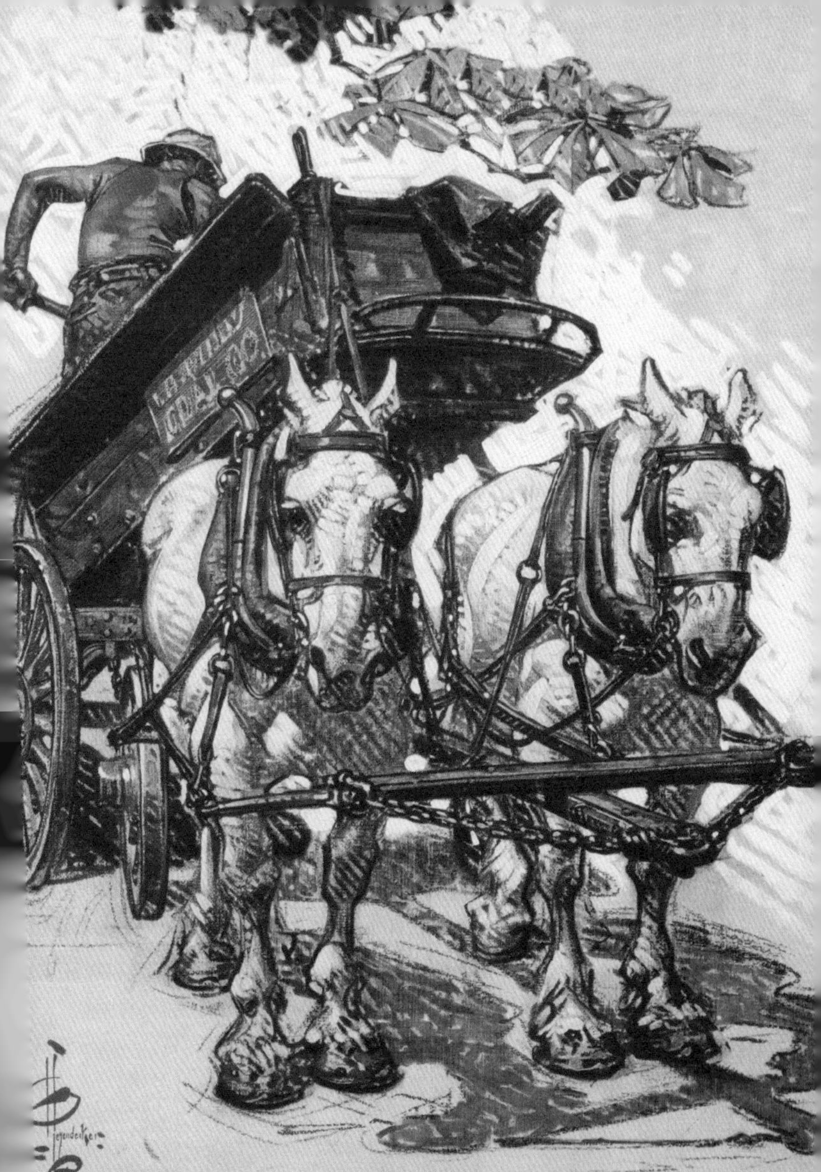

Laying and Raking Coal Fires

Very little has changed in the method of laying and lighting a coal fire since the nineteenth century. So we can still follow the method carefully outlined in 1861 by Mrs. Isabella Beeton in *The Book of Household Management*:

"Fire-lighting, however simple, is an operation requiring some skill; a fire is readily made by laying a few cinders at the bottom [of the grate] in open order; over this a few pieces of paper, and over that again, eight or ten pieces of dry wood; over the wood, a course of moderate-sized pieces of coal, taking care to leave hollow spaces between for air at the centre; and taking care to lay the whole well back in the grate, so that the smoke may go up the chimney, and not into the room. This done, fire the paper with a match from below, and, if properly laid, it will soon burn up; the stream of flame from the wood and paper soon communicating to the coals and cinders, provided there is plenty of air at the centre."

The debris left at the bottom of a coal fire after it had burned for some time could be divided into cinders and ashes. Cinders were good, ashes were useless. Saving the one and setting aside the other for the dustman were important tasks for thrifty housewives and housemaids.

The kitchen fire was usually raked late at night, just before the family went to bed. This was to ensure the cinders, which were the small remnants of coal that no longer burned with a flame, remained warm in the grate with any remaining lumps of coal. The ashes were removed so they did not smother the coal and stop the fire from burning properly.

In houses with drawing room and bedroom fires, the grate would be raked. The ashes and cinders that had fallen through the grate would be shoveled out every morning into a bucket or box with a wire sieve in it. The bucket was then shaken or rubbed so the ashes fell through the sieve, but the cinders remained on top. This method of separating the cinders and the ashes was called riddling. The cinders collected would then be put on the kitchen range fire to make a base for other fuel.

Some of the cinders collected may have been studied with extra care the evening before. Several superstitions were woven around the shapes of cinders that fell on the hearth. Young women were in the forefront of this sort of divination: spot a heart-shaped cinder on the hearth and a new lover would be expected to appear. A cinder shaped like a purse suggested that riches, or at least, some money, was in store. A coffin-shaped cinder was obviously a bad thing, while a round, hollow cinder indicated the arrival of a baby.

Cinderella's Fireside

The story of Cinderella, heroine of Charles Perrault's delightful fairy tale, is the perfect rags-to-riches romance. Cinderella, far more lovely than her step sisters, is banished to the kitchen to be a household drudge. Dirty from the dust and smoke of the kitchen fire, she is kept out of sight while her sisters go to balls and parties. Then appears a fairy godmother who magically converts a pumpkin to a coach and mice to footmen. She dresses Cinderella in beautiful clothes and sends her off to a ball, where, of course, a handsome prince falls in love with her—and loses her when the clock strikes midnight.

Cinderella is eventually found in the kitchen, and identified because only her dainty foot will fit the glass slipper that she lost when she fled the ballroom.

No matter that the glass slipper is a mistranslation of Perrault's original *pantoufle en vair* (fur slipper), the story continues to capture the imagination of children as much today as in the seventeenth century when it was written. It remains one of the most popular fairy tales of all time.

Much of this is, surely, because Cinderella is banished to the kitchen—a dirty, hellishly fiery and smoky place, which is, nevertheless, essential to a household's comfort and wellbeing. This gives it a particular resonance in a story of romantic love.

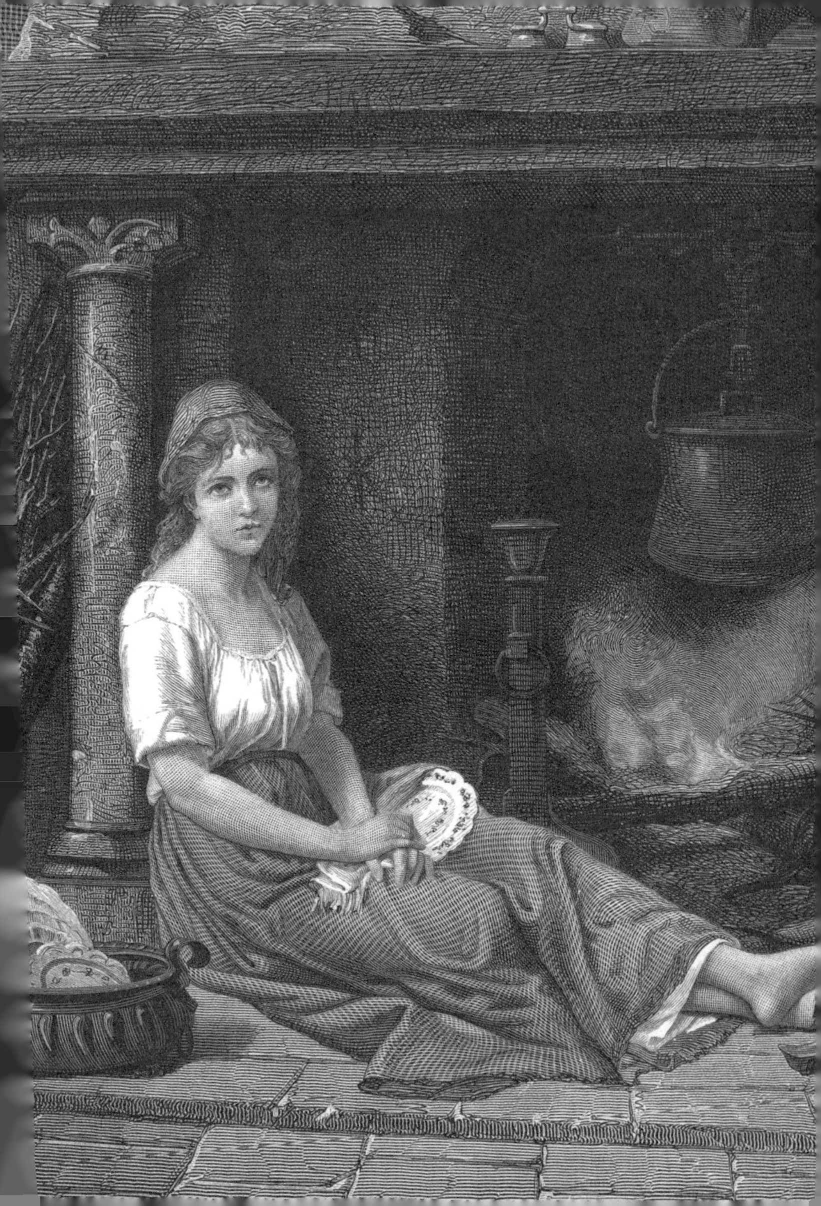

Cindererlla

by

CHARLES PERRAULT

She scoured the dishes, tables, etc., and cleaned madam's chamber, and those of misses, her daughters. She slept in a sorry garret, on a wretched straw bed, while her sisters slept in fine rooms, with floors all inlaid, on beds of the very newest fashion, and where they had looking glasses so large that they could see themselves at their full length from head to foot.

The poor girl bore it all patiently, and dared not tell her father, who would have scolded her; for his wife governed him entirely. When she had done her work, she used to go to the chimney corner, and sit down there in the cinders and ashes, which caused her to be called Cinderwench. Only the younger sister, who was not so rude and uncivil as the older one, called her Cinderella. However, Cinderella, notwithstanding her coarse apparel, was a hundred times more beautiful than her sisters, although they were always dressed very richly.

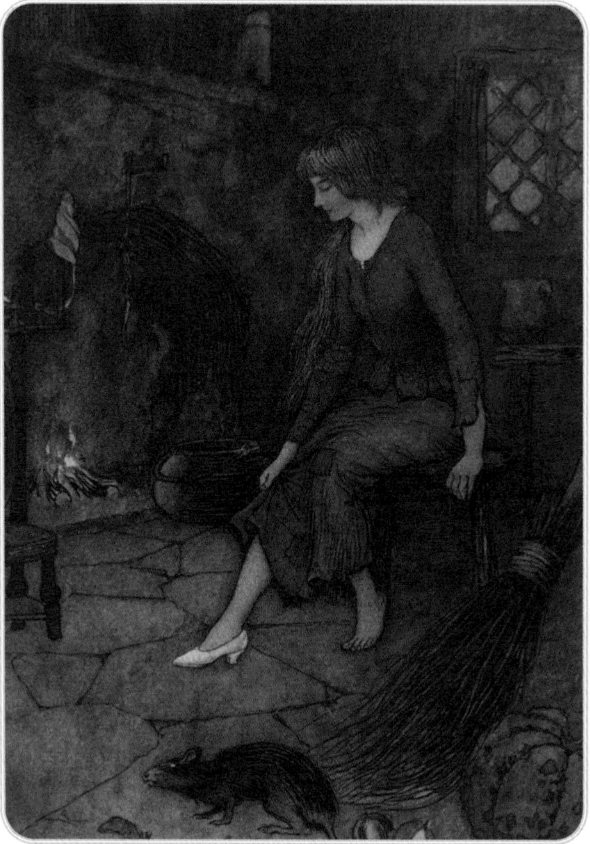

Coal Speak and Superstitions

There are many sayings in English that are given extra strength because they use coal as a metaphor. For instance:

- To "carry coals" means to be put upon. This is an allusion to the laborious and dirty occupation of coal-heavers.

- To "carry coals to Newcastle" means to do something superfluous or unnecessary: there is already plenty of coal in Newcastle since it sits on one of the world's great coal fields.

- In Victorian times "coal" was slang for cash in the sporting world. "To post the coal" meant to pay or put down the cash.

- "Coal brandy" was "burned brandy." An ancient way to set brandy on fire was to drop a live or red-hot coal in it.

- To "heap coals of fire" on someone means to wipe away animosity by doing deeds of kindness. The saying is based on verses from the second book of Proverbs in the King James Version of the Bible: "If thine enemy be hungry, give him bread to eat, and if he be thirsty, give him water to drink, for thou shalt heap coals of fire upon his head."

- To "rake someone over the coals" means to criticize their shortcomings, or to scold them. In medieval times in England it could mean a lot worse than this! Jews were "bled" if ever the king or barons needed money, and a common means of "persuading" those who resisted such demands was to haul them over the coals of a slow fire, to give them a "roasting."

- In Walter Scott's *Ivanhoe*, the villain Front-de-Boeuf threatened to rake Isaac over the coals.

As for coal and superstition, there are a couple of actions that could benefit us all if we followed them:

- One common superstition is that it is lucky to carry a lump of coal in your pocket. From burglars going out on a job to "first footers" at Hogmanay in Scotland (the first guests to arrive at midnight on New Year's Eve), carrying a piece of coal is considered the best chance of attracting good luck.

- Another common coal superstition is similar to a well-known superstition about salt: if a piece of coal is dropped on the road by a coalman delivering it, the first person who comes along should pick it up, spit on it, throw it over their left shoulder, and make a wish.

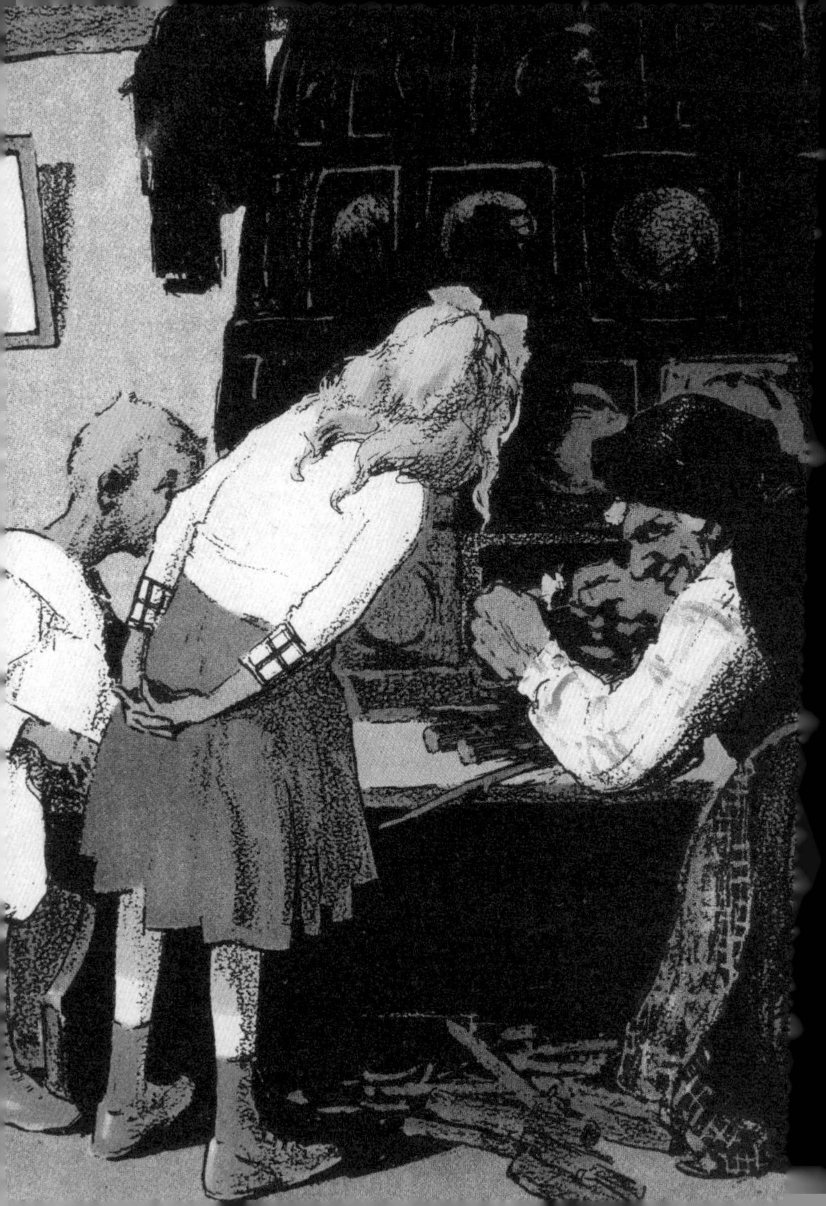

Fire Lighters

When man first made fire, he rubbed two sticks together until the friction caused one or both to smoke and then burst into flames. Since then, many ingenious ways of creating a flame have been invented. Here are a few of the most popular ways of lighting domestic fires.

MATCHES: Basically a flame on a small wooden, or sometimes wax, stick, the friction match was invented in England in the early nineteenth century. It involved tipping the stick with a chemical substance which, when rubbed on a rough surface, produced a flame. Although the match soon turned up in America as well, neither country used it much at first. It was expensive and not widely available. But it was not long before the safety match was being made in countless numbers and matchboxes became collectors' items.

BRANDS: Pieces of burning wood, taken from the fire with special brand tongs, and used to light candles or tapers.

TAPER: A very thin, candle-like wax stick with a wick down the center, used to take a flame from a fire or candle and use it to light other candles or lamps.

TINDER: A means of lighting a fire before matches. It involved using a material such as wood to catch the spark made by a flint and steel being struck together. Tinders were kept in a tinderbox, which was usually fitted with a flint and steel. Striking a light from the tinderbox was not easy, and most households preferred to keep their fire alive all night and blow the embers back to life with bellows in the morning.

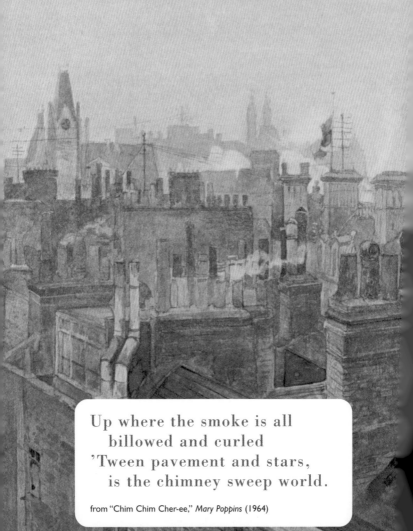

Up where the smoke is all
billowed and curled
'Tween pavement and stars,
is the chimney sweep world.

from "Chim Chim Cher-ee," *Mary Poppins* (1964)

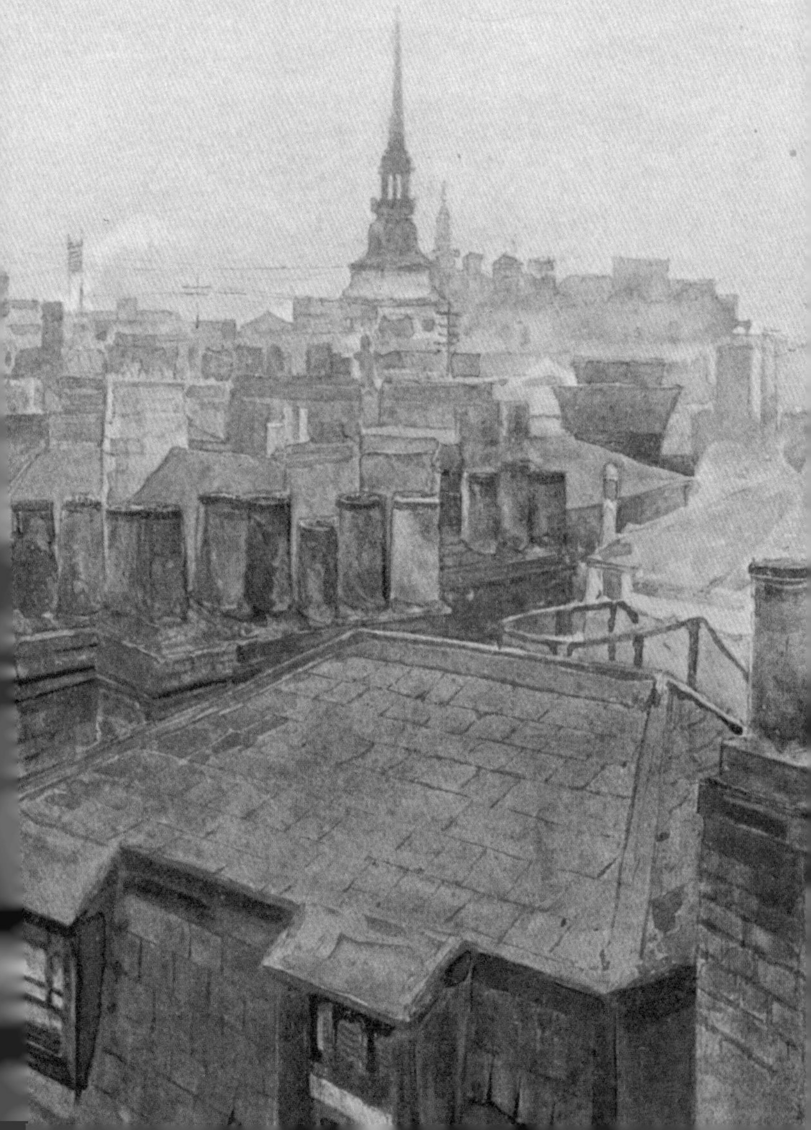

Sweeping the Chimney

"Sweep! Sweep Ho! Sweep!"
While quiet and warm in our beds we remain,
The Sweep trudges on, through the snow or the rain;
Though cold and half-naked, the storm he defies—
Employment his object—"Sweep! Soot ho!" he cries.

from Sam Syntax's Cries of London

The chimney sweep, his coal-blackened brushes over his shoulder, was a familiar figure trudging along city streets, shouting out his familiar cry of "Sweep Ho!" until well into the twentieth century—though by the outbreak of the First World War he had long been doing his rounds on a bicycle.

In the days when many houses, large and small, had open fires in the drawing room or living room, and also in bedrooms in winter, and all-year-round closed-fire cooking stoves in the kitchen, the chimney sweep was a busy man. Wintertime fires needed to have their flues swept every spring, and the flues of all-year-round fires were generally cleaned at least twice a year. Neglecting to sweep chimneys regularly, so that a layer of soot built up inside, could—and very often did—cause fires inside the chimney stack, often with disastrous consequences.

Many chimney sweeps had long lists of houses they visited

regularly, so they often became familiar figures in the home, known to both household staff and members of the family. The London *Daily Express* columnist Nathaniel Gubbins included a sweep as one of the regular characters in his column, which began appearing in Britain in 1930. He got the idea for the character partly from his mother's chimney sweep and partly from the sweep in his village, a "staunch Conservative" whose favorite oath was "Cor, stone the crows."

The sweep, having been banned from using very small boys as cleaners inside chimneys by a law of 1829, began using telescopic or expanding brushes, and by the mid-nineteenth century most chimney sweeping was done mechanically. Later, specially adapted vacuum cleaners took over the work of getting the soot and dust from the chimney and its flues.

People are often surprised to learn that there are many chimney sweeps working in America and Britain today. Their services are still in great demand to help prevent housefires related to fireplaces, heating systems, and chimneys. Now they are qualified members of large national organizations that encourage professionalism, ethical accountability, and high safety standards. Modern sweeps can now also attend conventions and trade shows to discuss new innovations in the industry.

Sweeps' Luck

"Now, as custom is, off went our bonnets...to a chimney sweep, sitting cross-legged, tailor-wise, on the rough plank of a shabby pony cart. It is said to bring luck...."

from *The Brighton Gazette*, September 1887

Chimney sweeps have long been a symbol of good luck. Meeting one in the street was thought by many to bring good fortune—provided certain customs were observed. A person who sees a chimney sweep must be very polite—bowing or taking off his hat or saying "Good morning" three times (and perhaps even turning around three times having said it).

Some people also believe that seeing a chimney sweep on their wedding day brings good luck. However, if the bride sees only the sweep's back before the marriage ceremony, then the couple will have bad luck instead.

Perhaps this is why, or so it was reported, that on the morning of the marriage of Princess Elizabeth (now Elizabeth II, queen of England) to Philip Mountbatten in 1947, a chimney sweep just happened to be walking up and down outside Kensington Palace, where the bridegroom was staying. Philip saw him and dashed out to shake his hand—for "sweep's luck."

In 1983 the *Daily Telegraph* newspaper reported that a chimney sweep named Mr. Cyril Buckland had discovered that he could make more money kissing brides than sweeping chimneys. He charged four pounds for a twenty-minute chimney-sweeping job and five pounds for a five-minute "good luck" appearance at a wedding.

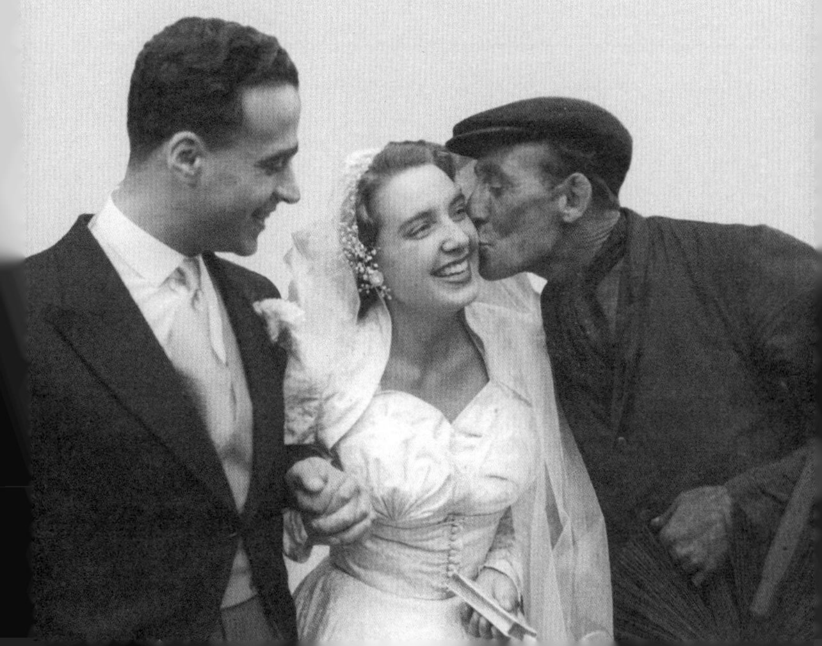

Original Sweeps

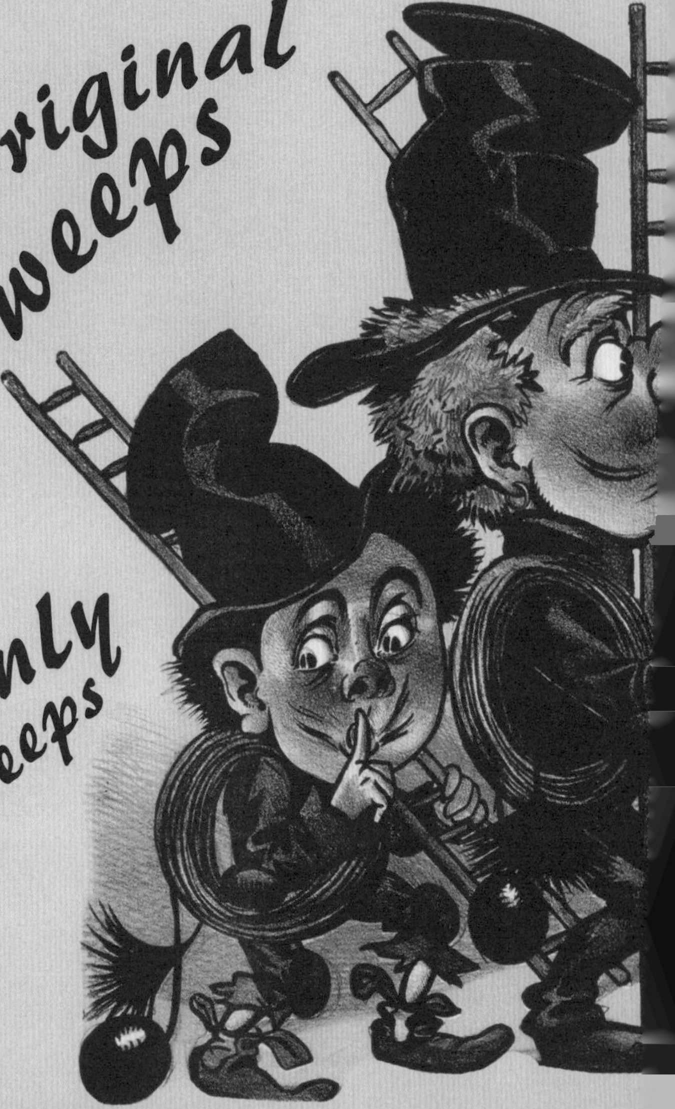

Only Sweeps

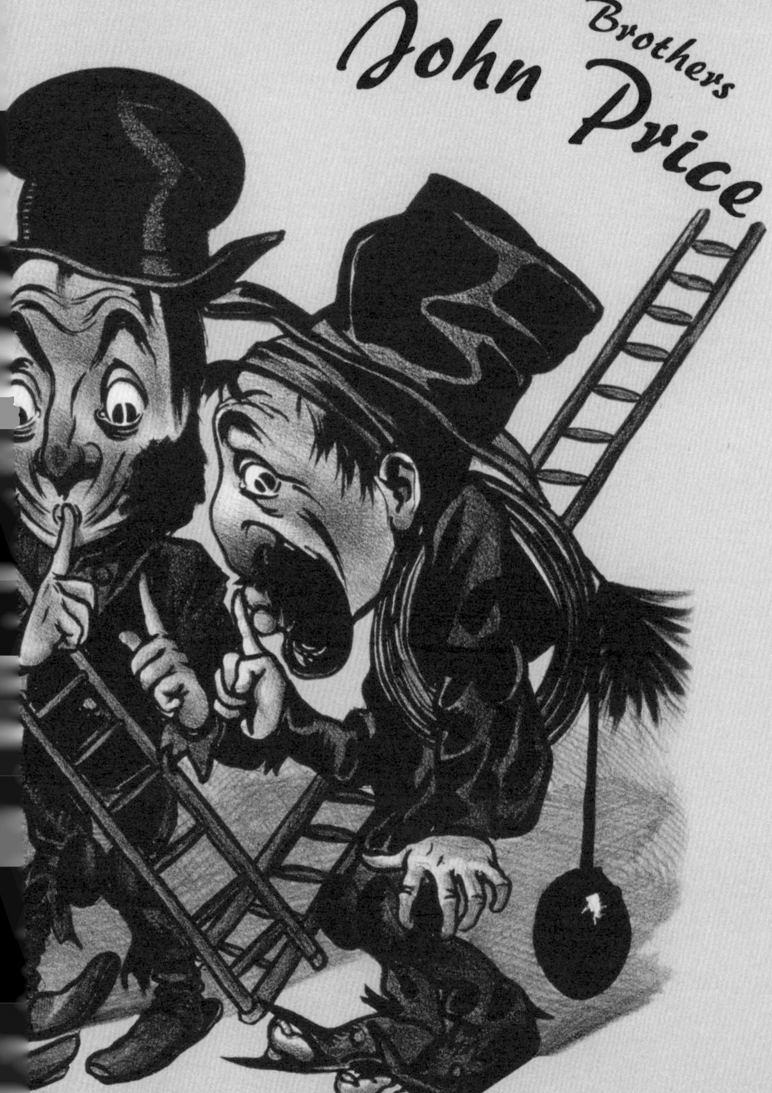
John Price
Brothers

Climbing Boys

For many years one of the great scandals of child labor was the apprenticing of small boys to climb chimneys. Many of them were orphans or poor children who had been abandoned by their families. Climbing boys' work involved climbing up the insides of chimneys to clean them. This was such appalling work that chimney sweeps would sometimes light fires under the boys to force them up the chimney—many boys were badly treated. There was often a fire lit somewhere in the house, even though the sweep was expected to do his work before the household was awake, so the boys were sometimes burned or overcome by smoke in the chimneys.

The numerous attempts to outlaw this abusive form of child labor in Britain were not very effective, until progressively stronger laws in 1840, 1846, and 1875 eventually began to affect a change. Similar working conditions existed in America until 1916, when the first federal child-labor law was passed.

Many people became aware of the horrors endured by boy sweeps when Charles Kingsley's fantasy fairy tale *The Water-Babies* was published in 1863. It gave a vivid account of the horrors endured by the young chimney sweep Tom at the hands of his brutal employer, Grimes. The book was a great success, and it was also made into a popular movie in 1978.

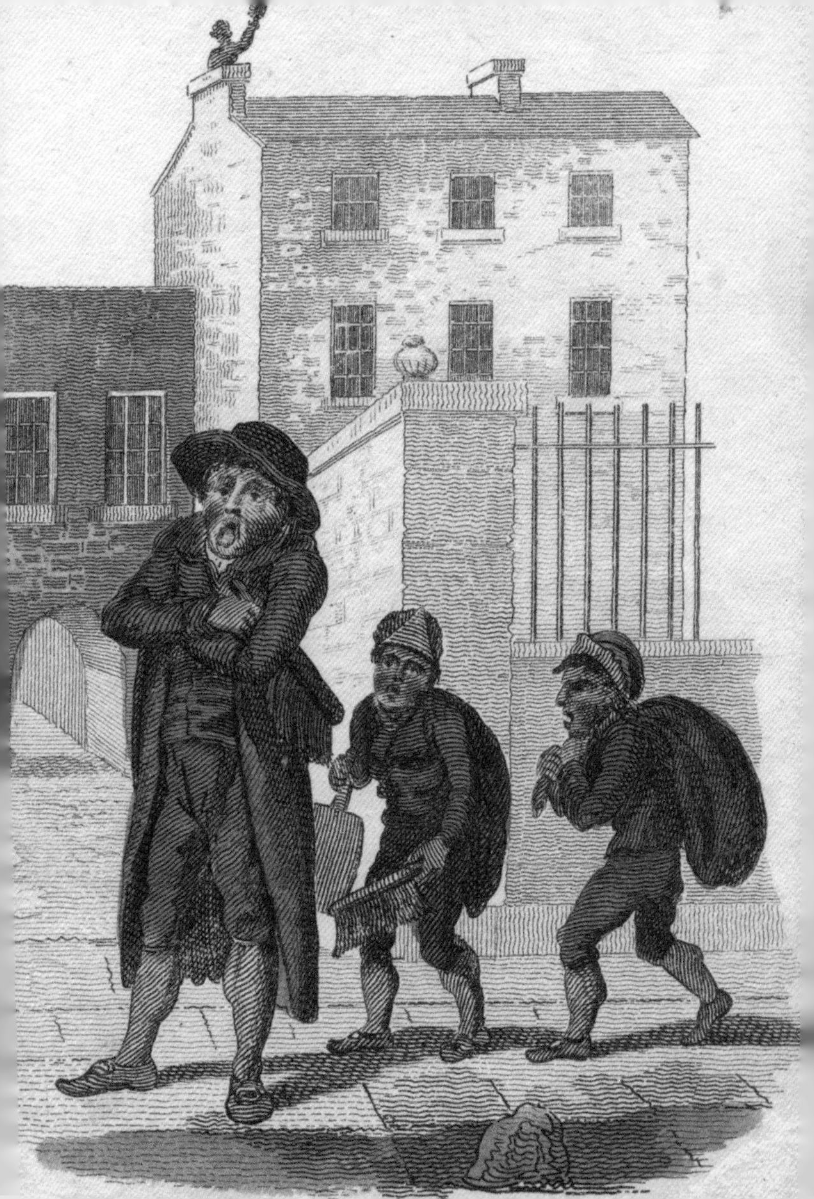

EXTRACT FROM

The Water-Babies

by

CHARLES KINGSLEY

Tom and his master [went] round the back way…and into a little back-door; …the housekeeper met them…and she gave Grimes solemn orders about "You will take care of this, and take care of that"…and then turned them into a grand room, all covered up in sheets of brown paper, and bade them begin…; and so after a whimper or two and a kick from his master, into the grate Tom went, and up the chimney, while a housemaid stayed in the room to watch the furniture….

How many chimneys Tom swept I cannot say; but he swept so many that he got quite tired, and puzzled too, for they were not like the town flues to which he was accustomed, but such as you would find—if you would only get up them and look, which perhaps you would not like to do—in old country-houses, large and crooked chimneys, which had been altered again and again, till they ran one into another…. So Tom fairly lost his way in them; not that he cared much for that, though he was in pitchy darkness, for he was as much at home in a chimney as a mole is underground; but at last, coming down as he thought the right chimney, he came down the wrong one, and found himself standing on the hearthrug in a room the like of which he had never seen before.

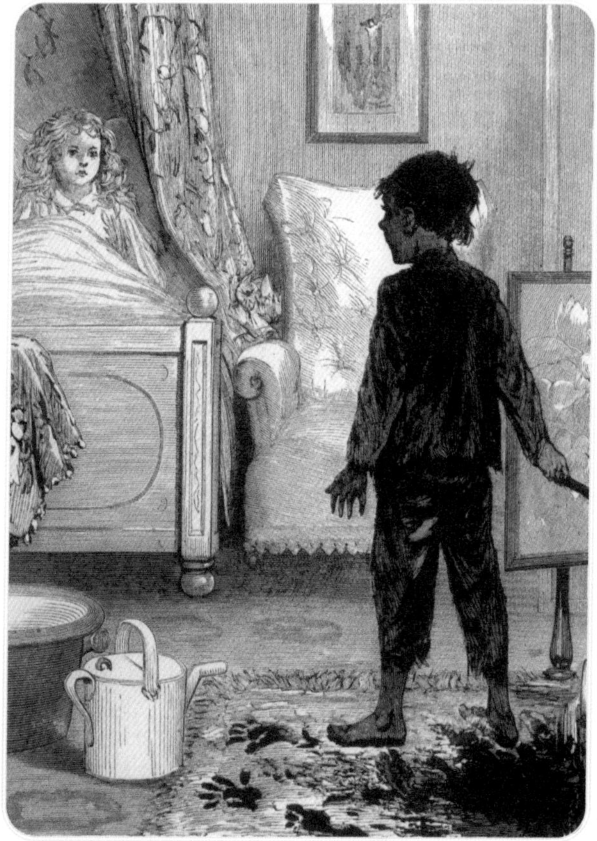

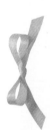

The Fireside Quilting Bee

Of all the romantic quilt stories, none is so cherished as the tradition of the "Quilting Bee." Some quilting bees lasted several days, especially when people came long distances, and guests often brought food. The fire would be lit, frames would be set up, and two or three women would sit on each side and one at each end. The hostess would usually supply the thread and scissors. Although these bees were usually women-only events, other family members could participate—husbands might draw patterns or cut out templates, and older children might cut out quilt patches or thread needles.

Quilting bees were once one of the most important types of neighborhood gatherings and social occasions. The women who made the quilts were making something that was most likely for their own families or close friends. Their quilts may have been beautiful or comforting, or simply warm and practical, but they certainly represented a labor of love.

One of the most famous of the patchwork quilt patterns was the Log Cabin, which was developed by pioneering women using every scrap of material they could find to make warm bedcovers for their families. Traditionally, the central patch of the pattern is red, to represent the hearth, and the dark and light sides of the pattern represent shadows and the firelight.

*"I have been at a 'Bee.' And if you would know
what this creature is in society here, then behold!
If a family is reduced to poverty by fire or sickness,
and the children are in want of clothes or anything
else, a number of ladies of the neighborhood who are
in good circumstances immediately get together at
some place and sew for them. Such an assembly is
called a bee!"*

from a letter Frederika Bremer sent home to Sweden in 1849

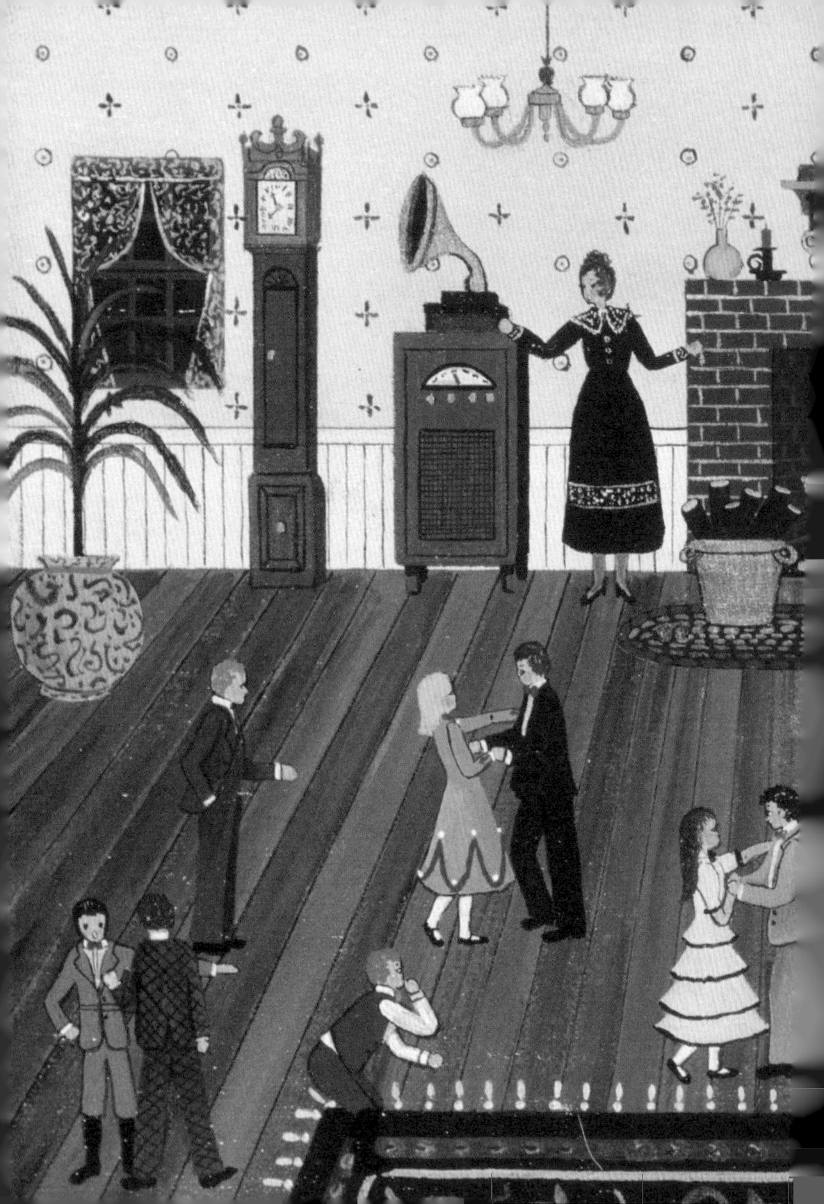

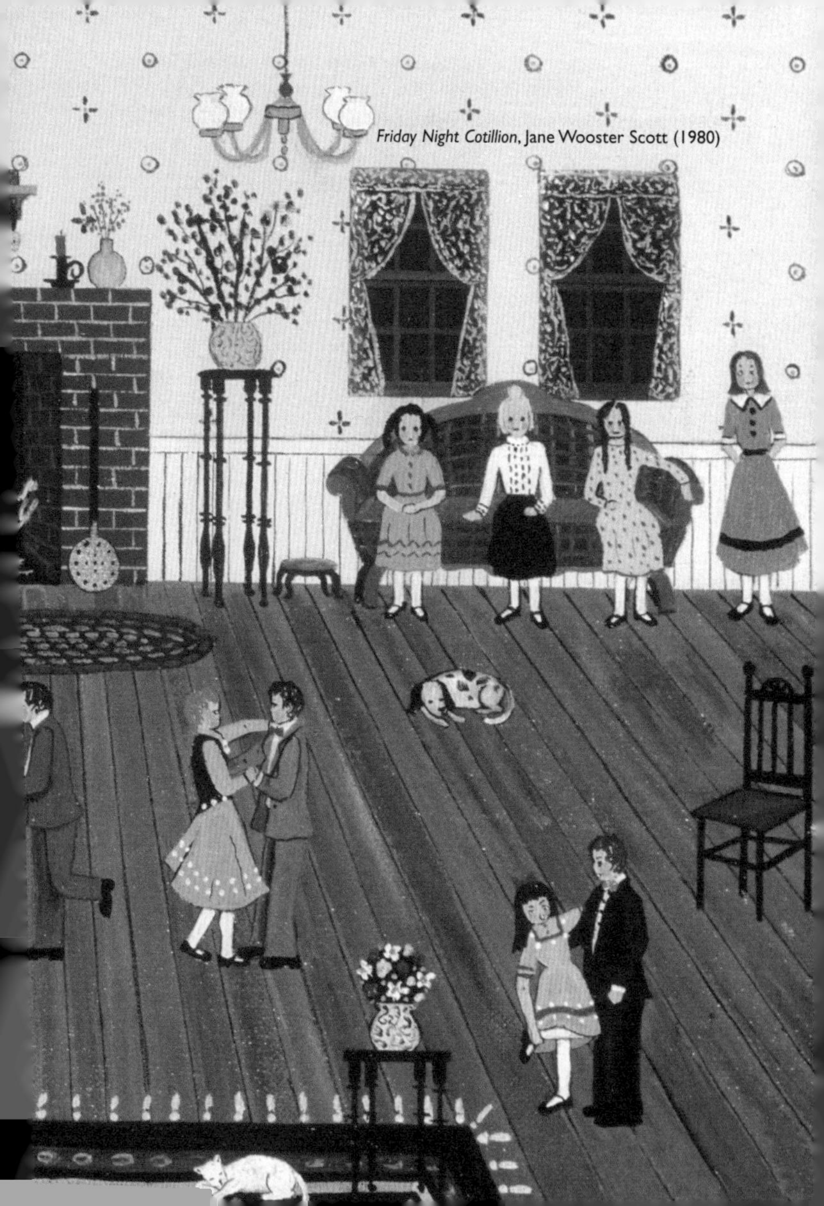

Friday Night Cotillion, Jane Wooster Scott (1980)

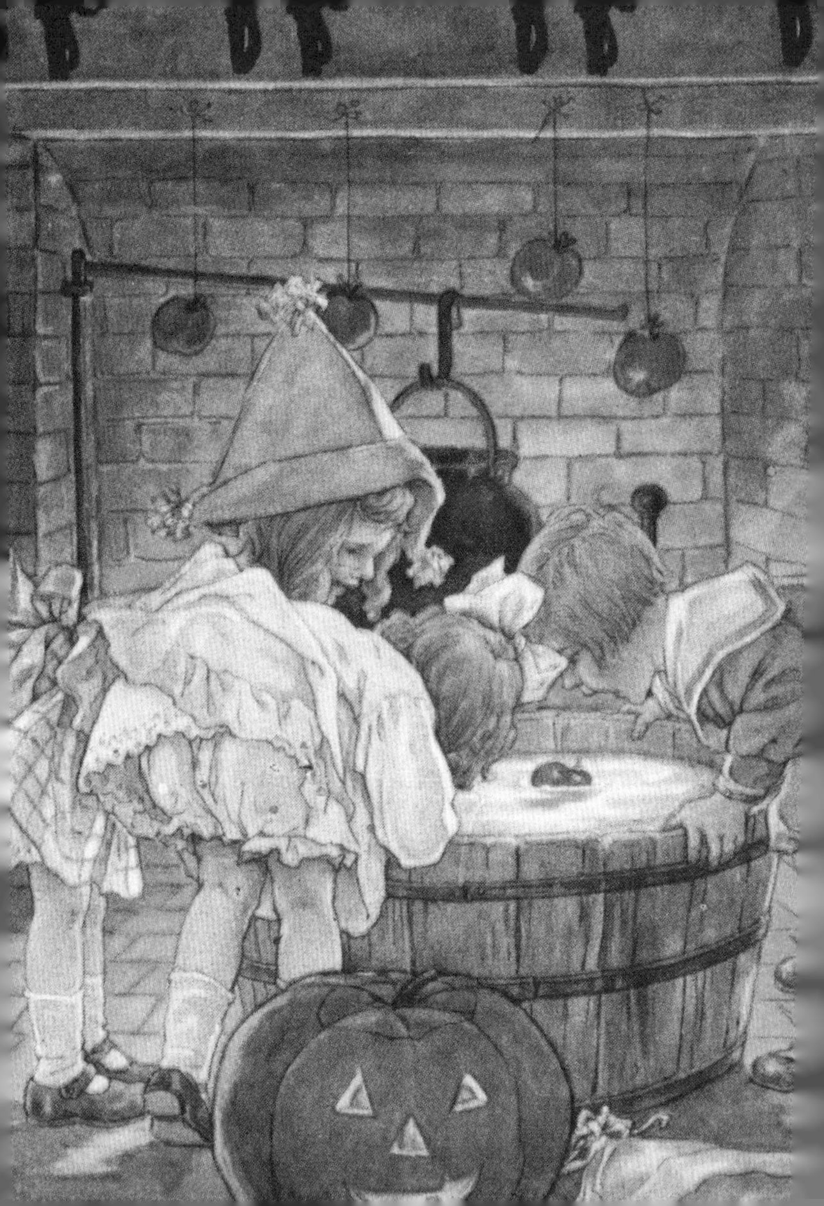

The Fireside at Halloween

Christmas, in the depths of winter, is the most traditional celebration associated with the cozy family pleasures of the fireside. But Halloween, coming at the very end of fall, is also a perfect time for the whole family to enjoy some fireside fun and play traditional Halloween games.

One of the best games, which is great fun for the whole family, is "bobbing for apples." It is one of the oldest Halloween games, and it comes from an ancient Celtic tradition for determining who would be the next person to marry. Simply fill a low, wide tub two-thirds full with water and carefully drop in ten to twenty medium-size apples, depending on the number of people playing. Then take turns putting your heads into the tub and trying to grab the apples out of the water using only your mouths—no hands! The winner is the person who manages to grab the most apples in a set period of time or just the first person to grab an apple at all!

If this game just sounds too wet for you, there is a dry alternative. You can tie apples to lengths of string by their stems and hang them from a beam on the ceiling or on a broom handle carefully supported by ladders or furniture, or just held by two tall adults. The contestants then try to grab the apples using only their mouths as they bob around on the string!

Fireside Punch

"Punch is a beverage made of various spirituous liquors or wine, hot water, the acid juice of fruits, and sugar. It is considered to be very intoxicating; but this is probably because the spirit, being partly sheathed by the mucilaginous juice and the sugars, its strength does not appear to the taste so great as it really is."

from *The Book of Household Management*, Mrs. Isabella Beeton

Punch became fashionable in England in the late seventeenth century and was popular enough throughout the eighteenth century for people to begin to form punch clubs. The making of the drink became something of a ritual. It was often served between the courses of a meal, but it was also a favorite fireside drink. Punch originated in India and the name comes from an Indian word, *punj*, meaning five. This refers to the five basic ingredients of the original drink: spirit, water, lemon, sugar, and spice.

The ritual of punch-making required the correct equipment. This included a deep punch bowl, made of silver or porcelain; long-handled ladles for serving it, their handles made of a material such as wood or whalebone that did not conduct heat; and many smaller items, including strainers, sugar bowls, sugar dredgers, and nutmeg graters. The punch was served in cup-shaped punch glasses. All these items, but especially the punch bowls and cups, are now valuable collectors' items.

Brandy Punch

Serves about 12

Ingredients:

juice of 8 lemons
juice of 2 oranges
10oz/285g sugar
ice cubes (2–3 freezer trayfuls)
4fl oz/120ml orange Curaçao
1 measure Grenadine
$1\frac{3}{4}$ pints/1 liter brandy
$1\frac{3}{4}$ pints/1 liter sparkling mineral water

1 Put the fruit juices together in a large jug.

2 Add the sugar and stir until the sugar has completely dissolved in the juices.

3 Put the ice in a punch bowl and pour over all the other ingredients.

4 If you like, float some orange and lemon slices on top as a decoration.

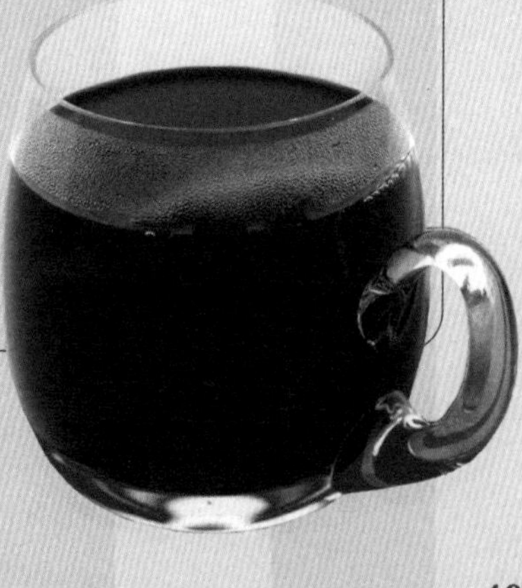

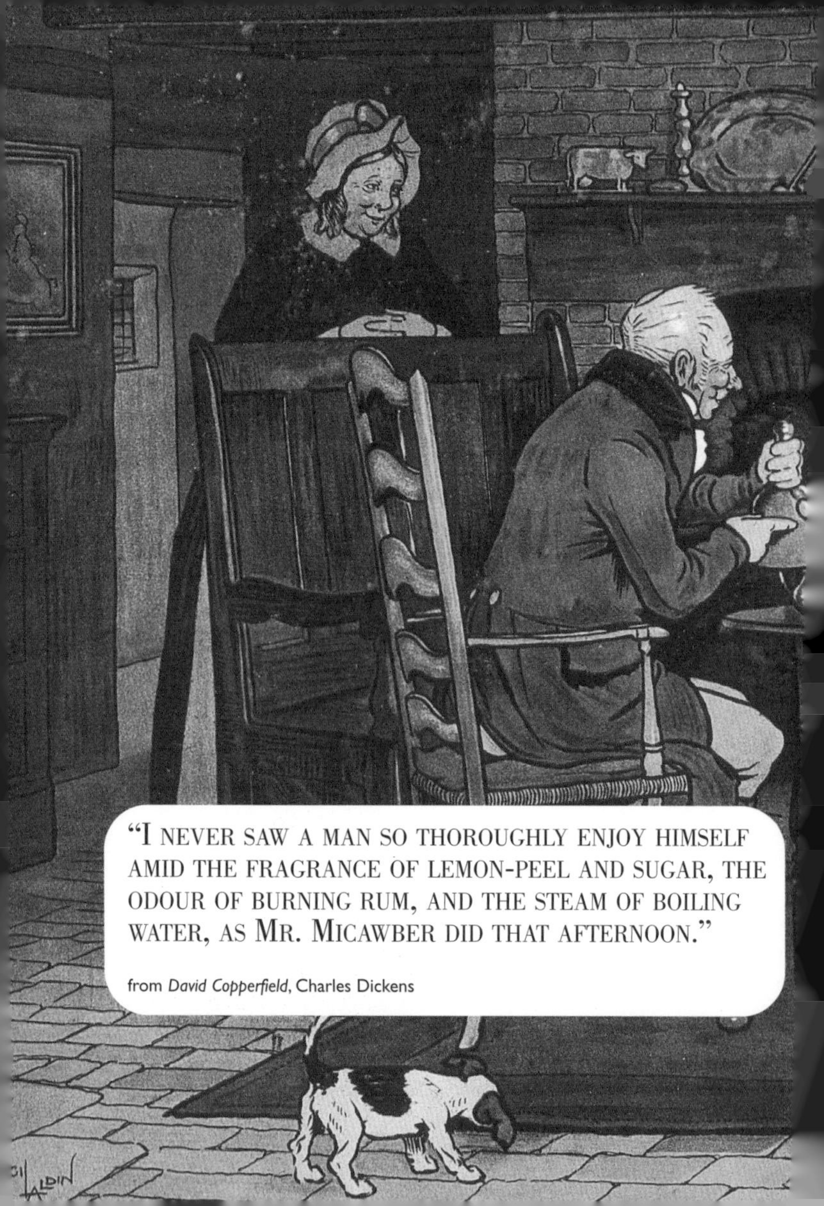

"I NEVER SAW A MAN SO THOROUGHLY ENJOY HIMSELF AMID THE FRAGRANCE OF LEMON-PEEL AND SUGAR, THE ODOUR OF BURNING RUM, AND THE STEAM OF BOILING WATER, AS MR. MICAWBER DID THAT AFTERNOON."

from *David Copperfield*, Charles Dickens

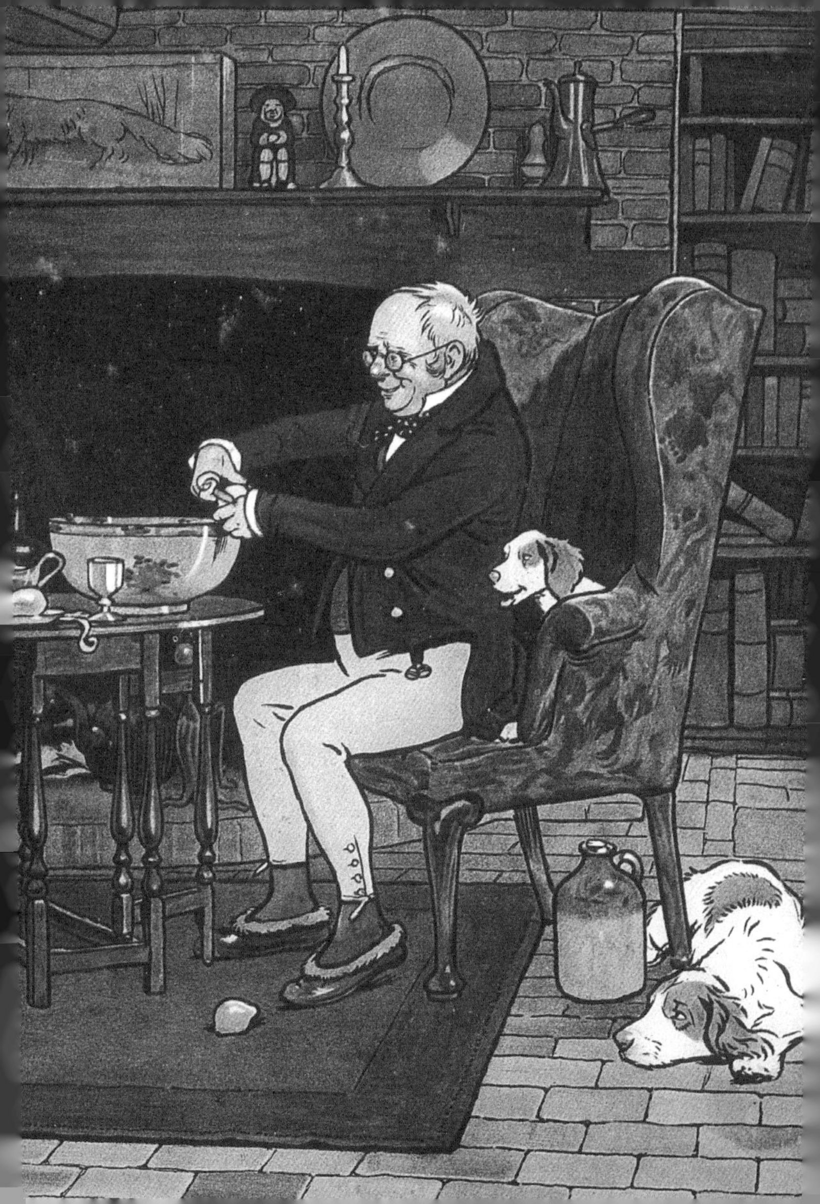

David Copperfield
by

CHARLES DICKENS

Peggotty and I were sitting one night by the parlour fire,
alone. I had been reading to Peggotty about crocodiles. I
must have read very perspicuously, or the poor soul must
have been deeply interested, for I remember she had a
cloudy impression, after I had done, that they were a sort of
vegetable. I was tired of reading, and dead sleepy; but having
leave, as a high treat, to sit up until my mother came home
from spending the evening at a neighbour's, I would rather
have died upon my post (of course) than have gone to bed. I
had reached that stage of sleepiness when Peggotty seemed
to swell and grow immensely large. I propped my eyelids
open with my two forefingers, and looked perseveringly at her
as she sat at work; at the little bit of wax-candle she kept for
her thread—how old it looked, being so wrinkled in all
directions!—at the little house with a thatched roof, where
the yard-measure lived; at her work-box with a sliding lid,
with a view of St. Paul's Cathedral (with a pink dome) painted
on the top; at the brass thimble on her finger; at herself,
whom I thought lovely. I felt so sleepy, that I knew if I lost
sight of anything for a moment, I was gone.

"Peggotty," says I, suddenly, "were you ever married?"

"Lord, Master Davy," replied Peggotty. "What's put marriage in your head?"

She answered with such a start, that it quite awoke me. And then she stopped in her work, and looked at me, with her needle drawn out to its thread's length.

"But *were* you ever married, Peggotty?" says I. "You are a very handsome woman, ain't you?"

I thought her in a different style from my mother, certainly; but of another school of beauty, I considered her a perfect example. There was a red velvet footstool in the best parlour, on which my mother had painted a nosegay. The ground-work of that stool, and Peggotty's complexion appeared to me to be one and the same thing. The stool was smooth, and Peggotty was rough, but that made no difference.

"Me handsome, Davy!" said Peggotty. "Lawk, no, my dear! But what put marriage in your head?"

"I don't know!—You mustn't marry more than one person at any time, may you, Peggotty?"

"Certainly now," says Peggotty, with the promptest decision.

"But if you marry a person, and the person dies, why then you may marry another person, mayn't you, Peggotty?"

"You *may*," says Peggotty, "if you choose, my dear. That's a matter of opinion."

"But what is your opinion, Peggotty?" said I.

I asked her, and looked curiously at her, because she looked so curiously at me. 👉

"My opinion is," said Peggotty, taking her eyes from me, after a little indecision and going on with her work, "that I never was married myself, Master Davy, and that I don't expect to be. That's all I know about the subject."

"You an't cross, I suppose, Peggotty, are you?" said I, after sitting quiet for a minute.

I really thought she was, she had been so short with me; but I was quite mistaken: for she laid aside her work (which was a stocking of her own), and opening her arms wide, took my curly head within them, and gave it a good squeeze. I know it was a good squeeze, because, being very plump, whenever she made any little exertion after she was dressed, some of the buttons on the back of her gown flew off. And I recollect two bursting to the opposite side of the parlour, while she was hugging me.

"Now let me hear some more about the Crorkindills," said Peggotty, who was not quite right in the name yet, "for I an't heard half enough."

I couldn't quite understand why Peggotty looked so queer, or why she was so ready to go back to the crocodiles. However, we returned to those monsters, with fresh wakefulness on my part...but I had my doubts of Peggotty, who was thoughtfully sticking her needle into various parts of her face and arms, all the time.

We had exhausted crocodiles, and begun with alligators, when the garden-bell rang. We went out the door; and there was mother, looking unusually pretty, I thought, and with her a gentleman with beautiful black hair and whiskers...

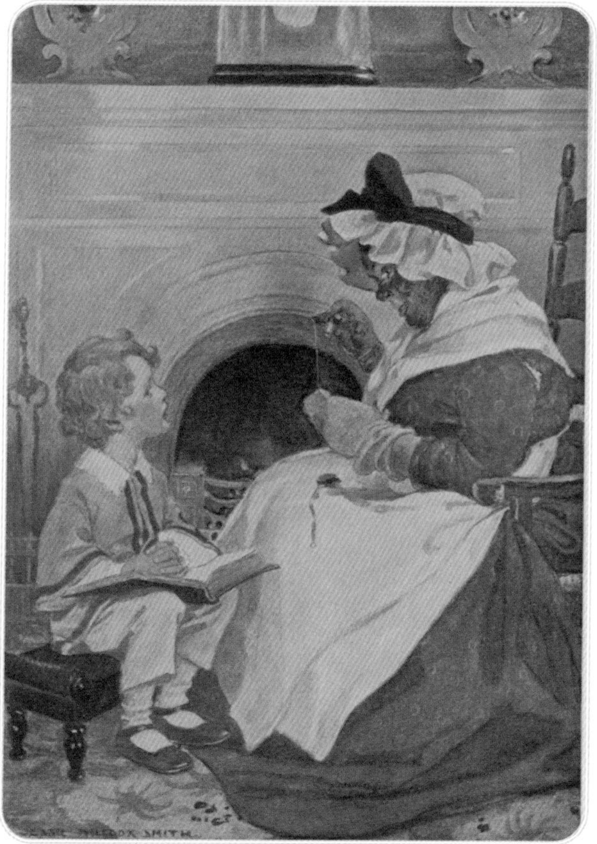

The Proverbial Cat

Cats love the fireside with a fierce passion: they gaze into the flames
until they are overcome with drowsiness. Then they curl up with their
tails over their noses, and go to sleep, in their famous imitation of a
hearthrug. The more extrovert characters stretch out in front of the
hearth, displaying their bellies with sensuous abandon. They've been
making themselves comfortable among humans since they were first
domesticated in Egypt, more than five thousand years ago. The ancient
Egyptians elevated them into little gods because they protected their
valuable grain stores from marauding rats. Given their superior status, it's
no wonder they are the subject of proverbial sayings all over the world.

"HAPPY IS THE HOME WITH AT LEAST ONE CAT." *Italian Proverb*

"BOOKS AND CATS AND FAIR-HAIRED LITTLE GIRLS MAKE
THE BEST FURNISHING FOR A ROOM." *French Proverb*

"YOU WILL ALWAYS BE LUCKY IF YOU KNOW HOW TO MAKE
FRIENDS WITH STRANGE CATS." *Colonial Proverb*

"IN A CAT'S EYE, ALL THINGS BELONG TO CATS." *English Proverb*

"BEWARE OF PEOPLE WHO DISLIKE CATS." *Irish Proverb*

"AFTER DARK ALL CATS ARE LEOPARDS." *Native American Proverb*

"A CAT MAY LOOK AT A KING." *English Proverb*

"HAPPY OWNER, HAPPY CAT. INDIFFERENT OWNER,
RECLUSIVE CAT." *Chinese Proverb*

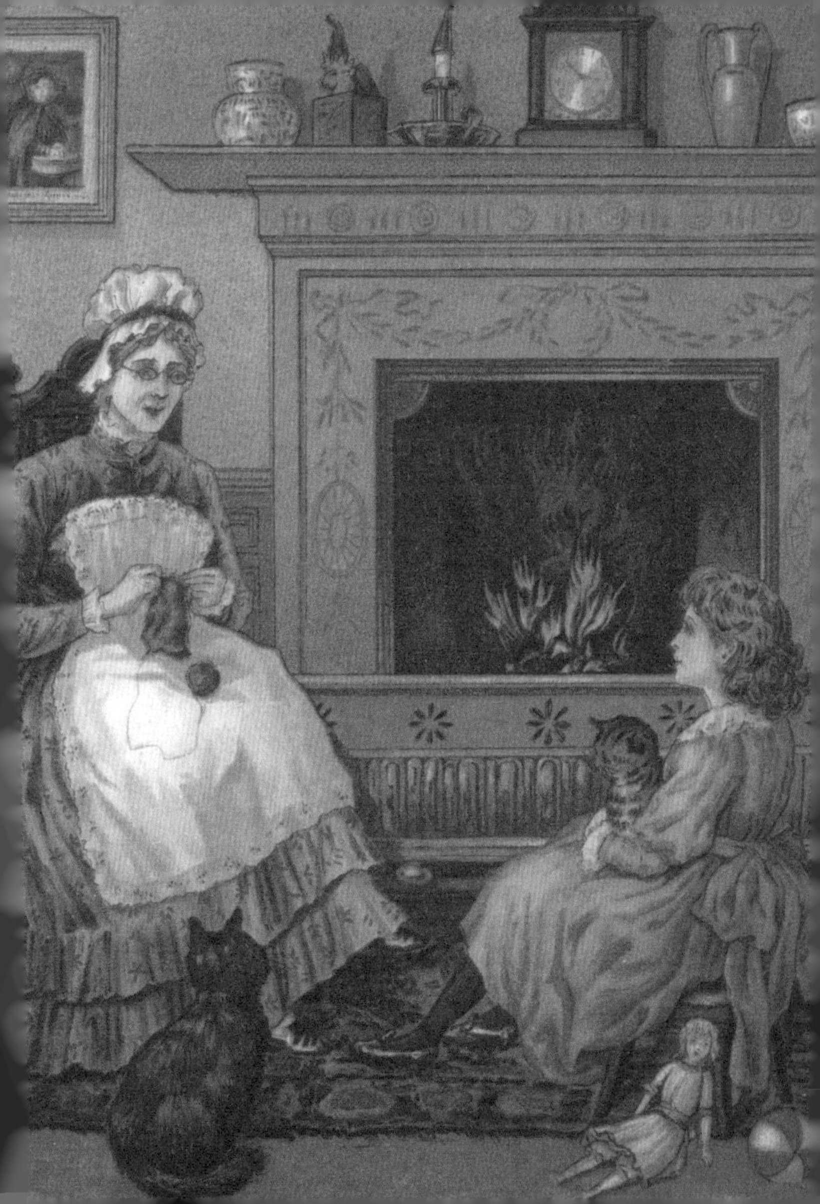

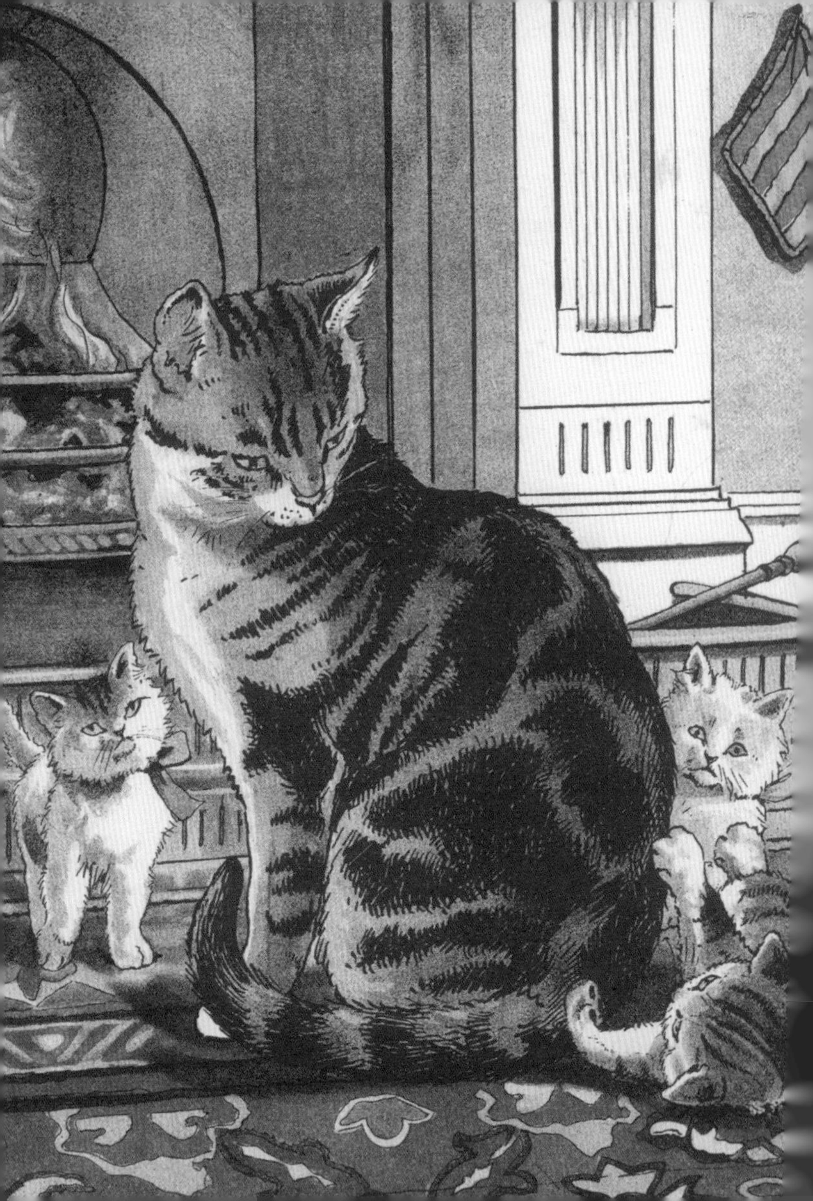

Cats' Tails

Considering the amount of time that cats spend sleeping as near to a fire as they can get, it is perhaps not surprising that several superstitions have grown up around the cat and the hearth, many of them to do with the weather.

- **A cat sitting with its tail pointing toward the fire was once believed by many to indicate that a hard frost was on its way.**

- **For other people, a cat's tail pointing at the fire signified a change in the weather.**

- **Yet others believed that it was generally unlucky for the cat to sit with its tail pointing toward the fire.**

- **Even today, many people say they have noticed that when their cat sits with its back to the fire it is a sign that the weather is going to turn cold, stormy, or wet.**

- **An inside-out version of this belief in some countries of Eastern Europe is that cats attract lightning bolts. Supposedly gods or angels throw them at cats to exorcise the evil spirits said to take possession of cats during thunderstorms. Some poor cats still get scooped up from in front of warm fires to be thrown out during thunderstorms so their owners' houses are not struck by lightning.**

- **In the more remote parts of the Scottish Highlands, witches were said to draw a cat through the fire to raise winds that would influence the course of ships at sea.**

Make Your Own Knitted Throw

Knitting has long been a favorite fireside activity. It can be picked up and put down at any stage, so it's the perfect way to spend a few spare minutes with your family in front of the fire. This knitted throw is based on a simple Shaker design and, once made, it is an ideal item to keep on the couch or on the back of a chair where it can easily be grabbed to put around your shoulders when you are cold.

The Shaker community learned a diverse range of practical skills, and the Sisters regularly fit their knitting around other work. They spun and dyed their own wool, winding it into balls using a table swift. They produced a range of knitted goods such as mittens, socks, stockings, sweaters, and rugs.

This knitted throw is made from 100% pure new wool and is the size of a square blanket. The wool was chosen in a quiet tweed color, which suits the utilitarian nature of the article, although you can choose any color you wish. The overall pattern is a simple check made from two basic knitting stitches—moss stitch and stocking stitch—knitted on a circular needle. Both moss and stocking stitch are worked using simple knit and purl stitches to create a richly textured design for the throw.

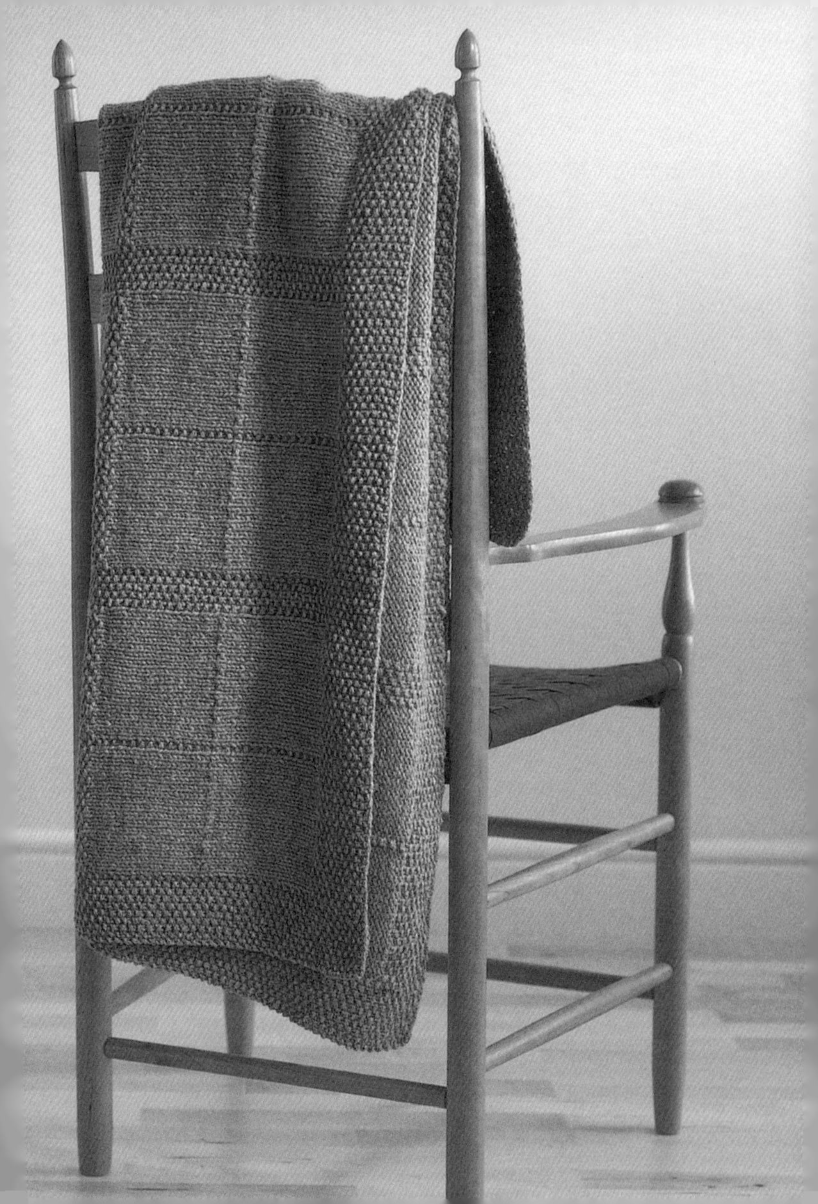

This throw is knitted in one piece on circular knitting needles. These can accommodate a large number of stitches (make sure you buy an extra long variety), but you knit in the same way as with straight needles. Check your knitting often, correcting any mistakes before continuing.

MATERIALS:

- Circular knitting needles US 8 (31½in-long)/UK 5mm (80cm-long)
- Scissors
- Eight 4oz/100g skeins of 100% pure new wool Rowan Magpie Tweed
- Large tapestry needle

Finished size: about 43in/110cm square

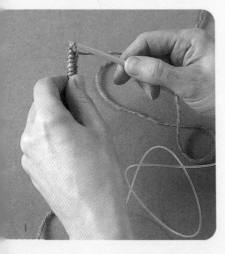

1 Cast on 175 stitches.

2 Work 16 rows of moss stitch. To do this, knit one, purl one across the row, beginning with a knit stitch on every row.

3 Work 10 stitches in moss stitch to make the border. Pattern row 1: knit 17 stitches, purl 1, knit 17, work 5 stitches in moss stitch. Repeat the pattern three times and then finish the row in moss stitch.

4 Work 10 stitches in moss stitch. Pattern row 2: purl 35 stitches, moss stitch 5. Repeat the pattern three times and then finish the row in moss stitch.

5 Continue alternating the two pattern rows until 25 rows have been completed, ending on the second pattern row. Work a row of moss stitch.

6 Work the two pattern rows alternately for a further 25 rows, ending on the second pattern row. Work 6 rows of moss stitch.

7 This forms the check pattern for the entire throw. Continue until there are four rows of four large check squares. Tie in new skeins of wool on the wrong side.

8 End on a second pattern row and then work 16 rows of moss stitch. Cast off loosely.

9 Untie the knots and sew the ends of the wool into the throw on the wrong side. Using a damp cloth, lightly iron on the wrong side.

The Swedish Stove

"Here I experienced that unspeakably sweet feeling of seclusion from the clamor and noise of the world."

from *Ett Hem (A Home)*, Carl Larsson

Carl Larsson's serene watercolor of his wife Karin's bedroom (shown on the following page) is a perfect example of his exquisite paintings. His delight in the day-to-day life of his household is beautifully conveyed. Karin's bedroom is both spacious and comfortable and is warmed by a gloriously tiled Swedish fireplace that houses a cozy wood-burning stove. There is also a characteristically romantic note in the flower garland over the door and the border around the ceiling, which was painted by Carl in 1894 as a special present for his wife.

Porcelain tile stoves like the one in Larsson's picture are called *kakelugnar* in Swedish, and are the perfect combination of beauty and practicality. They originated in fifteenth-century Germany; but by the seventeenth century, Swedish factories were making them too, and eventually achieved a crucial technical breakthrough in their design. Up until 1767, the tiled cladding had been a decorative shell that acted as a hollow container for the iron wood-burner—the smoke went straight up the chimney through the stovepipe.

Effectively, this also meant much of the heat was escaping along with the smoke! It was Swedish stove masons Fabian Wrede and Carl Johan Cronstedt who solved the problem. They made a brilliant improvement by directing the smoke from the wood-burner through a network of long flues winding up and down inside the tiled stove surround. This made the stove about eight times more efficient than before.

Tiled stoves were the standard means of heating in Swedish town houses right up to the early 1900s. They were mainly made by two factories—the Uppsala-Ekeby and Rörstrand Porcelain companies. Each stove could be designed to coordinate with the interior design of a particular room. They varied in their size, shape, and the motifs used for the tiles. Householders could choose styles that included shells, fleur-de-lis, and floral patterns. The styles of the wood-burners also varied immensely—some had ornate handles; others had arched or square brass double doors.

Nowadays, historic stoves are prized antiques—and due to the ecology movement, there has been a revival in their popularity. Meanwhile, Larsson continues to enchant—he is not only Sweden's most famous artist, but his beloved house has become a national icon. It is now open to the public, and there you can see Karin's bedroom stove in all its glory.

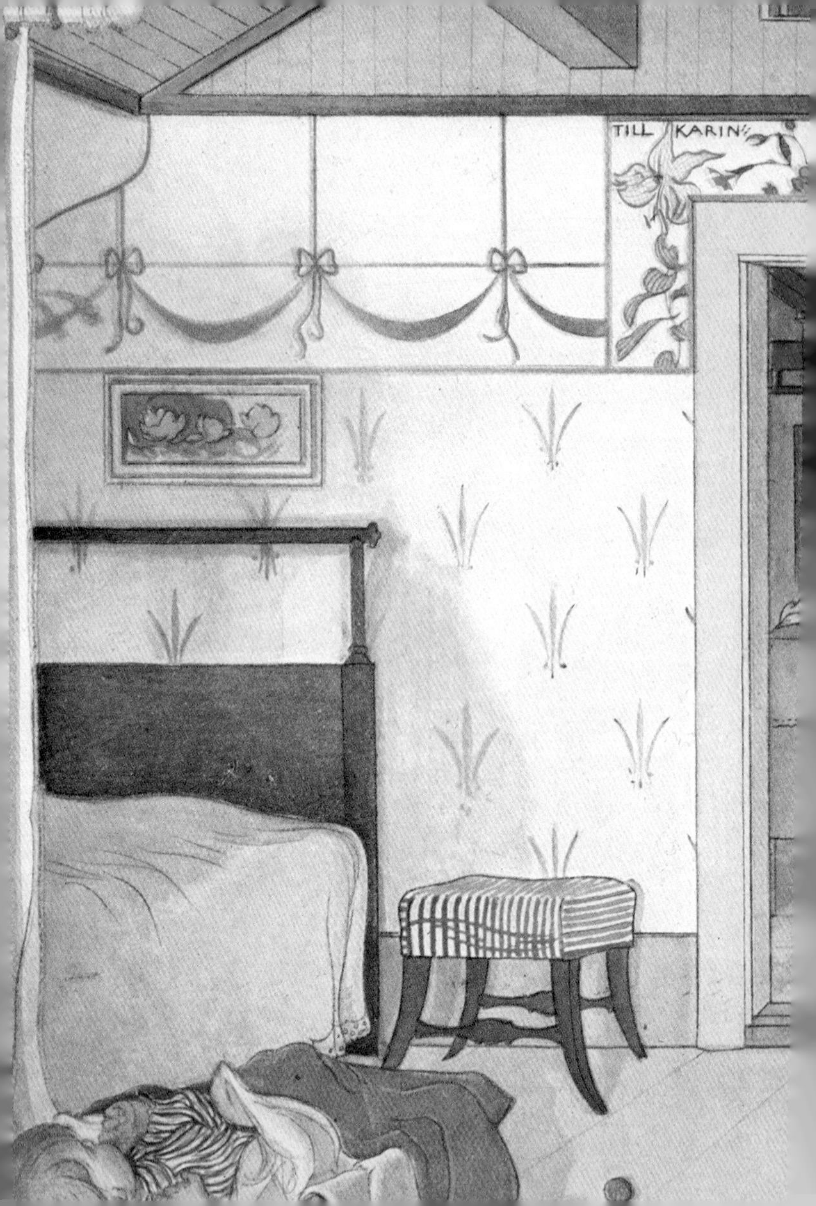
TILL KARIN

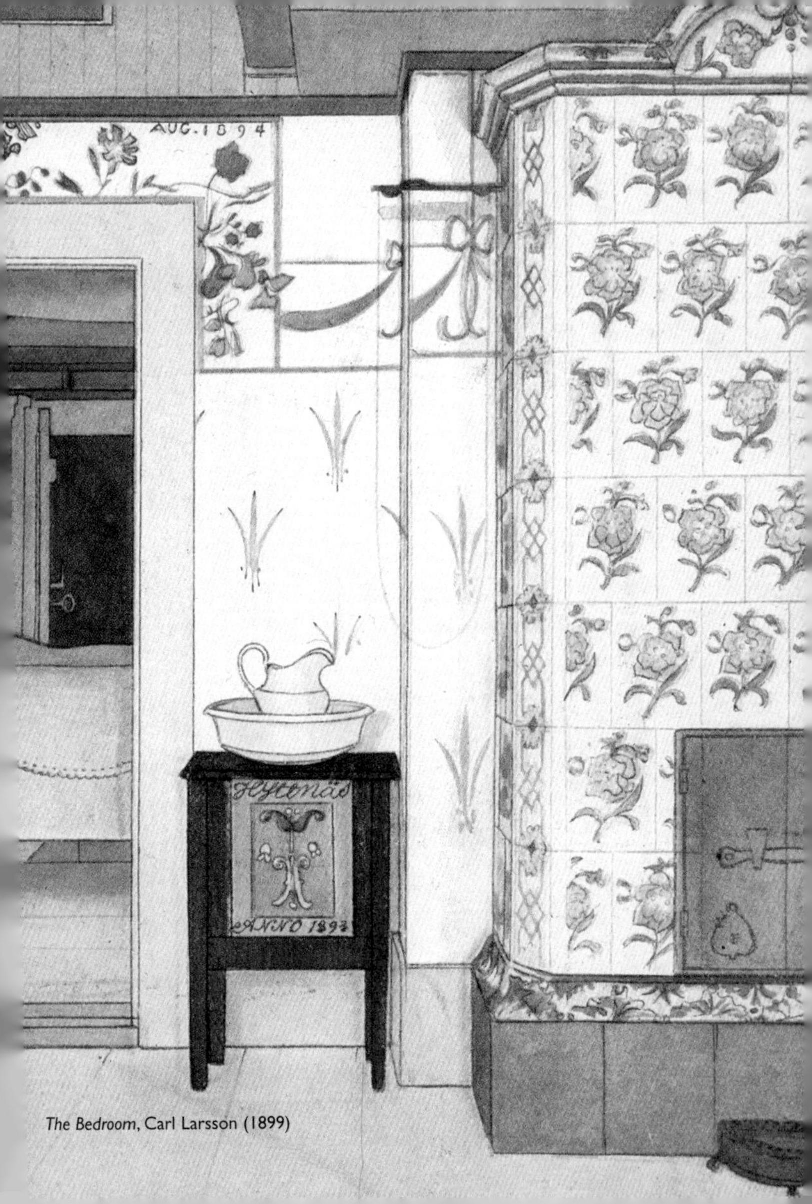
AUG. 1894

The Bedroom, Carl Larsson (1899)

Acrostic: Around my lonely hearth to-night

by

LEWIS CARROLL

Around my lonely hearth to-night,
    Ghostlike the shadows wander:
Now here, now there, a childish sprite,
Earthborn and yet as angel bright,
    Seems near to me as I ponder.

Gaily she shouts: the laughing air
    Echoes her note of gladness—
Or bends herself with earnest care
Round fairy-fortress to prepare
Grim battlement or turret-stair—
    In childhood's merry madness!

New raptures still hath youth in store.
    Age may but fondly cherish
Half-faded memories of yore—
Up, craven heart! Repine no more!
Love stretches hands from shore to shore:
    Love is, and shall not perish!

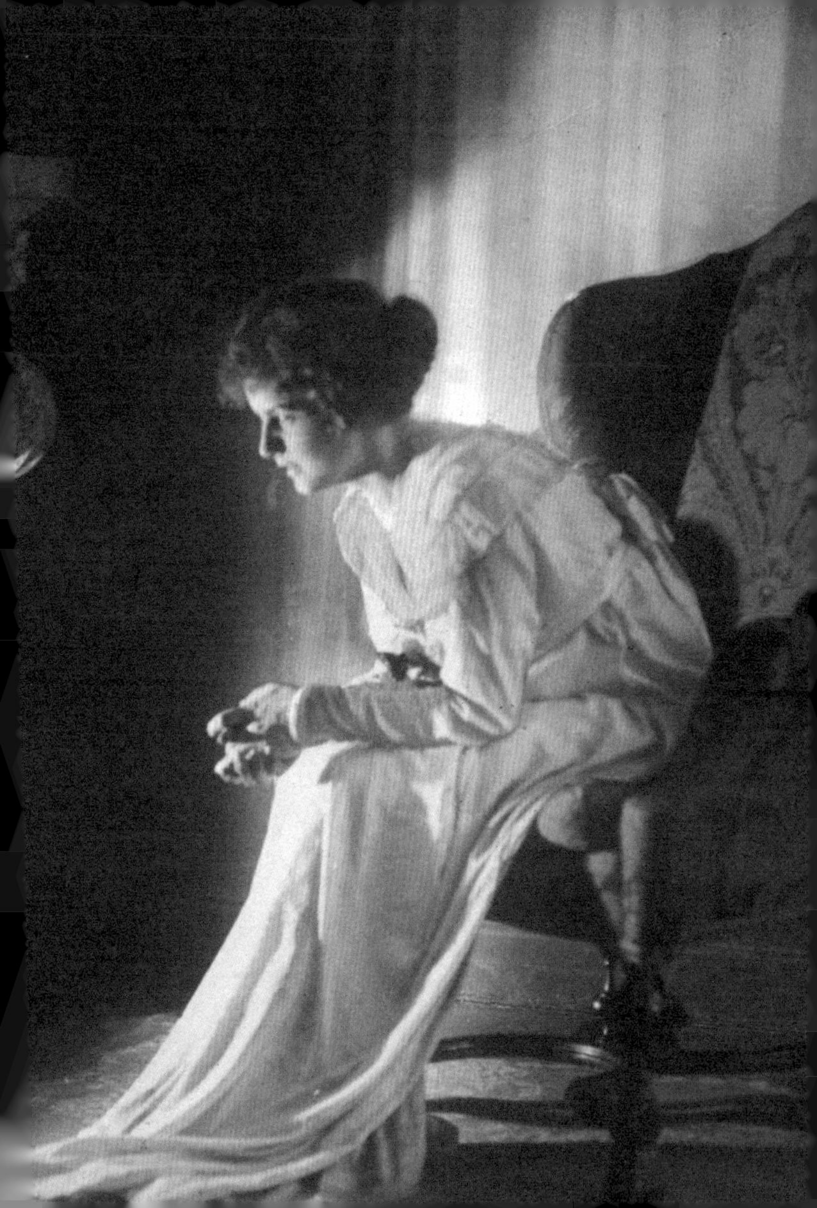

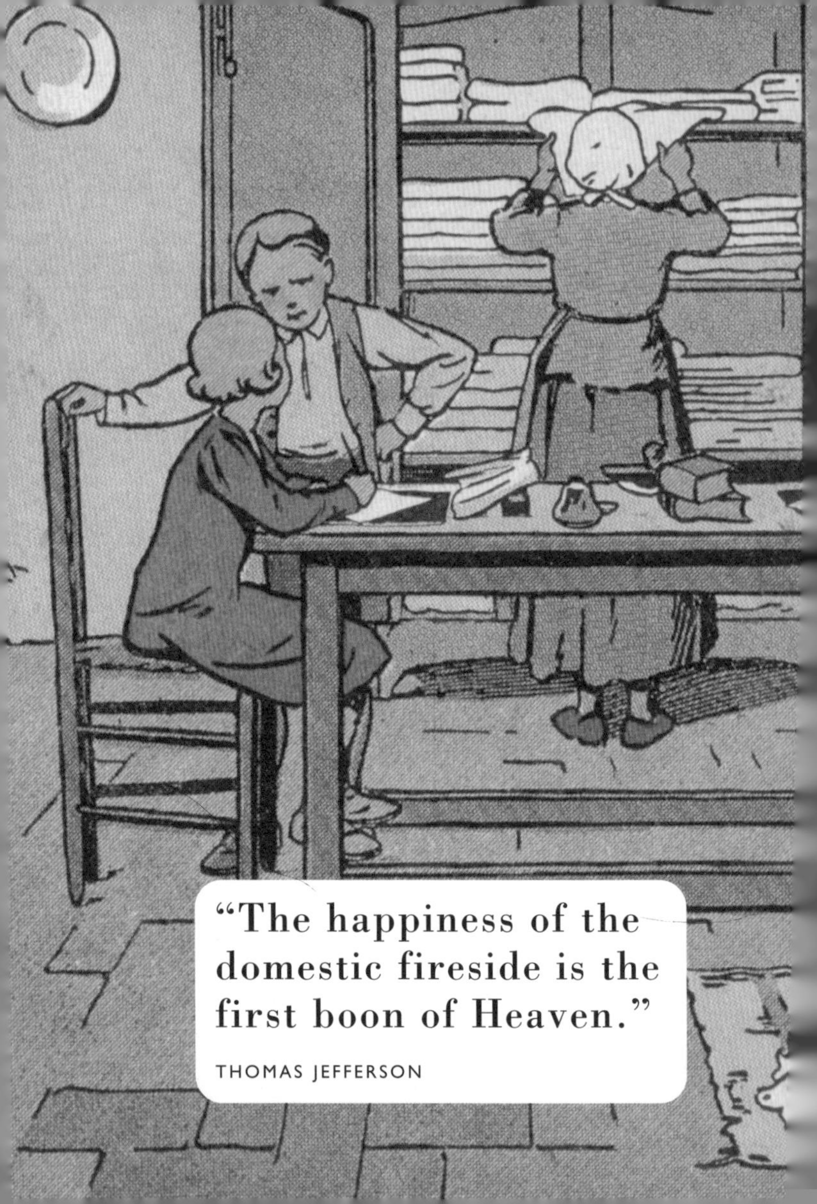

"The happiness of the domestic fireside is the first boon of Heaven."

THOMAS JEFFERSON

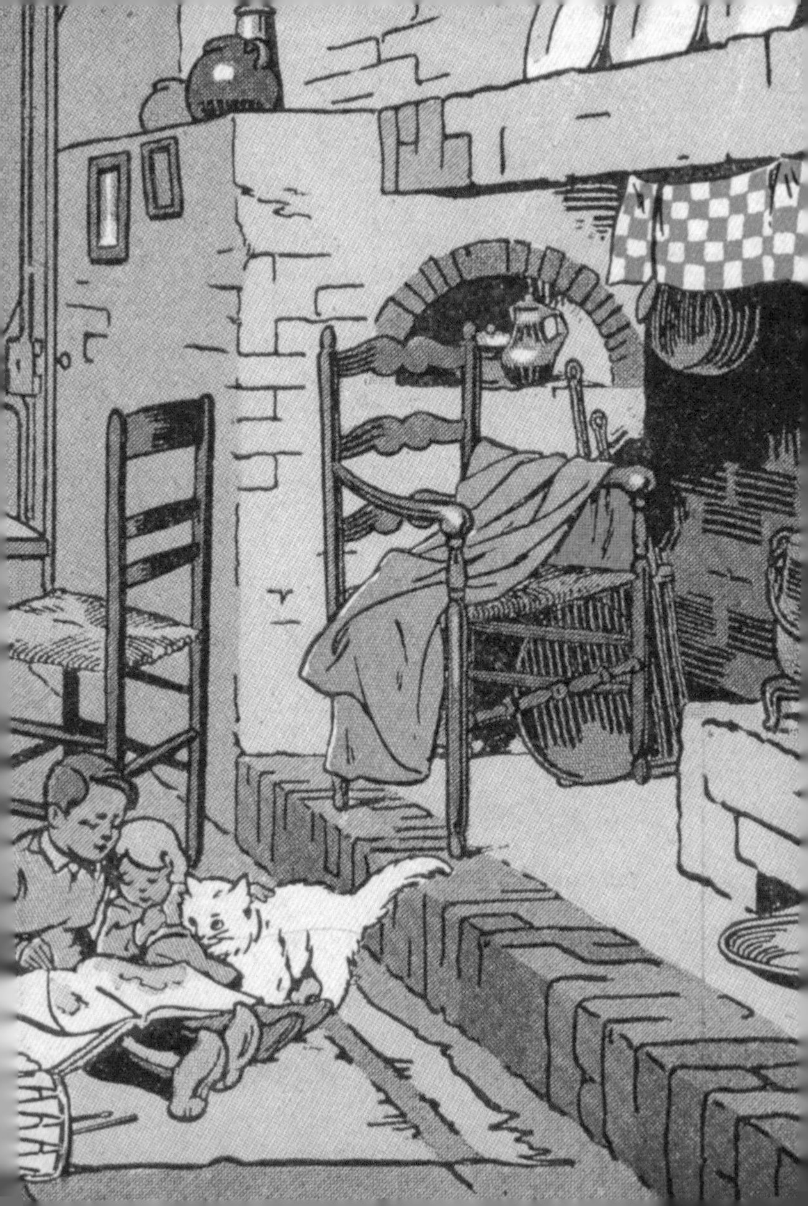

The Wonderful Aga Saga

Throughout Britain, splendidly large and handsomely enameled stoves, colored black, deep royal blue, or stylish green, take up whole walls of country kitchens. Within their numerous ovens, whole meals can be cooked easily and perfectly. Sometimes, in a crisis during the lambing season on farms, newborn motherless lambs can be given a good start in life warmed in the cooker's bottom oven—with the door left open, of course. And, more often than not, there is likely to be someone nonchalantly warming his bottom against the front of the stove while chatting about this and that to anyone else in the kitchen.

The oven is the Aga, a stove beloved by Britain's country-dwelling middle-classes. The Aga is actually Swedish. It was the invention of Nobel-Prize-winning physicist Dr. Gustaf Dalen. He lost his sight in an accident in his laboratory and set about inventing a stove safe enough for blind people to use.

The Aga was first made under licence in Britain in the 1920s, at a time when domestic servants were becoming increasingly difficult to find —working-class girls could have a much easier life with shorter working hours in factories, shops, and offices. The Aga's great attraction was that wonderful cooking could be done in the oven, instead of just on the stove top or by roasting meats on a spit. There was no coal or wood to worry about because Agas were fueled by oil, gas, or electricity.

The Aga was not just reliable and practical, it also was expensive. The middle-class housewife accustomed to giving orders to her cook or housemaid, experienced no loss of face at doing her own cooking at such a splendid looking stove.

Today, the Aga is the stove of choice in big country kitchens and some town kitchens. The Aga has even given its name to a genre of best-selling novels—the "Aga Saga"—a label first attached to the early novels of Joanna Trollope.

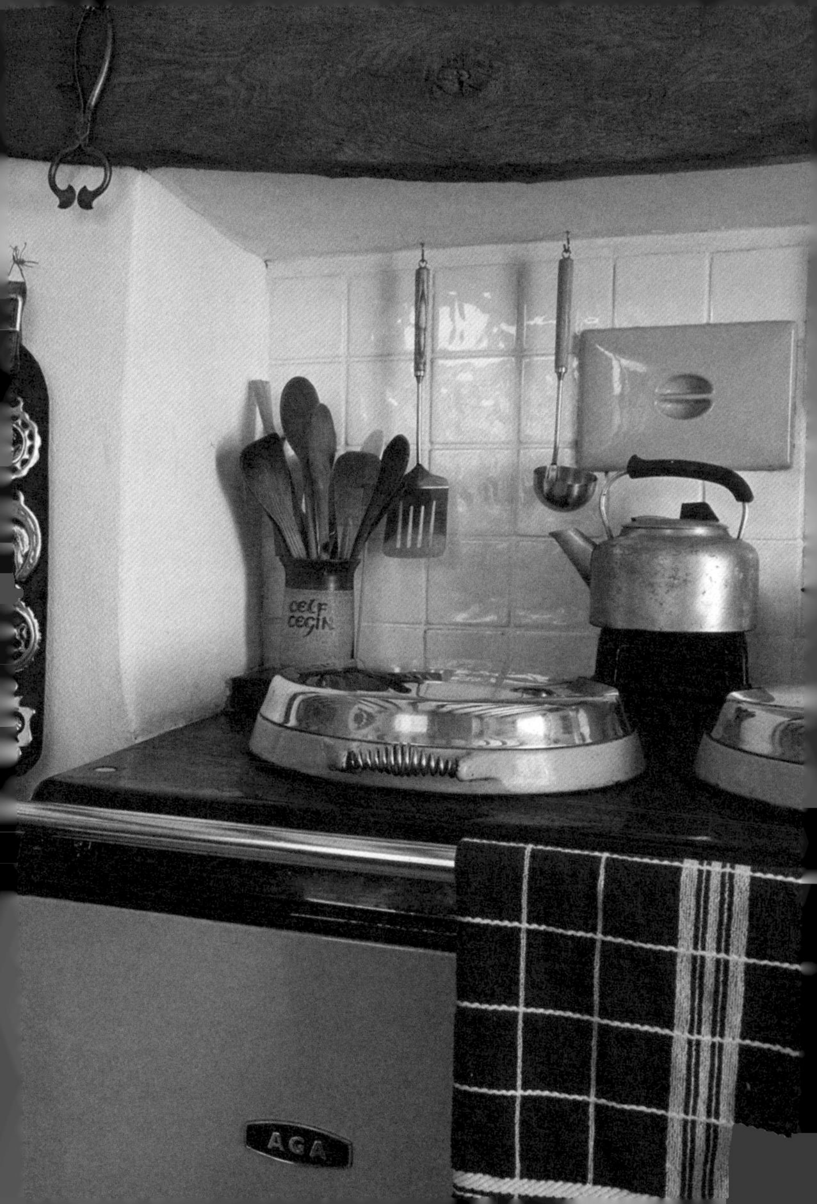
AGA

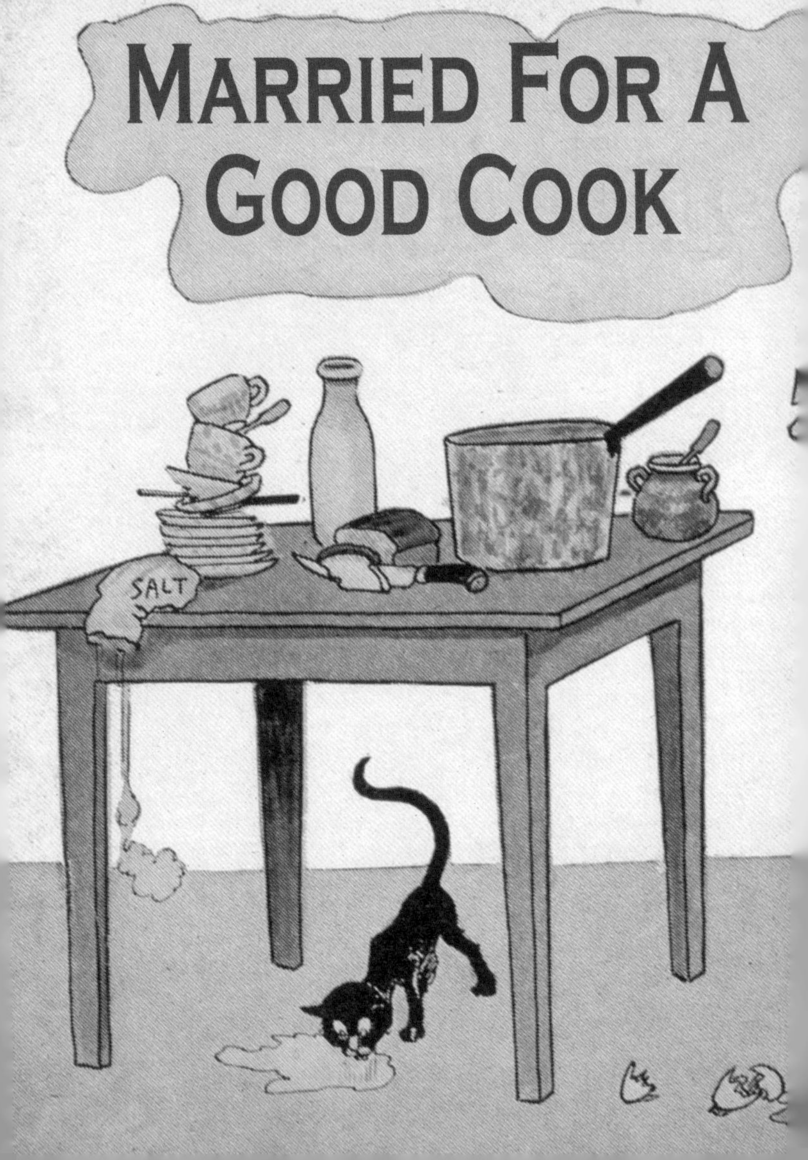
MARRIED FOR A GOOD COOK
SALT

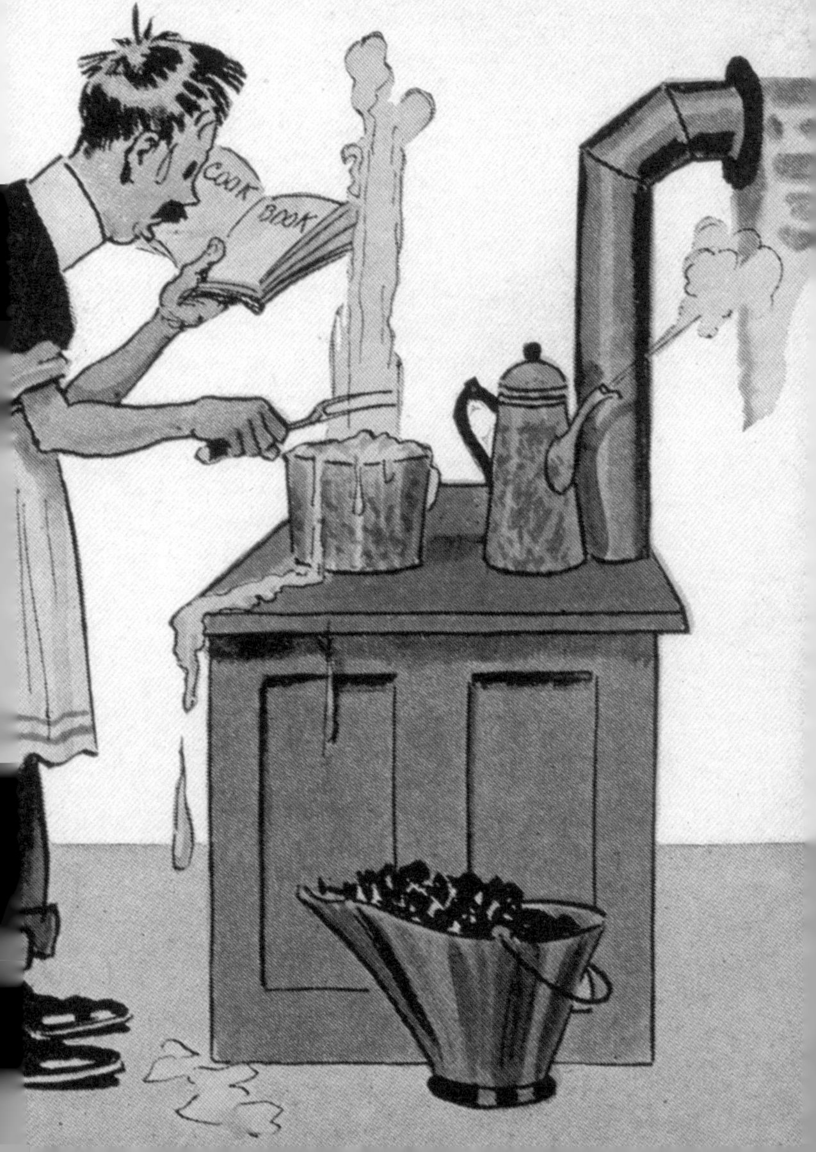
COOK
BOOK

Alice in Wonderland

by

LEWIS CARROLL

"There's certainly too much pepper in that soup!" Alice said to herself, as well as she could for sneezing.

Even the Duchess sneezed occasionally; and, as for the baby, it was sneezing and howling alternately without a moment's pause. The only things in the kitchen that did not sneeze were the cook, and a large cat which was sitting on the hearth and grinning from ear to ear.

…The cook took the cauldron of soup off the fire, and at once set to work throwing everything within her reach at the Duchess and the baby—the fire-irons came first; then followed a shower of saucepans, plates, and dishes. The Duchess took no notice even when they hit her; and the baby was howling so much already, that it was quite impossible to say whether the blows hurt it or not.

"Oh, please mind what you're doing!" cried Alice, jumping up and down in an agony of terror. "Oh, there goes his precious nose;" as an unusually large saucepan flew close by it, and very nearly carried it off.

"If everybody minded their own business," the Duchess said in a hoarse growl, "the world would go round a deal faster than it does."

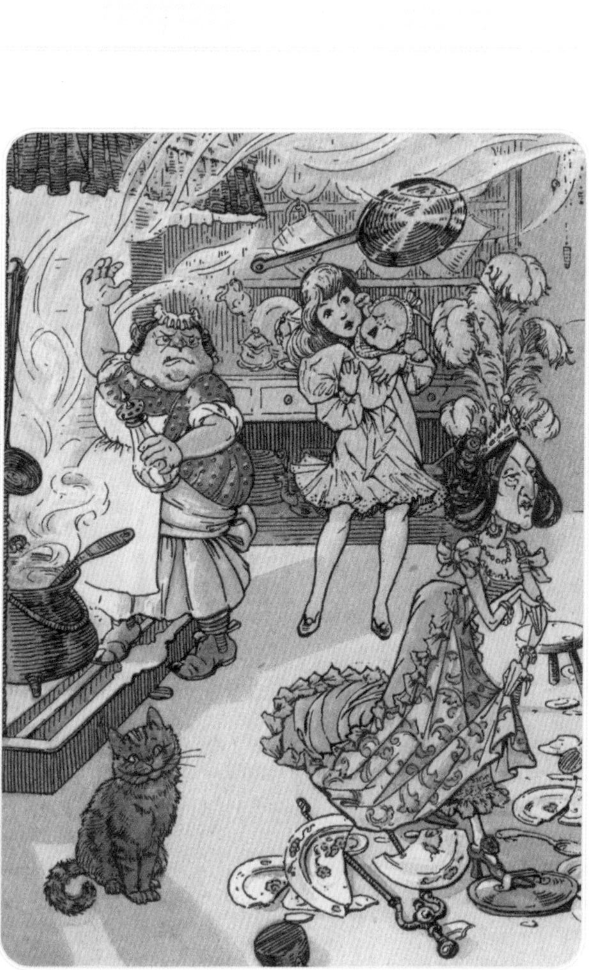

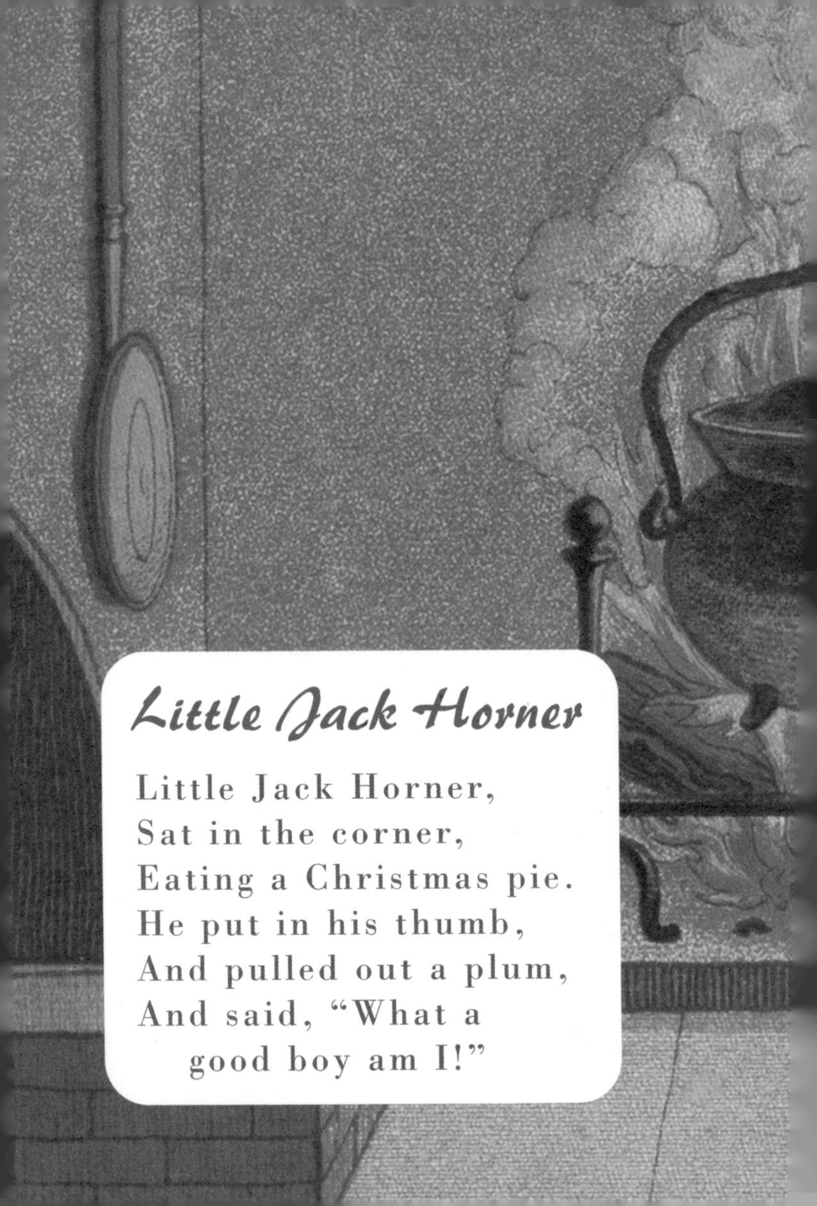

Little Jack Horner

Little Jack Horner,
Sat in the corner,
Eating a Christmas pie.
He put in his thumb,
And pulled out a plum,
And said, "What a
good boy am I!"

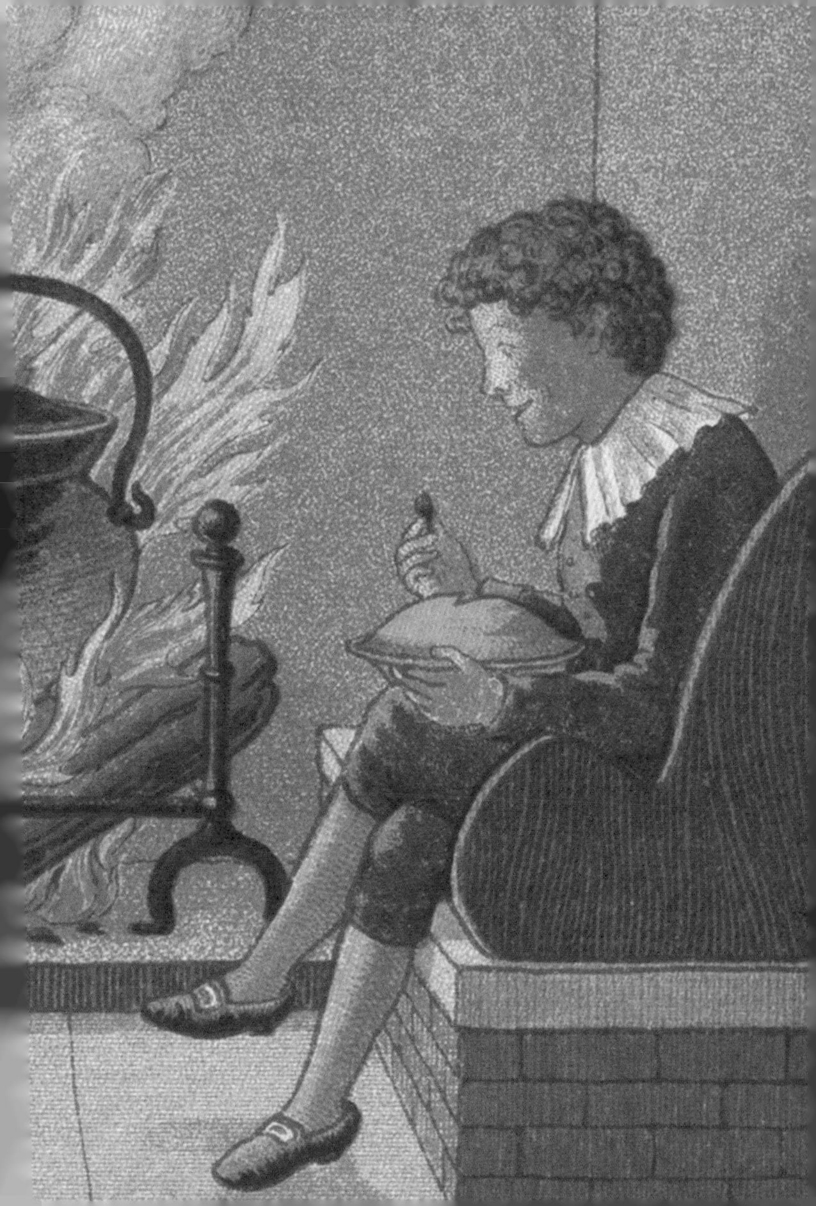

President's Fireside Chats

America's thirty-first President, Franklin Delano Roosevelt, was the first head of state to master the art of using radio. At that time, radio was still a relatively new technique of mass communication for using as an effective political device.

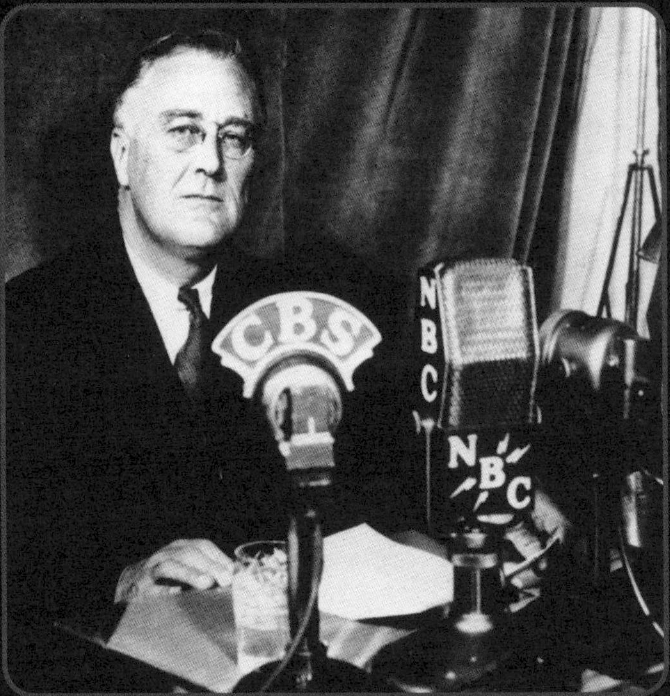
CBS
NBC
NBC

FDR began giving radio talks to the people of New York state shortly after he was elected Governor in 1928. Sitting in front of the microphone in his study in the Governor's Mansion, in Albany, he spoke to his fellow citizens, as they sat by their firesides listening to their radios. It was as if they were neighbors having a chat. FDR told them about what was going on in the current session of the state legislature. After each session ended, his radio talk would sum up its successes and failures.

By 1933, when FDR was first inaugurated as President, the radio talks, soon to be referred to as his "fireside chats," were such an important part of his way of making contact with his fellow Americans that he continued them.

FDR prepared most of the talks himself, although he did ask his aides to give him much background material. Because he made sure he was thoroughly familiar with everything he talked about, his fireside chats always sounded as if they were his own thoughts, not those of a team of aides and speech writers. He could discuss the most complicated legislation in a way that was easily understood by his listeners. He never talked down to them, and he never sounded as if he were reading or reciting a speech.

Today, despite the overwhelming importance of television as a means of communication, US presidents still follow in FDR's footsteps and make regular radio broadcasts to their fellow Americans.

The fire upon the hearth is low.

And there is stillness everywhere,

And, like winged spirits, here and there

The firelight shadows fluttering go.

from *In the Firelight*, Eugene Field

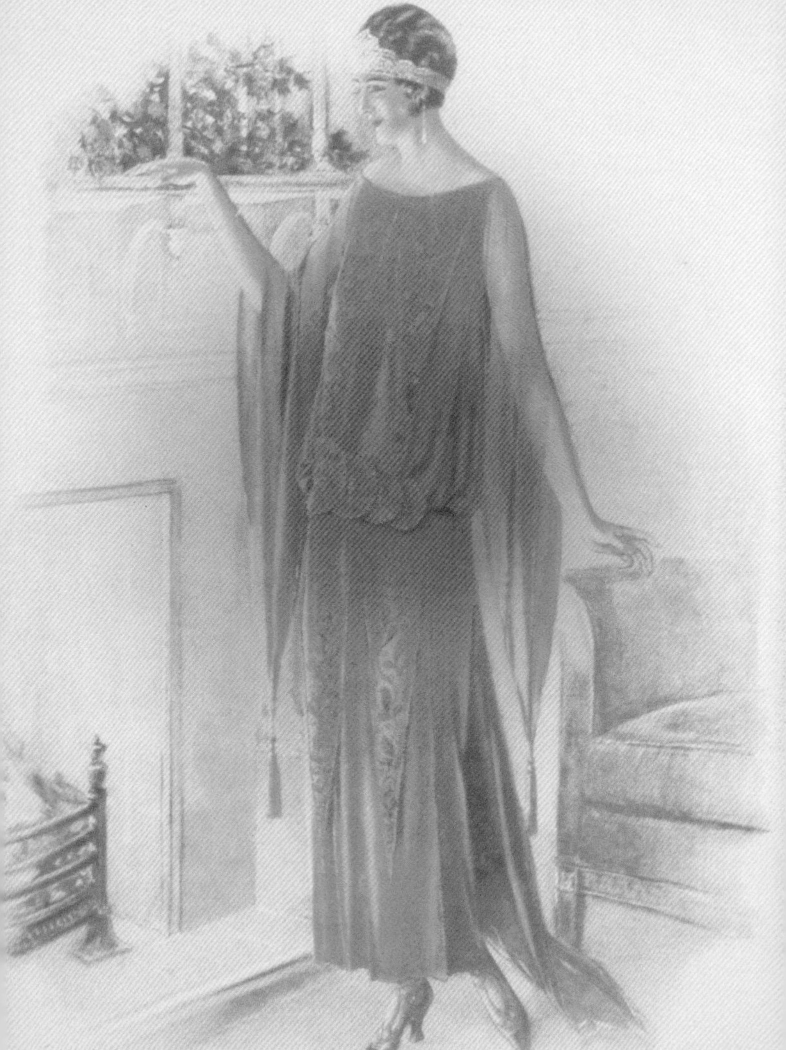

Hot Toddy

Think of sitting next to a blazing fire on a winter's night with the aroma from the warm drink in your hand wafting under your nose. In such circumstances, the hot toddy in your glass is more than just a drink. It is a satisfying heady experience.

A toddy is a mixture of a spirit and hot water, sweetened with sugar and flavored with lemon, honey, or spices such as cloves, nutmeg, cinnamon, or ginger. Whisky is a favorite spirit for a hot toddy, but brandy and rum are also good choices.

Hot Chocolate

A mug of delicious hot chocolate, slowly sipped while curled up on the fireside sofa, is the ultimate just-before-bed experience. For complete enjoyment, the ingredients must be of the highest quality. Use whole milk and the finest bittersweet chocolate to create the true, rich flavor of the drink. Four or five squares of an organic chocolate with 70 percent cocoa solids are ideal.

Chop the chocolate into small pieces so it will melt quickly. Gently heat the milk to just below boiling point, then stir the chocolate into the pan. When the chocolate has melted, pour the drink into a pretty mug, find a cozy spot in front of the fire, sit back, and enjoy.

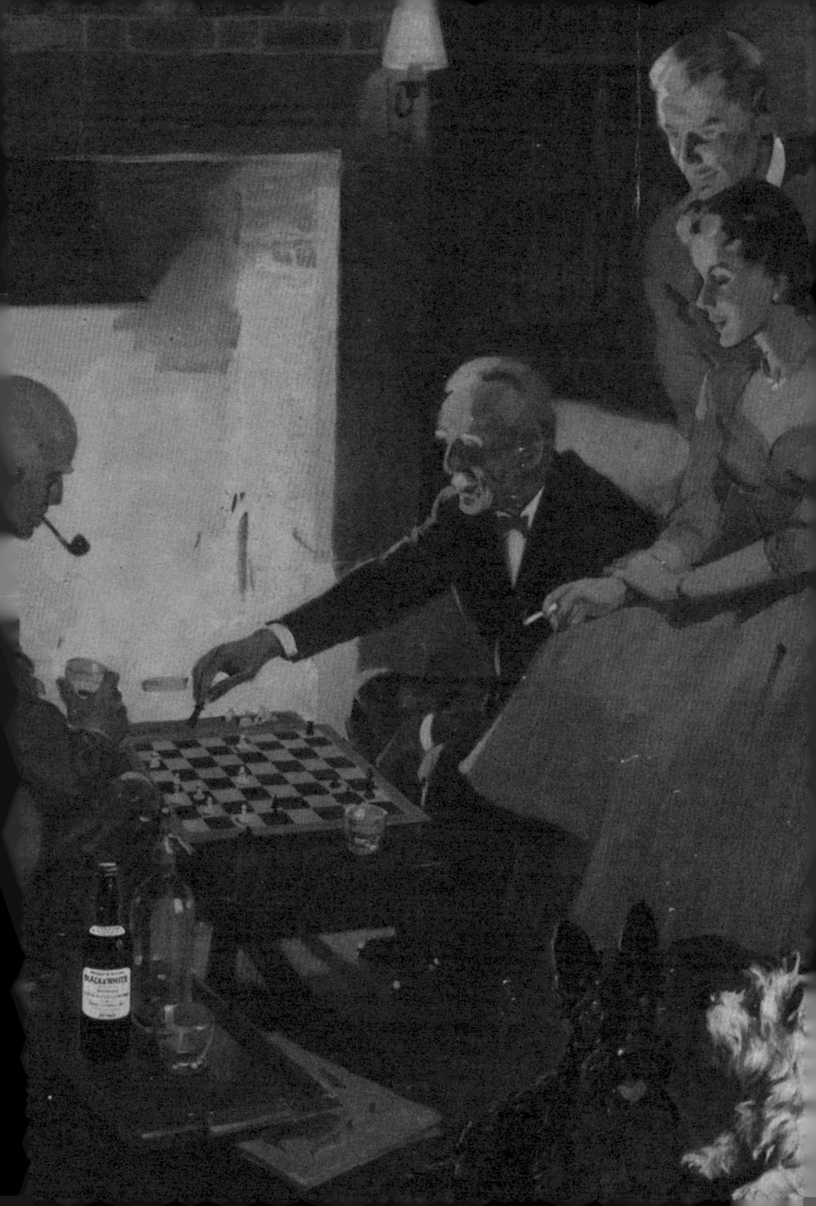
BLACK & WHITE

The Inglenook Fireplace

"Inglenooks" were originally sitting areas built inside large stone fireplaces during the medieval period. The wood-burning area stood in the center of a recess in the wall, leaving space for a bench or other seating on either side of the fire. There people could drink, talk, and relax sheltered from the drafts whistling through the hall.

As houses got smaller, their fireplaces were built in proportion. The openings for them were reduced to the size of the grate within them. The inglenook became the sort of fire most often encountered by travelers in old inns.

The inglenook made a comeback in houses on both sides of the Atlantic at the end of the nineteenth century. In America, the inglenook fireplace was usually at the very heart of the shingle-style houses and cottages that many rich industrialists built away from the turmoil of the city. These shingled retreats were built for summer-resort holidays, where the family could gather together in carefree safety around the warm and glowing fire.

In Britain, the inglenook fireplace was revived as a result of the success of the Arts and Crafts Movement, with its emphasis on domestic design and architecture.

Of course, in many old houses in England the inglenook was never removed and is today a highly desirable asset in the competitive business of buying and selling country cottages. What people are looking for is the snug little room within a room that English author Flora Thompson conjured up so vividly in *Candleford Green*.

Recalling life in rural Oxfordshire in the 1890s, Thompson described a former inglenook fireplace in which a "small sitting room grate with hobs had replaced the fire on the hearth of a few years before." The household called this little room within a room the "hearthplace."

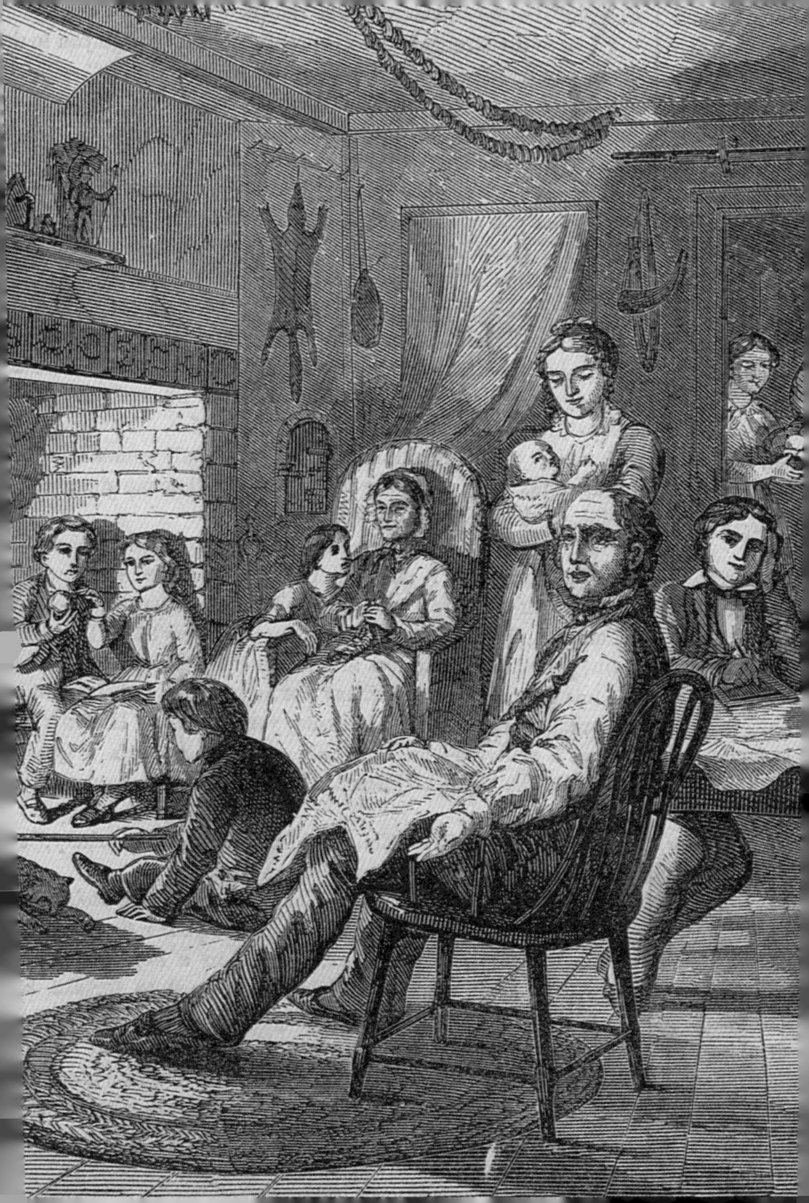

Gaudi's Fireplace

This spectacular mushroom-shaped fireplace was designed by renowned Spanish architect Antoni Gaudi. It can be found in the vestibule of the beautiful Casa Battlo apartment building in Barcelona. Like a traditional inglenook fireplace, Gaudi's fireplace has small seats within it—on one side of the fire, there is a seat large enough for a young couple and, on the other side, a smaller seat for their chaperone.

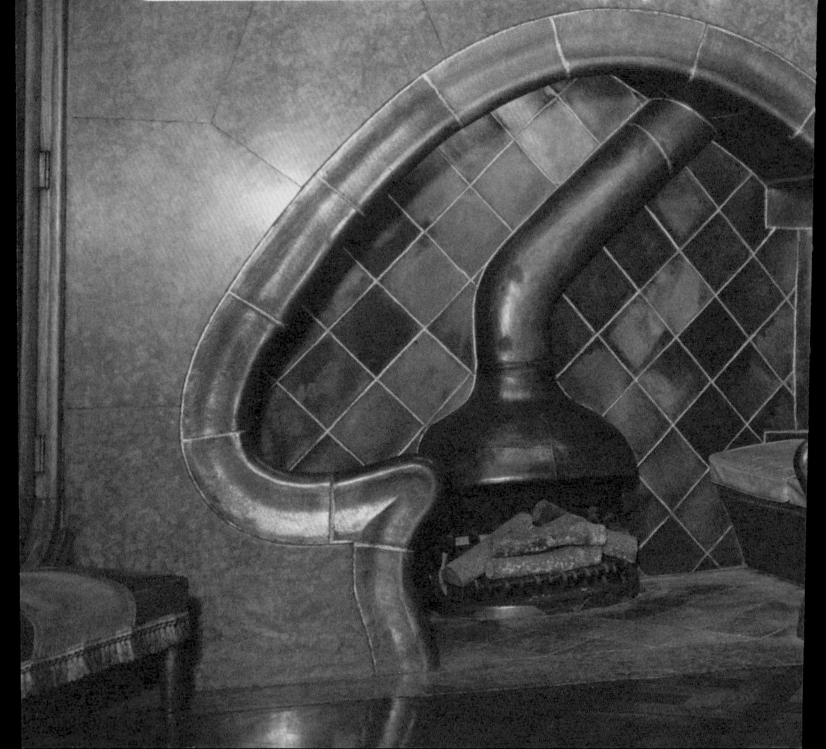

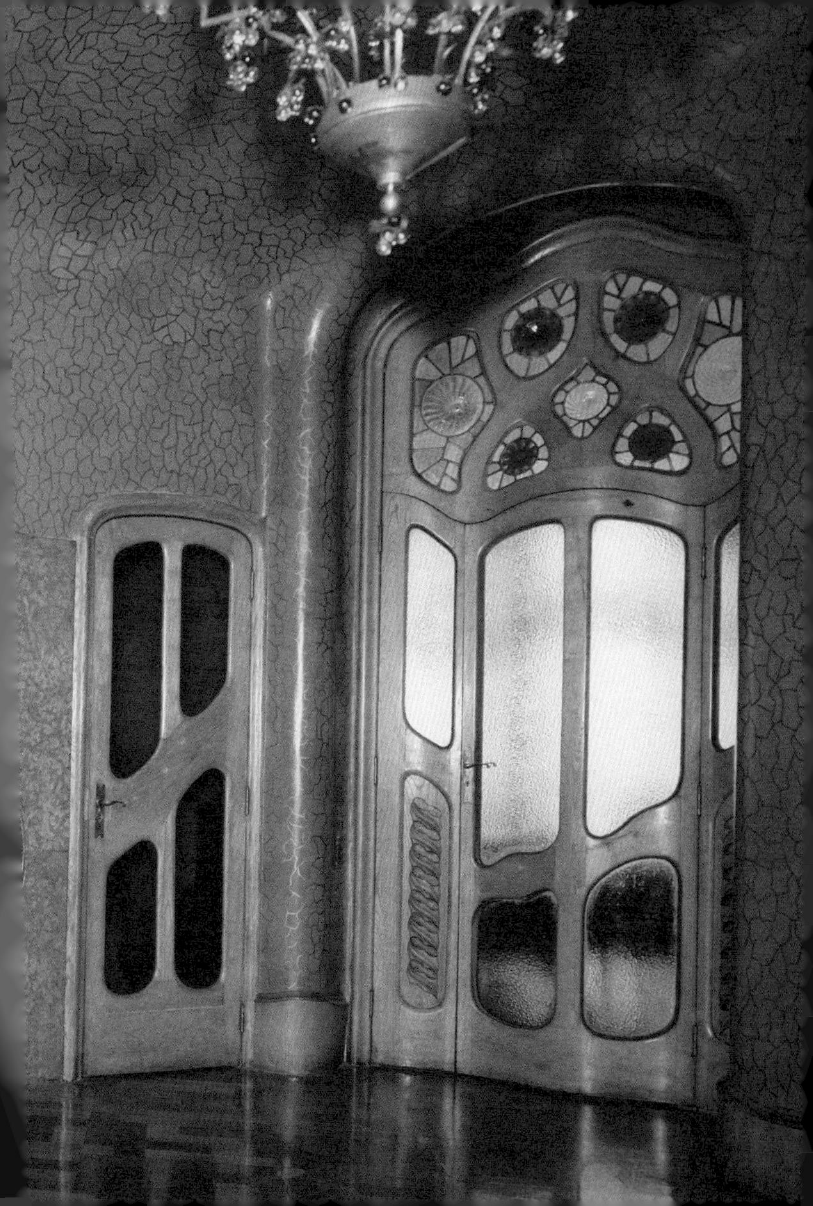

Little Polly Flinders

Little Polly Flinders
Sat among the cinders
Warming her
    pretty little toes.
Her mother came
    and caught her
And whipped her
    little daughter
For spoiling her
    nice new clothes.

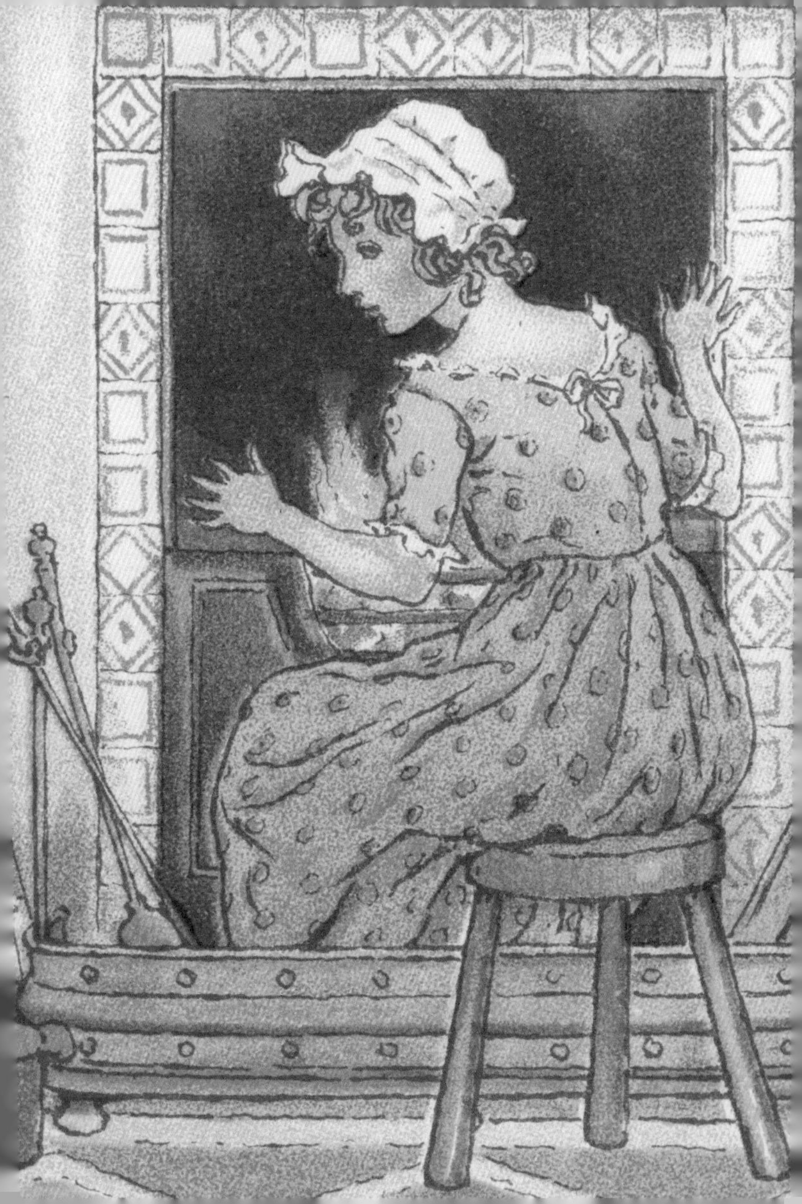

Benjamin Franklin's Fire

Among the many inventions and scientific experiments of the great American patriot, diplomat, and amateur scientist Benjamin Franklin, few were more beneficial than his Pennsylvania Fireplace. It is now more widely known as the "Franklin Stove."

Benjamin Franklin was unhappy with the way the living room fire burned the shins of anyone sitting in front of it, but left their backs in cold drafts. His solution to the problem was simple. He designed a stove in which the fire burned in front of an enclosed chamber that was divided vertically by a baffle. The baffle was sealed off from the fire itself and was connected to a space under the floor on which the stove sat. The underfloor (or cellar) space also gave the fire its air, thus eliminating the drafts (from under doors and through windows) that had previously kept the fire going.

When the fire was lit in the stove, radiant heat from it flowed into the living room, as did warm air from the baffle. Smoke from the fire was drawn up the stove, over and behind the baffle and into the chimney flue.

RIGHT: **Diagrams of Franklin Stove, circa 1760, from *Oeuvres de M. Franklin*, 1773, Vol. II.**

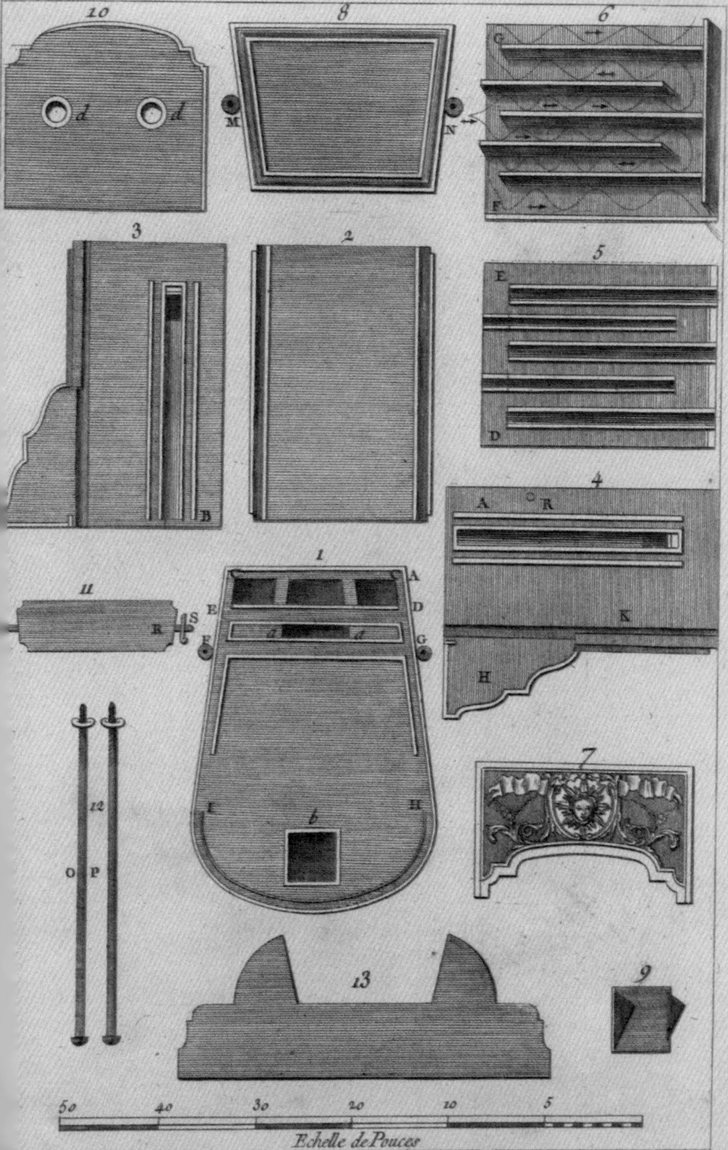
10
d
d
8
M
N
6
G
F
3
B
2
5
E
D
4
A
R
K
H
1
A
E
D
F
G
d
d
I
H
b
11
R
S
12
O
P
7
13
9
50
40
30
20
10
5
Echelle de Pouces

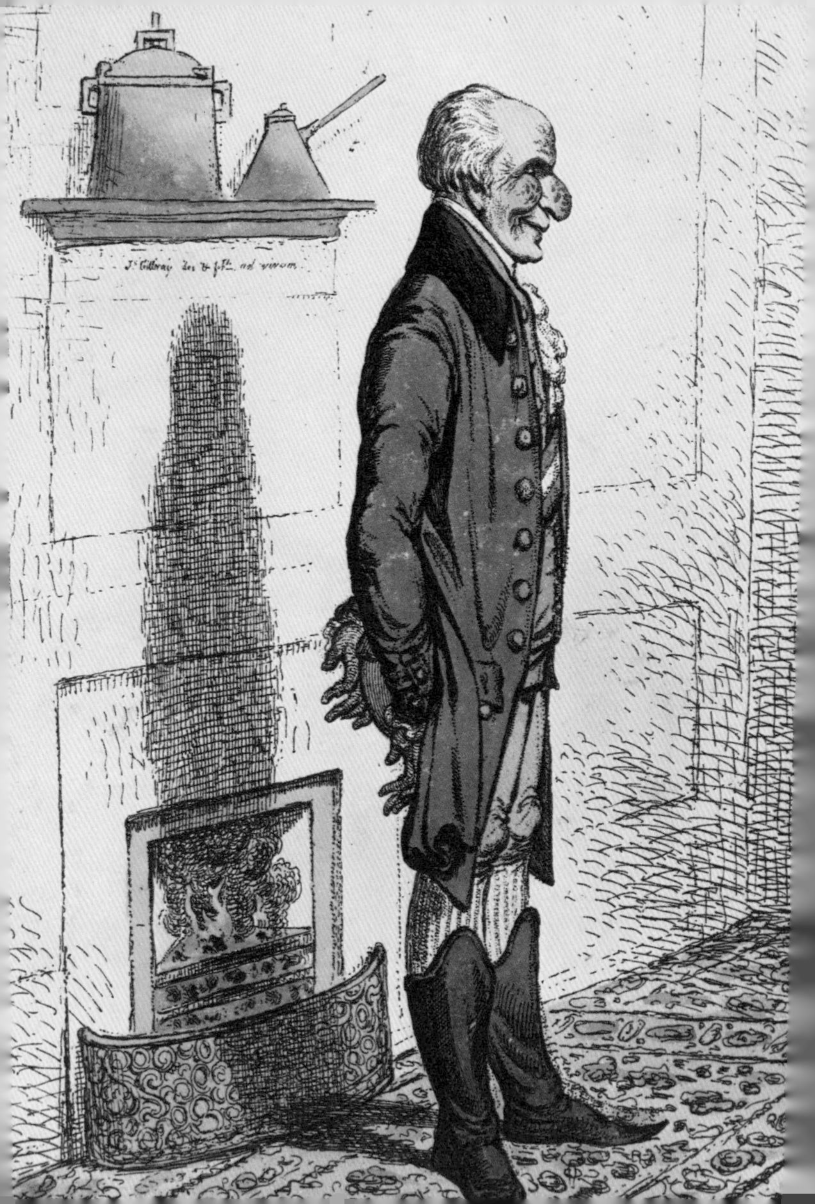
Js Gillray des & fect ad vivum

Count Rumford's Fire

The first true cooking-stove, which rapidly replaced hearth fires and charcoal ranges, was based in part on an invention by American Benjamin Thomson. But Thompson called himself Count Rumford. In London at the end of the eighteenth century, Count Rumford was horrified by the fuel-wasting smoke that hung over the city and set about redesigning its living room fireplaces and kitchen cooking fires.

Count Rumford's fireplace had a deep back wall, built of brick, and constructed so that its face sloped forward. In the throat of the chimney, which was as wide as the chimney but very shallow, he put a rotating metal plate allowing the chimney to be closed, opened fully, or set at positions in between. This arrangement helped prevent down drafts from the chimney forcing smoke into the living room. It also improved control of the burning rate of the fire. At the same time, the forward-sloping back wall of the fireplace pushed radiant heat out into the room. Count Rumford's more efficiently designed "register" grate and fireplace used fuel more efficiently and burned less of it, while also heating rooms much more effectively.

For the kitchen, he produced the first design for an enclosed, coal-fired range. It was to be called the "kitchener." By the mid-nineteenth century the old open-hearth cooking fires were becoming a thing of the past. Cast-iron ranges, whose heat could be controlled, replaced the open fire in everything from castle to cottage. By this time, Count Rumford himself was so famous that even Mrs. Isabella Beeton could describe him as "the celebrated philosopher and physician, who wrote so learnedly on all subjects connected with domestic economy and architecture."

LEFT: *The Comforts of a Rumford Stove*; Rumford standing in front of his invention, 1800.

Fire Screens

*"Before her removing from Norland, Elinor
had painted a very pretty pair of screens for her
sister-in-law, which being now just mounted
and brought home, ornamented her present
drawing room; and these screens, catching the
eye of John Dashwood on his following the
other gentlemen into the room, were officiously
handed by him to Colonel Brandon for
his admiration."*

from *Sense and Sensibility*, Jane Austen

Several kinds of fire screen were used in drawings rooms at
the beginning of the nineteenth century. The type of screens
that Elinor Dashwood painted in *Sense and Sensibility* had been
used in Europe since the late Middle Ages. They were small
screens on a pole, set between someone—usually a lady—and
the fire to provide protection from its direct heat. A circular
screen on what looks like an iron pole can be seen in a
fifteenth-century painting called *The Virgin and Child*, by the
Flemish artist Robert Campin. The earliest such screens ☞

238

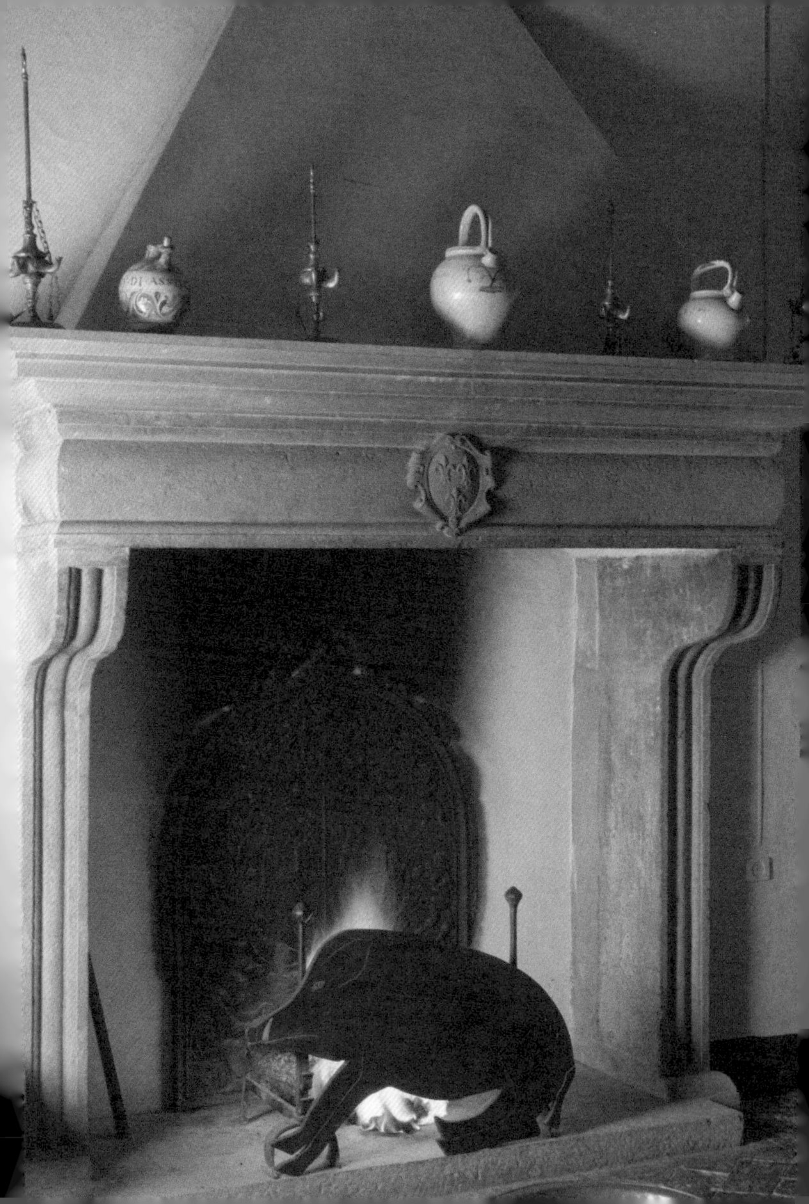

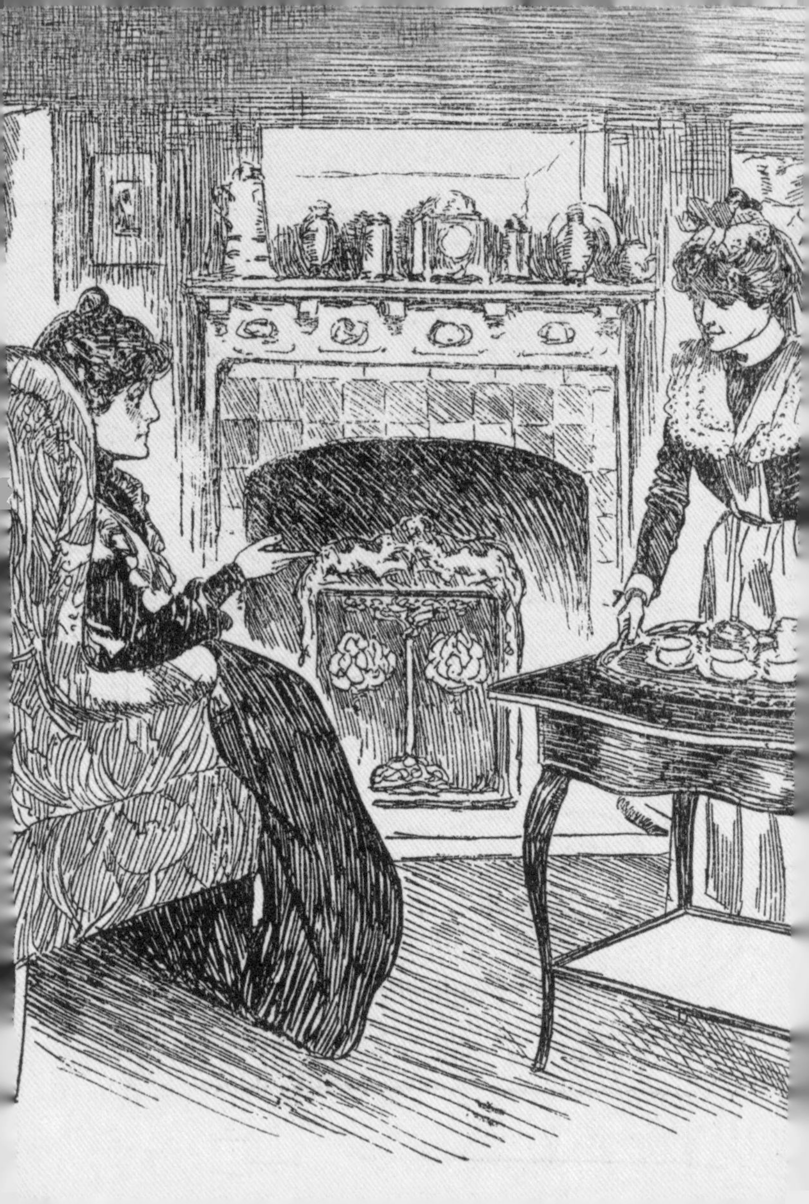

☞ known in England date from Elizabeth I's reign. By the mid-seventeenth century, the poles were always metal, though their feet and stands were wood, and the screens, which could be slid up and down the pole to adjust their height, were often decorated with tapestry, needlework or painted panels made by the ladies of the house.

Many Victorian and Edwardian drawing rooms had a larger variation of the pole screen in the form of a large screen on a wooden shaft and stand, often with a tripod foot.

Larger still were the free-standing square or rectangular fire screens, sometimes with folding sides, which were made in a variety of materials including, wood, metal, and glass. They were set in front of the hearth and were large enough to hide the grate. First seen in England during the reign of William and Mary, these screens can still be found in many homes, often with a tapestry or needlepoint panel sewn by the owner.

Fire screens are now sought-after antiques, commanding high prices if in good condition. If Elinor Dashwood's screens had been mounted on mahogany, they might have fetched thousands at auction a couple of centuries after she made them.

Even today fire screens don't have to be boring. Modern homeowners can accessorize their fireplaces with custom-made screens. Contemporary metal shops and blacksmiths can outdo any factory-made product with their innovative designs.

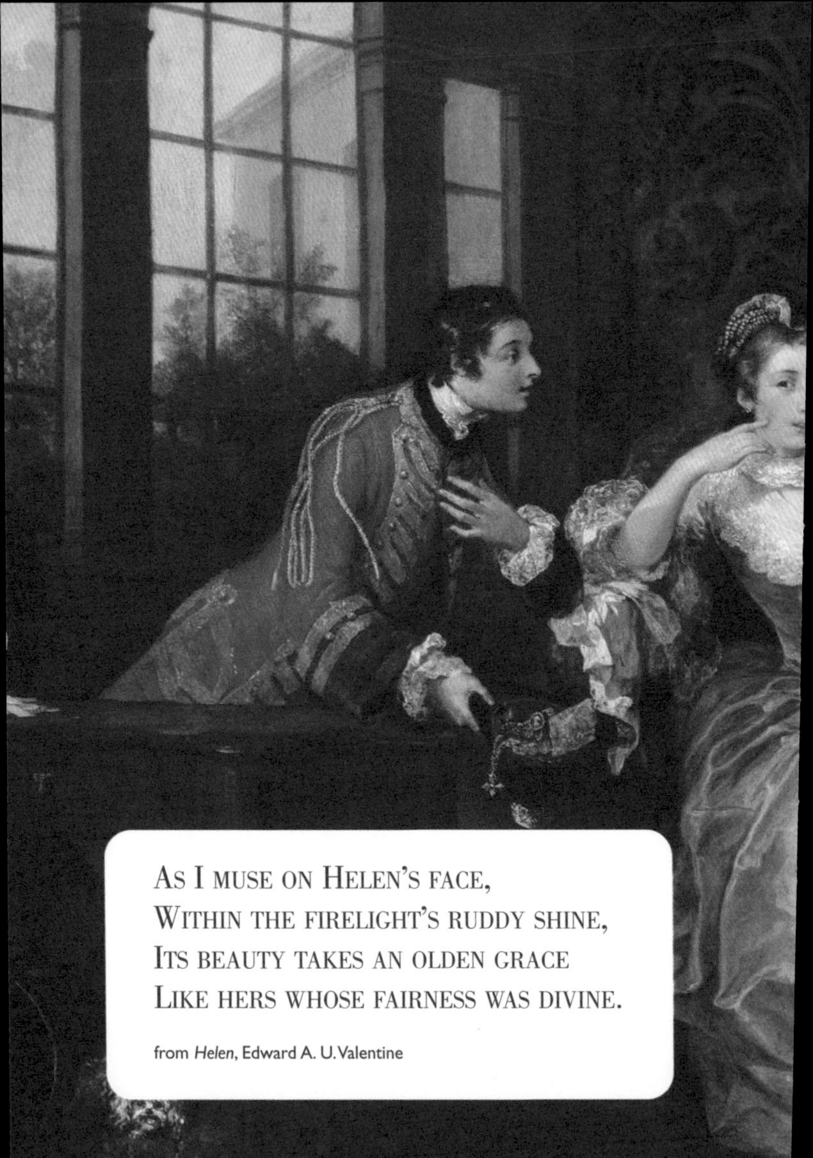

As I muse on Helen's face,
Within the firelight's ruddy shine,
Its beauty takes an olden grace
Like hers whose fairness was divine.

from *Helen*, Edward A. U. Valentine

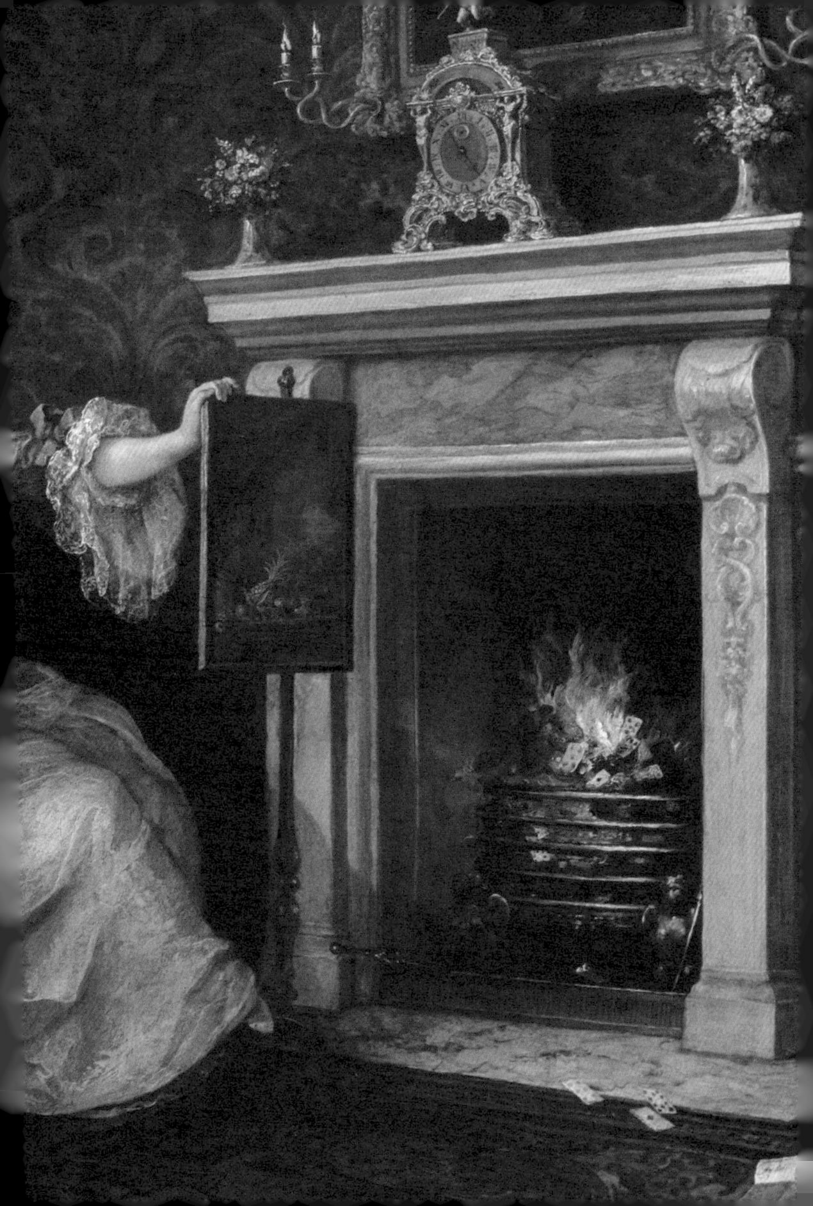

EXTRACT FROM

Three Weeks

by

ELINOR GLYN

A bright fire burnt in the grate, and some palest orchid-mauve silk curtains were drawn in the lady's room when Paul entered from the terrace. And loveliest sight of all, in front of the fire, stretched at full length, was his tiger—and on him—also at full length—reclined the lady, garbed in some strange clinging garment of heavy purple crepe, its hem embroidered with gold, one white arm resting on the beast's head, her back supported by a pile of the velvet cushions, and a heap of rarely bound books at her side, while between her red lips was a rose not redder than they—an almost scarlet rose. Paul had never seen one as red before.

The whole picture was barbaric. It might have been some painter's dream of the Favourite in a harem. It was not what one would expect to find in a sedate Swiss hotel.

She did not stir as he stepped in, dropping the heavy curtains after him. She merely raised her eyes, and looked Paul through and through. Her whole expression was changed; it was wicked and dangerous and *provocante*. It seemed quite true, as she had said—she was evidently in the devil's mood.

Paul bounded forward, but she raised one hand to stop him.

"No! you must not come near me, Paul. I am not safe to-day. Not yet. See, you must sit there and we will talk."

And she pointed to a great chair of Venetian workmanship and wonderful old velvet which was new to his view.

"I bought that chair in the town this morning at the curiosity shop on the top of Weggisstrasse, which long ago was the home of the Venetian envoy here—and you bought me the tiger, Paul. Ah! that was good. My beautiful tiger!" And she gave a movement like a snake, of joy to feel its fur under her, while she stretched out her hands and caressed the creature where the hair turned white and black at the side, and was deep and soft.

"Beautiful one! beautiful one!" she purred. "And I know all your feelings and your passions, and now I have got your skin—for the joy of my skin!" And she quivered again with the movements of a snake.

It is not difficult to imagine that Paul felt far from calm during this scene—indeed he was obliged to hold on to his great chair to prevent himself from seizing her in his arms.

"I'm—I'm so glad you like him," he said in a choked voice. "I thought probably you would. And your own was not worthy of you. I found this by chance. And oh! good God! if you knew how you are making me feel—lying there wasting your caresses upon it!"

She tossed the scarlet rose over to him; it hit his mouth.

"I am not wasting them," she said, the innocence of a 👉

kitten in her strange eyes—their colour impossible to define to-day. "Indeed not, Paul! He was my lover in another life—perhaps—who knows?"

"But I," said Paul, who was now quite mad, "want to be your lover in this!"

Then he gasped at his own boldness.

With a lightning movement she lay on her face, raised her elbows on the tiger's head, and supported her chin in her hands. Perfectly straight out her body was, the twisted purple drapery outlining her perfect shape, and flowing in graceful lines beyond—like a serpent's tail. The velvet pillows fell scattered at one side.

"Paul—what do you know of lovers—or love?" she said. "My baby Paul!"

"I know enough to know I know nothing yet which is worth knowing," he said confusedly. "But—but—don't you understand, I want you to teach me—"

"You are so sweet, Paul! when you plead like that I am taking in every bit of you. In your way as perfect as this tiger. But we must talk—oh! such a great, great deal—first."

A rage of passion was racing through Paul, his incoherent thoughts were that he did not want to talk—only to kiss her—to devour her—to strangle her with love if necessary.

He bit the rose.

"You see, Paul, love is a purely physical emotion," she continued. "We could speak an immense amount about souls, and sympathy, and understanding, and devotion. All beautiful things in their way, and possible to be enjoyed at a distance from one another. All the things which make passion noble—but without love—which is passion—these things dwindle and become duties presently, when the hysterical exaltation cools. Love is tangible—it means to be close—close—to be clasped—to be touching—to be One!"

Her voice was low—so concentrated as to be startling in contrast to the drip of the rain outside, and her eyes—half closed and gleaming—burnt into his brain. It seemed as if strange flames of green darted from their pupils.

"But that is what I want!" Paul said, unsteadily.

"Without counting the cost? Tears and—cold steel—and blood!" she whispered. "Wait a while, beautiful Paul!"

He started back chilled for a second, and in that second she changed her position, pulling the cushions around her, nestling into them and drawing herself cosily up like a child playing on a mat in front of the fire, while with a face of perfect innocence she looked up as she drew one of her great books nearer, and said in a dreamy voice:

"Now we will read fairy-tales, Paul."

But Paul was too moved to speak. These rapid changes were too much for him, greatly advanced though he had become in these short days since he had known her. He leant back in his chair, every nerve in his body quivering, his young fresh face almost pale.

Chocolate Truffles

Chocolate truffles are an extravagant indulgence—just the thing for one of those evenings when the time beside the fire is earmarked for special relaxation: low lights, soft music, a good wine. Considering how sinfully delicious they are, chocolate truffles are very easy to make. They should be made with the best ingredients possible, choosing a high-quality bittersweet chocolate with at least 70 percent cocoa solids.

Ingredients:
7fl oz/200ml light cream
1oz/25g butter
1lb/450g organic bittersweet chocolate, broken into pieces
2 tbsp rum, brandy, or other liqueur of your choice (optional)

Coatings:
4 tbsp cocoa sifted with 1 tbsp confectioners' sugar
chocolate vermicelli
2–3oz/50–75g chocolate

1 Line a shallow baking pan with waxed paper.

2 For the truffles, heat the cream and butter together in a heavy-based pan until the mixture reaches a rolling boil. Remove the pan from the heat and stir in the chocolate pieces, stirring until the chocolate has melted and the mixture is smooth. Add the liqueur, if using. Pour the mixture into the prepared pan, spreading it out with a spatula. Leave in a cool place, uncovered, for 24 hours to firm up.

3 The next day, remove pieces of the mixture, large enough to make truffles the size of large marbles, from the baking pan and roll them into balls in the palms of your hands. Put them back in the pan while you prepare the coatings.

4 For the three coatings, shake the sifted cocoa and confectioners' sugar onto a sheet of waxed paper; sprinkle the chocolate vermicelli onto a plate; put the chocolate into a bowl set over gently simmering water, making sure the bowl does not touch the water, and leave until the chocolate has melted.

5 Coat each truffle in one of the three coatings, rolling them in the cocoa and sugar mixture or the vermicelli, or using a fork to dip them into the melted chocolate. When each truffle is coated, put it in the baking pan, lined with fresh waxed paper. When the coatings have set, put the truffles in a covered container, separating the layers with waxed paper, and store in the refrigerator. They will keep in the refrigerator for up to 2 weeks.

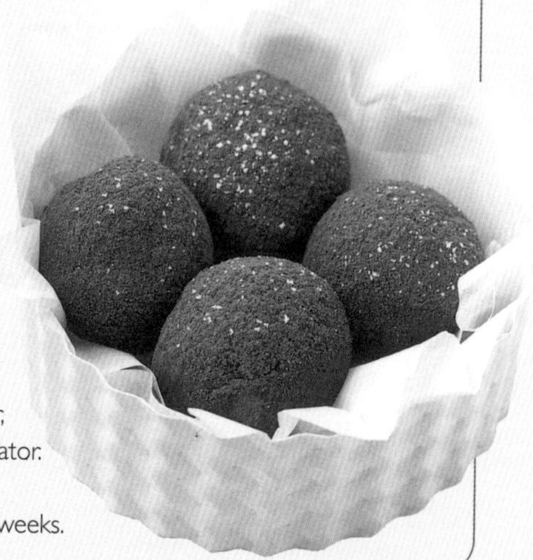

Mantel Clocks

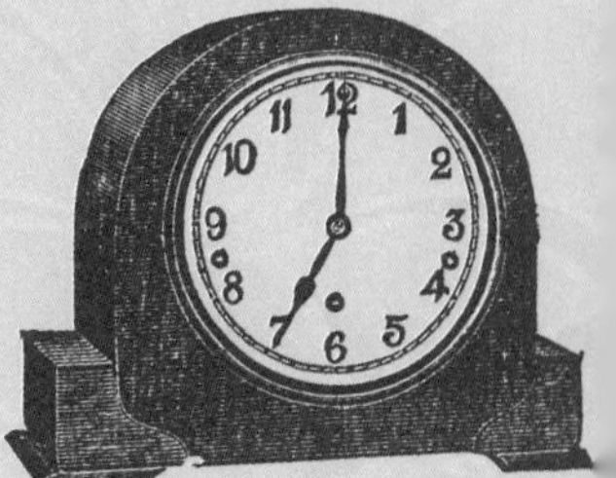

12
1
2
3
4
5
6
7
8
9
10
11

When the fireplace was basically a hole in the wall, domestic clocks were made to hang from beams (the lantern clock), on a bracket attached to the wall (bracket clocks), or on the floor (the longcase clock). Once the chimneypiece, or mantelpiece, had become an important focus of attention in living rooms, the question of what to set upon it also became important. One obvious answer was a clock.

The earliest mantel clocks first appeared in Europe in the seventeenth century, and were mainly bracket clocks adapted to stand on a table or mantelpiece. The true mantel clock was a spring-wound device designed specially to be set on the mantelpiece. Rather than being squarish in shape, like bracket clocks, they tended to have a greater width than depth and were often designed with ornate backplates or other adornment that enhanced the clock's appearance when it was reflected in a mantel mirror. While mantel and table clocks could be wound from the front or the back, clocks intended specifically for the mantelpiece tended to be wound from the front via a key inserted into a hole in the dial plate.

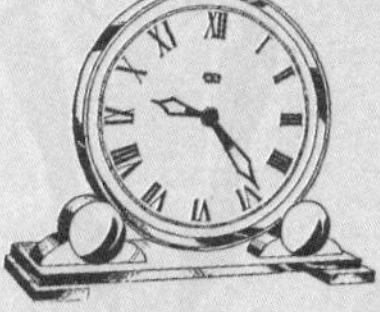

The design of the clock on the mantelpiece became splendidly exuberant, influenced in England by the fashion for Oriental style. The clocks were often veneered in ebonized pearwood or in walnut, kingwood, or tortoiseshell. Clock cases were covered in ornate applied decoration, with chased and gilded mounts, heavily engraved dial plates, and ornate handles, capitals, and bases.

For nearly a century and a half, French taste influenced mantel-clock styles across Europe. Toward the end of the nineteenth century, exquisitely designed and decorated clocks and "mantel sets"—a clock set between matching vases—in Boulle and rococo styles faced out into rooms filled with the heavy Germanic- and Victorian-style furniture and drapes that dominated European domestic taste.

Thanks to a Boston family of clockmakers, the Willard family, American mantel-clock design took an attractive turn toward the end of the eighteenth century. One of the four Willard brothers turned his back on the traditional longcase clock and came up with the forerunner of what became known as the Massachusetts shelf clock.

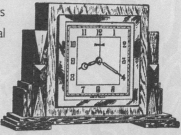

Fireplace Mirrors

In *Through the Looking Glass*, Lewis Carroll introduced his young heroine Alice to a magical mode of transport that would not have been possible a couple of centuries before.

The mirror, or "looking-glass" as well-bred Victorians liked to refer to it, first found a place over the fire in the late seventeenth century, when a French architect, Robert de Cotte, designed what he called a "chimney-glass." These mirrors were made up of several pieces of small glass joined together within a frame, and so it was not until ways were found to make larger inexpensive sheets of glass that the mantelpiece mirror became an established item in most homes.

In the eighteenth century, carefully placed and beautifully framed mirrors became essential items in the living and drawing rooms of the affluent. As the renowned English furniture-designer Thomas Sheraton wrote in *The Cabinet Dictionary* in 1803, well-placed mirrors, providing "reflection or perspective representation of the room" were among the furnishings requisite for "elegant drawing rooms receiving persons of the highest rank."

The frame around the mirror became a work of art in itself, its design reflecting the fashions of the period. The frames around mirrors came in recognizable styles, from Baroque and rococo to Gothic, Adam, and Regency.

By the time Alice was scrambling through the looking-glass in her warm Victorian home, mirror frames were less ornate than in Georgian times and much heavier and more solid-looking than before.

The wheel of fashion, influenced by new movements in art and design, continued to turn. The design and style of mantelpiece mirrors changed as much as other home furnishings, with the Arts and Crafts movement, Art Nouveau, Art Deco, Modernism, and other styles all influencing the appearance of the mirror over the fireplace.

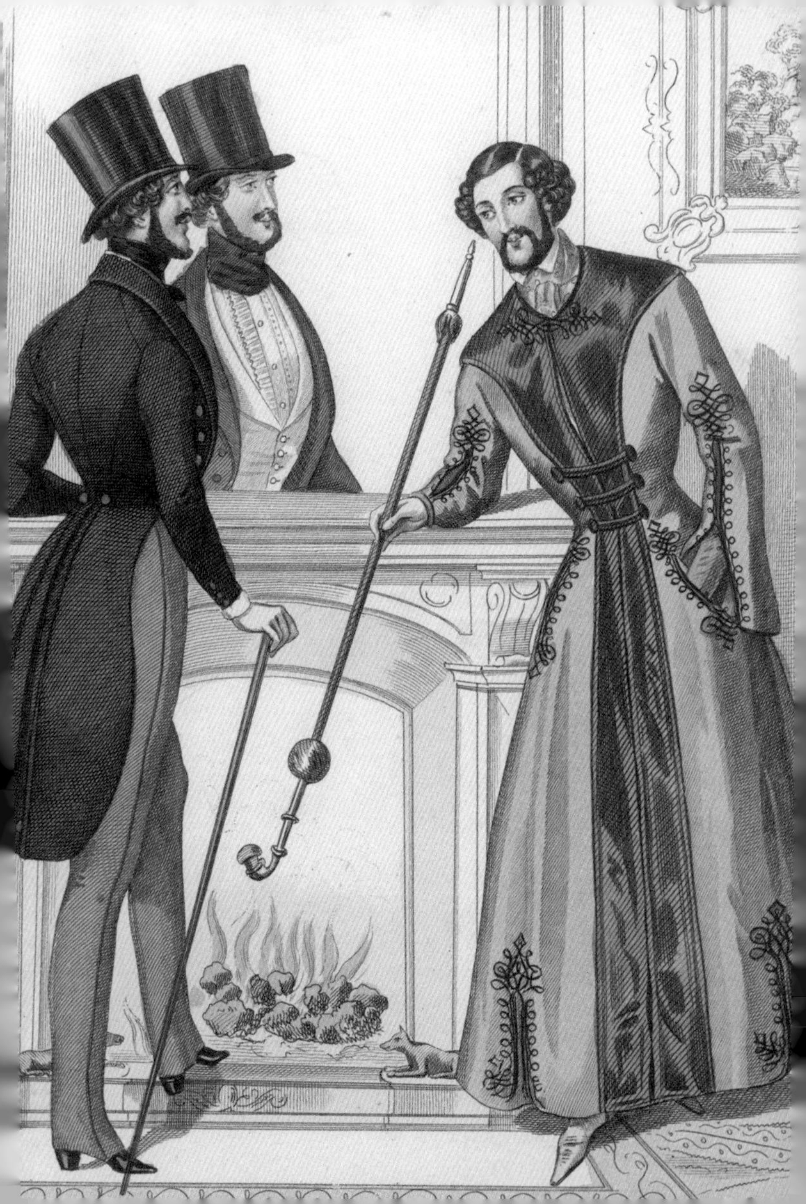

Through the Looking Glass

by

LEWIS CARROLL

"I'll tell you all my ideas about Looking-glass House. First, there's the room you can see through the glass—that's just the same as our drawing room, only the things go the other way. I can see all of it when I get upon a chair—all but the bit behind the fireplace. Oh! I do so wish I could see *that* bit! I want so much to know whether they've a fire in the winter: you never *can* tell, you know, unless our fire smokes, and then smoke comes up in that room too—but that may be only pretence, just to make it look as if they had a fire.

"Oh, Kitty! how nice it would be if we could only get through into Looking-glass House…Let's pretend there's a way of getting through into it, somehow, Kitty. Let's pretend the glass has got all soft like gauze, so that we can get through. Why it's turning into a sort of mist now…."

In another moment Alice was through the glass, and had jumped lightly down into the Looking-glass room. The very first thing she did was to look whether there was a fire in the fireplace, and she was quite pleased to find that there was a real one, blazing away as brightly as the one she had left behind. "So I shall be as warm here as I was in the old room," thought Alice.

The Goblins' Blessings

Yon Elves of fire, eyes all aglow
In flicker and in flame delight—
They flutter round when lamps are low,
To tinker, toil, and mend all night.
While Mary dreams on mother's chair
By morn the goblins' blessings will be there.

CÉLINE DIXON

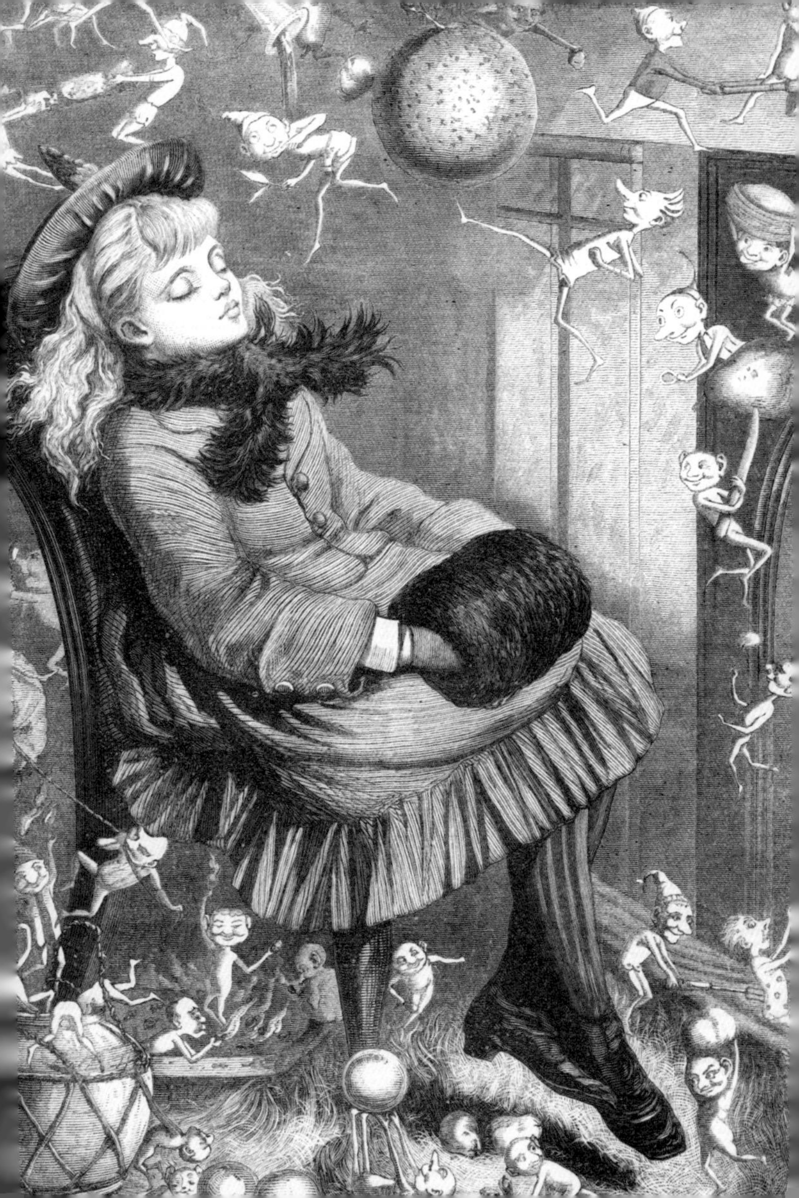

EXTRACT FROM

A Christmas Carol

by

CHARLES DICKENS

[Scrooge] took off his cravat; put on his dressing-gown and slippers, and his nightcap; and sat down before the fire to take his gruel.

It was a very low fire indeed; nothing on such a bitter night. He was obliged to sit close to it, and brood over it, before he could extract the least sensation of warmth from such a handful of fuel. The fireplace was an old one, built by some Dutch merchant long ago, and paved all round with quaint Dutch tiles, designed to illustrate the Scriptures. There were Cains and Abels, Pharaohs' daughters; Queens of Sheba, Angelic messengers descending through the air on clouds like feather-beds, Abrahams, Belshazzars, Apostles putting off to sea in butter-boats, hundreds of

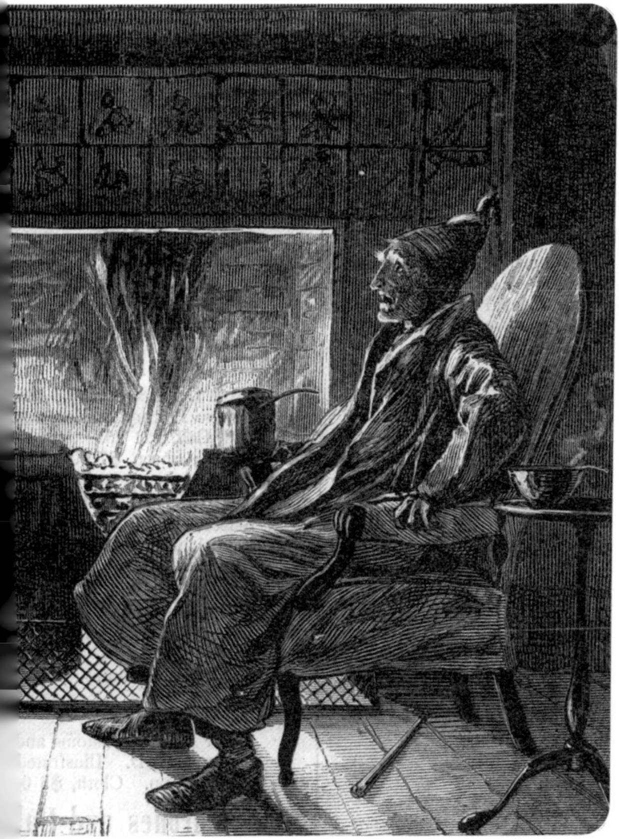

 figures to attract his thoughts—and yet that face of Marley, seven years dead, came like the ancient Prophet's rod, and swallowed up the whole. If each smooth tile had been a blank at first, with power to shape some picture on its surface from the disjointed fragments of his thoughts, there would have been a copy of old Marley's head on every one.

"Humbug!" said Scrooge; and walked across the room.

After several turns, he sat down again. As he threw his head back in the chair, his glance happened to rest upon a bell, a disused bell, that hung in the room, and communicated for some purpose now forgotten with a chamber in the highest story of the building. It was with great astonishment, and with a strange, inexplicable dread, that as he looked, he saw this bell begin to swing. It swung so softly in the outset that it scarcely made a sound; but soon it rang out loudly, and so did every bell in the house.

This might have lasted half a minute, or a minute, but it seemed an hour. The bells ceased as they had begun, together. They were succeeded by a clanking noise, deep down below; as if some person were dragging a heavy chain over the casks in the wine merchant's cellar. Scrooge then remembered to have heard that ghosts in haunted houses were described as dragging chains.

The cellar-door flew open with a booming sound, and then he heard the noise much louder, on the floors below; then coming up the stairs; then coming straight towards his door.

"It's humbug still!" said Scrooge. "I won't believe it."

His colour changed though, when, without a pause, it came on through the heavy door, and passed into the room before his eyes. Upon its coming in, the dying flame leaped up, as though it cried "I know him; Marley's Ghost!" and fell again.

The same face: the very same. Marley in his pigtail, usual waistcoat, tights and boots; the tassels on the latter bristling, like his pigtail, and his coat-skirts, and the hair upon his head. The chain he drew was clasped about his middle. It was long, and wound about him like a tail; and it was made (for Scrooge observed it closely) of cash-boxes, keys, padlocks, ledgers, deeds, and heavy purses wrought in steel. His body was transparent; so that Scrooge, observing him, and looking through his waistcoat, could see the two buttons on his coat behind.

Scrooge had often heard it said that Marley had no bowels, but he had never believed it until now.

No, nor did he believe it even now. Though he looked the phantom through and through, and saw it standing before him; though he felt the chilling influence of its death-cold eyes; and marked the very texture of the folded kerchief bound about its head and chin, which wrapper he had not observed before; he was still incredulous, and fought against his senses.

"How now!" said Scrooge, caustic and cold as ever. "What do you want with me?"

"Much!"—Marley's voice, no doubt about it.

Delft Blue Around the Fire

The town of Delft in The Netherlands has produced its inimitable blue earthenware for centuries, with mantel vases and other ornaments being high on the list of its products. Although glazed wall and fireplace tiles were only a side-line of the Dutch ceramics industry, they were made in huge numbers.

The Dutch tiles that paved Ebeneezer Scrooge's fireplace in England could well have been in place since the seventeenth century. By the end of that century, a quarter of a million Dutch tiles were selling every year in northern Germany alone, and they were sent all over Europe and to colonial America. Delft glazed earthenware became even more fashionable in England with the accession to the throne of the Dutch William III in 1688.

In America, where much fireplace and chimneypiece design was inspired by pattern books from England. Many of the basic materials, such as marble and tiles, came from Europe, with Delft tiles being particularly popular.

The Philipse Manor Hall in Yonkers, New York, has a large open fireplace, originally lined with blue and white Dutch tiles depicting Biblical scenes. The manor is a graceful and mellow eighteenth-century house, now in the care of a preservation society. A few of the original Dutch tiles still remain around the fireplace today, with the gaps filled with modern copies.

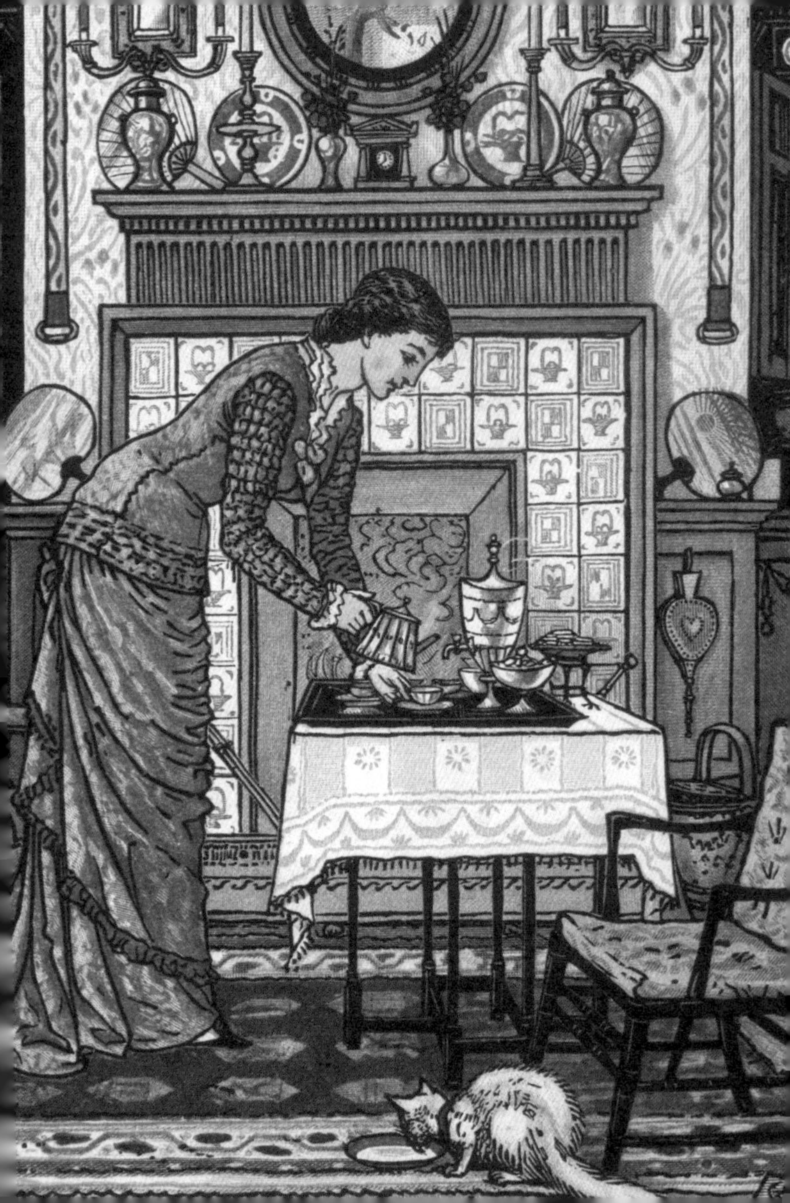

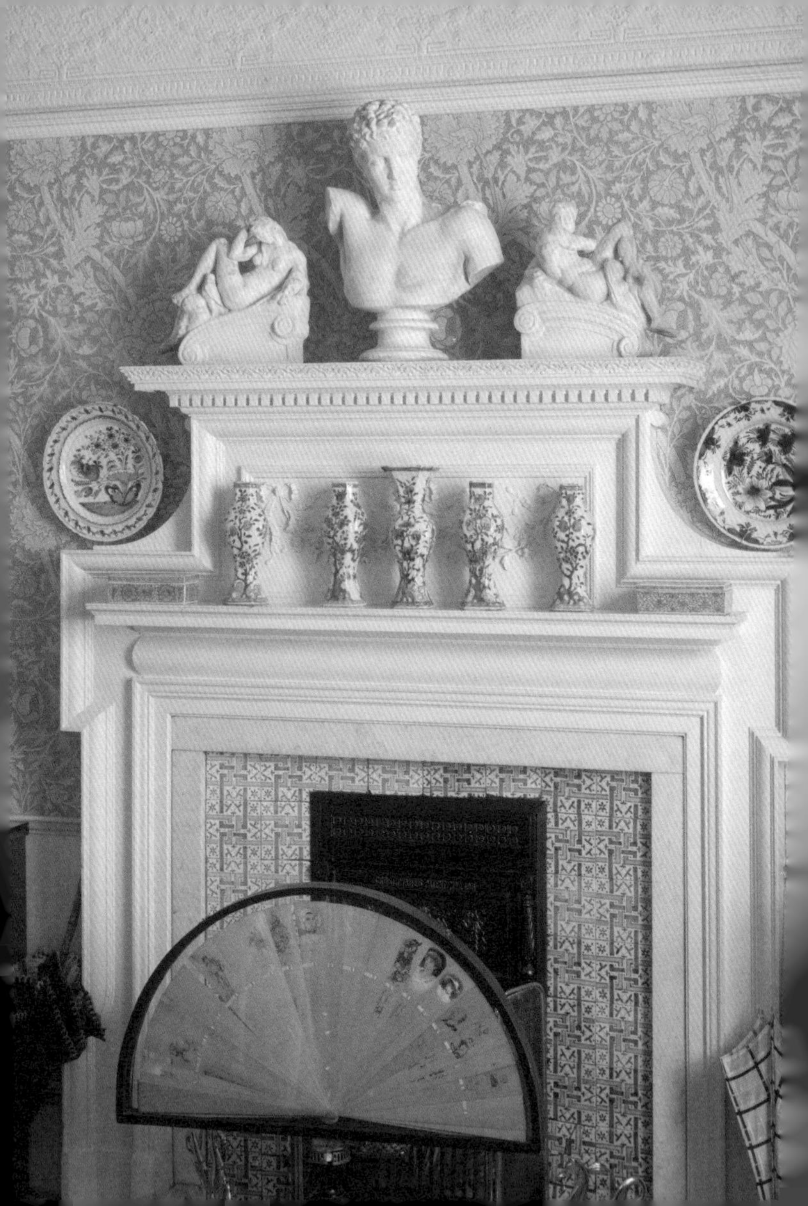

Garnitures de Cheminée

In the seventeenth century, the increasingly affluent upper classes of Europe were beginning to indulge in what is known in our time as "conspicuous consumption." Where better than on the mantelpiece or by the hearth of one's drawing room fireplace to display large pieces of fashionable and expensive earthenware and porcelain?

A *garniture de cheminée* set could consist of three, five, or seven usually vase-shaped ornaments, either of Chinese export porcelain or Delft pottery. The Dutch pottery industry was influenced by the arrival in Amsterdam in 1602 of two shiploads of Ming porcelain from China. Soon, Europe was flooded with Dutch pottery decorated in the *chinoiserie* style.

In Britain, after 1688, royal palaces and the great houses of the noble supporters of the Glorious Revolution began displaying large collections of Dutch pottery ornaments—from towering tulip stands shaped like Chinese pagodas to huge jars and great platters, as well as the popular sets of vases.

King William III and Queen Mary led the way in importing Delft ware into Britain. They commissioned a Delft factory to create tiles for an entire room, including the fireplace. They also commissioned many ornamental objects, such as tulip vases decorated with the motto and coats of arms of the royal family.

Modern Rustic Fireside Style

The need to relax in front of an open fire may be even more pressing in today's stressed-out world. This may be the reason why the decorating style widely known as "modern rustic" became so appealing. Every designer knows that the heart of today's country interior is the fireplace: this provides a welcoming, relaxed focus for a serene, comfortable rural home. The fireplace may include an embedded rustic beam for a mantle, stone or tile details, and a brick or clay tile hearth area—the choice is extensive.

Modern rustic style has its roots in the rural life of various country cultures—whether they originate within America, England, Sweden, Spain, or France. The style is generously broad and includes looks derived from humble farmhouses as well as grander country houses and chateaus. In general, however, the overall feel is rural, warm, cozy, and appealing.

Natural materials play an important part in modern rustic rooms, and may be applied in carved wood details, woven rush chair seats, rough plaster walls, or natural stone floors. Further details such as distressed ceiling beams, rough stone walls or floors, and coarse plaster walls all add to the peaceful, timeless atmosphere.

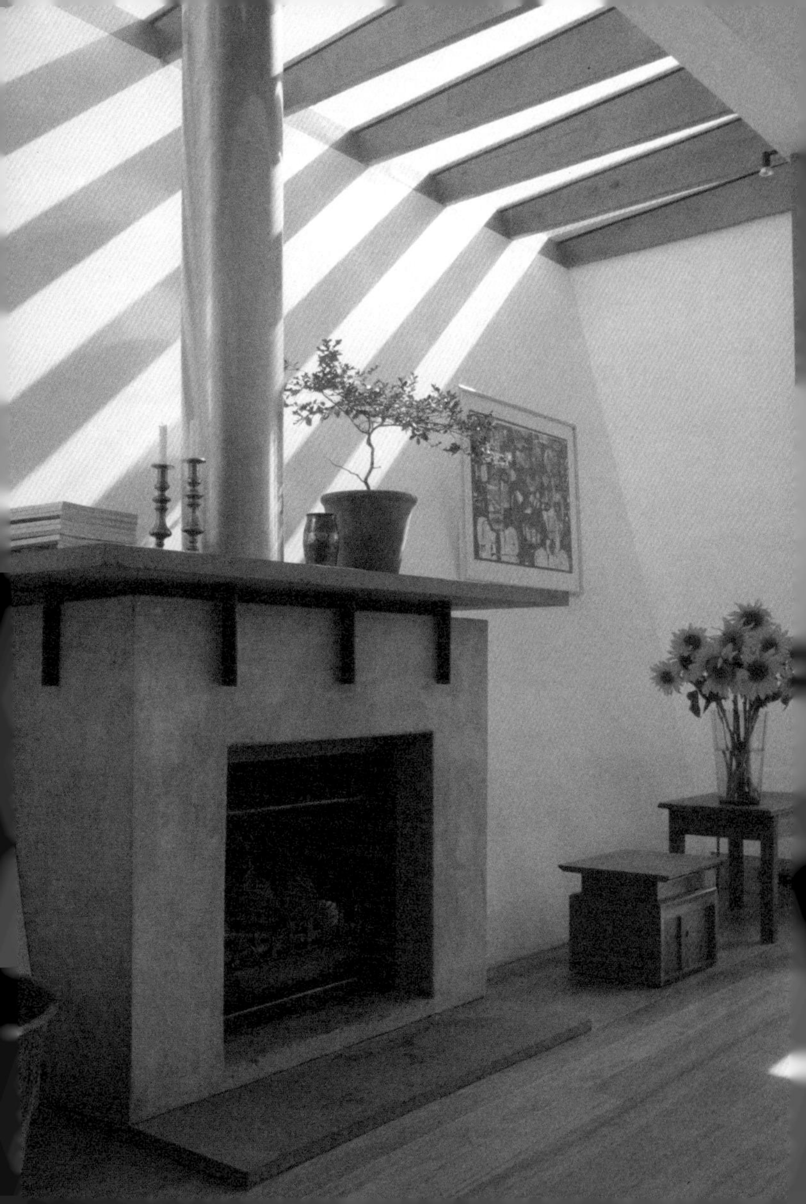

Snow-Bound: A Winter Idyl

by

JOHN GREENLEAF WHITTIER

Shut in from all the world without,
We sat the clean-winged hearth about,
Content to let the north-wind roar
In baffled rage at pane and door,
While the red logs before us beat
The frost-line back with tropic heat;
And ever, when a louder blast
Shook beam and rafter as it passed,
The merrier up its roaring draught
The great throat of the chimney laughed:
The house-dog on his paws outspread
Laid to the fire his drowsy head,
The cat's dark silhouette on the wall
A couchant tiger's seemed to fall;
And, for the winter fireside meet,
Between the andirons' straddling feet,
The mug of cider simmered slow,
The apples sputtered in a row,
And, close at hand, the basket stood
With nuts from brown October's wood.

What matter how the night behaved?
What matter how the north-wind raved?
Blow high, blow low, not all its snow
Could quench our hearth-fire's ruddy glow.

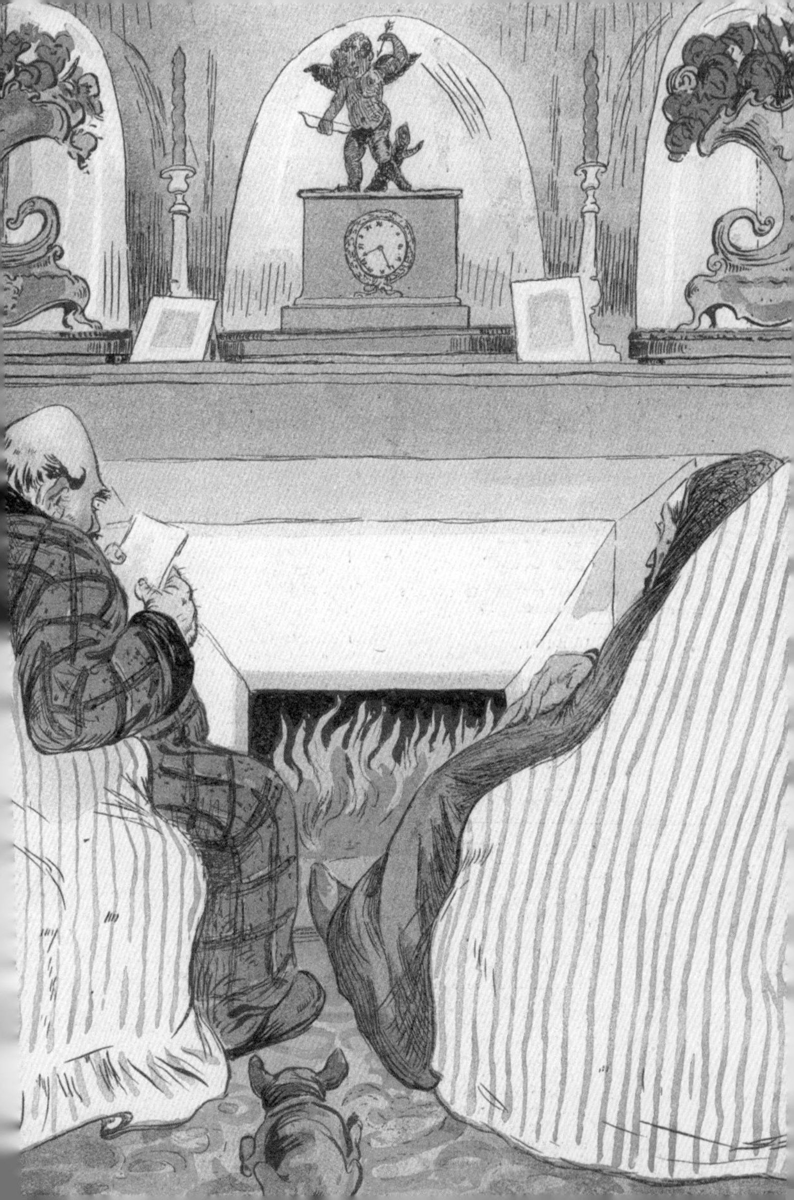

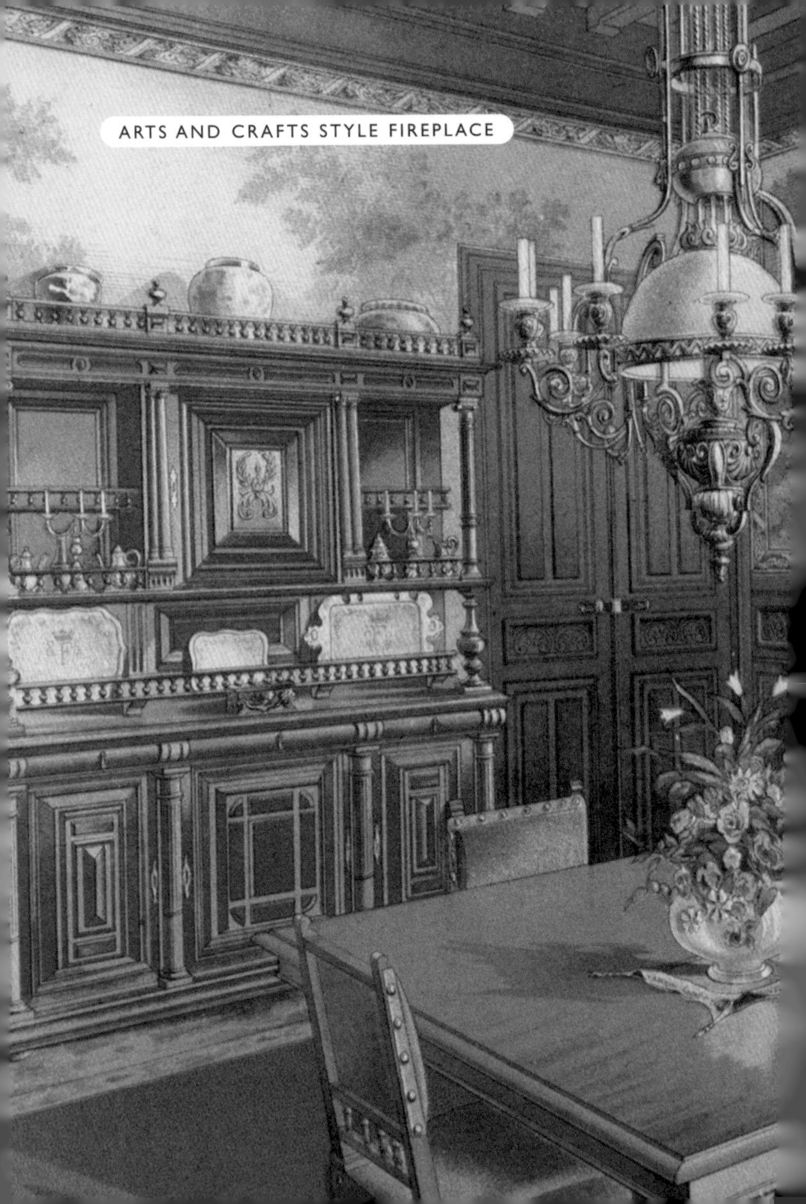

ARTS AND CRAFTS STYLE FIREPLACE

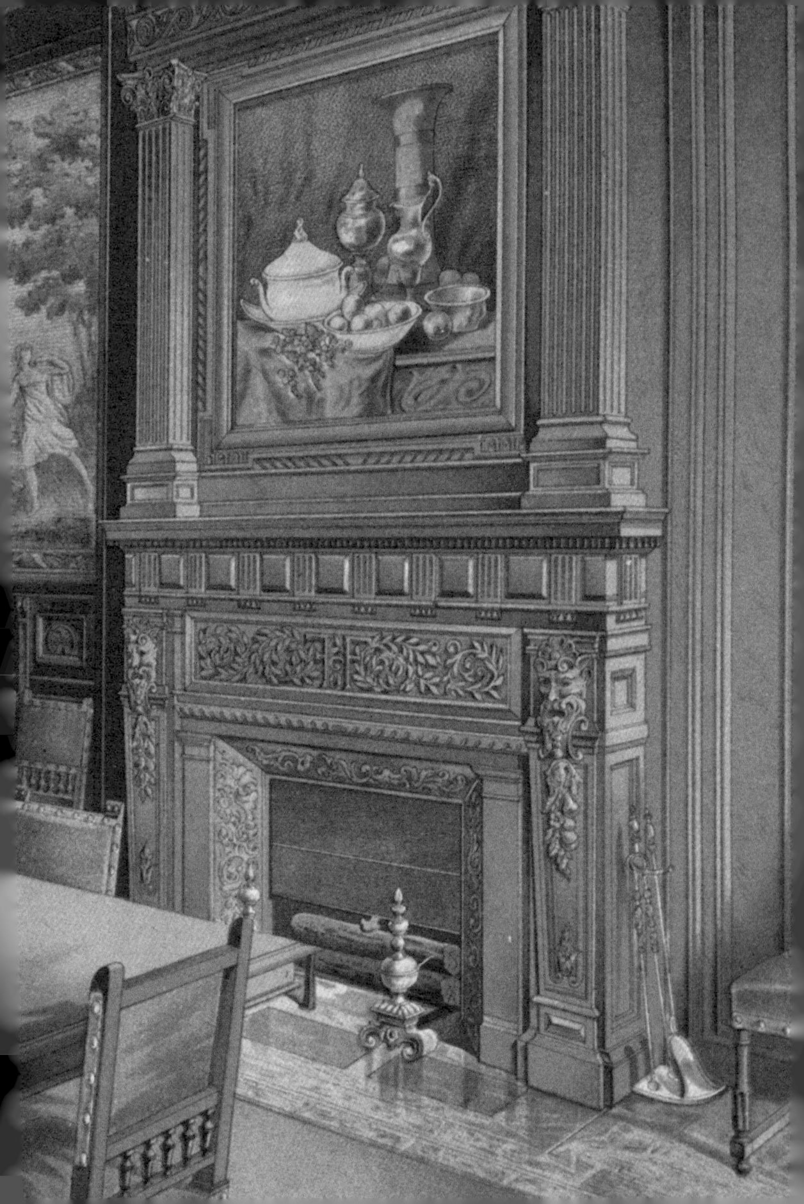

The Blithedale Romance

by

NATHANIEL HAWTHORNE

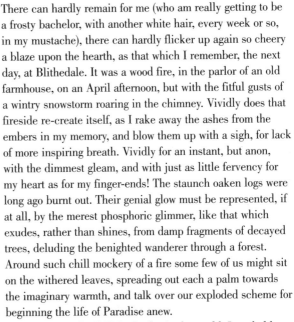

There can hardly remain for me (who am really getting to be a frosty bachelor, with another white hair, every week or so, in my mustache), there can hardly flicker up again so cheery a blaze upon the hearth, as that which I remember, the next day, at Blithedale. It was a wood fire, in the parlor of an old farmhouse, on an April afternoon, but with the fitful gusts of a wintry snowstorm roaring in the chimney. Vividly does that fireside re-create itself, as I rake away the ashes from the embers in my memory, and blow them up with a sigh, for lack of more inspiring breath. Vividly for an instant, but anon, with the dimmest gleam, and with just as little fervency for my heart as for my finger-ends! The staunch oaken logs were long ago burnt out. Their genial glow must be represented, if at all, by the merest phosphoric glimmer, like that which exudes, rather than shines, from damp fragments of decayed trees, deluding the benighted wanderer through a forest. Around such chill mockery of a fire some few of us might sit on the withered leaves, spreading out each a palm towards the imaginary warmth, and talk over our exploded scheme for beginning the life of Paradise anew.

Paradise, indeed! Nobody else in the world, I am bold to

affirm—nobody, at least, in our bleak little world of New England—had dreamed of Paradise that day except as the pole suggests the tropic. Nor, with such materials as were at hand, could the most skilful architect have constructed any better imitation of Eve's bower than might be seen in the snow hut of an Esquimaux. But we made a summer of it, in spite of the wild drifts.

It was an April day, as already hinted, and well towards the middle of the month. When morning dawned upon me, in town, its temperature was mild enough to be pronounced even balmy, by a lodger, like myself, in one of the midmost houses of a brick block—each house partaking of the warmth of all the rest, besides the sultriness of its individual furnace—heat. But towards noon there had come snow, driven along the street by a northeasterly blast, and whitening the roofs and sidewalks with a business-like perseverance that would have done credit to our severest January tempest. It set about its task apparently as much in earnest as if it had been guaranteed from a thaw for months to come. The greater, surely, was my heroism, when, puffing out a final whiff of cigar-smoke, I quitted my cosey pair of bachelor-rooms—with a good fire burning in the grate, and a closet right at hand, where there was still a bottle or two in the champagne basket and a residuum of claret in a box— quitted, I say, these comfortable quarters, and plunged into the heart of the pitiless snowstorm, in quest of a better life.

The better life! Possibly, it would hardly look so now;

it is enough if it looked so then. The greatest obstacle to being heroic is the doubt whether one may not be going to prove one's self a fool; the truest heroism is to resist the doubt; and the profoundest wisdom to know when it ought to be resisted, and when to be obeyed.

Yet, after all, let us acknowledge it wiser, if not more sagacious, to follow out one's daydream to its natural consummation, although, if the vision have been worth the having, it is certain never to be consummated otherwise than by a failure. And what of that? Its airiest fragments, impalpable as they may be, will possess a value that lurks not in the most ponderous realities of any practicable scheme. They are not the rubbish of the mind. Whatever else I may repent of, therefore, let it be reckoned neither among my sins nor follies that I once had faith and force enough to form generous hopes of the world's destiny—yes!—and to do what in me lay for their accomplishment; even to the extent of quitting a warm fireside, flinging away a freshly lighted cigar, and travelling far beyond the strike of city clocks, through a drifting snowstorm.

There were four of us who rode together through the storm; and Hollingsworth, who had agreed to be of the number, was accidentally delayed, and set forth at a later hour alone. As we threaded the streets, I remember how the buildings on either side seemed to press too closely upon us, insomuch that our mighty hearts found barely room enough to throb between them. The snowfall, too, looked inexpressibly dreary

(I had almost called it dingy), coming down through an atmosphere of city smoke, and alighting on the sidewalk only to be moulded into the impress of somebody's patched boot or overshoe. Thus the track of an old conventionalism was visible on what was freshest from the sky. But when we left the pavements, and our muffled hoof-tramps beat upon a desolate extent of country road, and were effaced by the unfettered blast as soon as stamped, then there was better air to breathe. Air that had not been breathed once and again! air that had not been spoken into words of falsehood, formality, and error, like all the air of the dusky city!

"How pleasant it is!" remarked I, while the snowflakes flew into my mouth the moment it was opened. "How very mild and balmy is this country air!"

"Ah, Coverdale, don't laugh at what little enthusiasm you have left!" said one of my companions. "I maintain that this nitrous atmosphere is really exhilarating; and we can never call ourselves regenerated men till a February northeaster shall be as grateful to us as the softest breeze of June!"

So we all of us took courage, riding fleetly and merrily along, by stone fences that were half buried in the wave-like drifts; and through patches of woodland, where the tree-trunks opposed a snow-incrusted side towards the northeast; and within ken of deserted villas, with no footprints in their avenues; and passed scattered dwellings, whence puffed the smoke of country fires, strongly impregnated with the pungent aroma of burning peat. Sometimes, encountering

 a traveller, we shouted a friendly greeting; and he, unmuffling his ears to the bluster and the snow-spray, and listening eagerly, appeared to think our courtesy worth less than the trouble which it cost him. The churl! He understood the shrill whistle of the blast, but had no intelligence for our blithe tones of brotherhood. This lack of faith in our cordial sympathy, on the traveller's part, was one among the innumerable tokens how difficult a task we had in hand for the reformation of the world. We rode on, however, with still unflagging spirits, and made such good companionship with the tempest that, at our journey's end, we professed ourselves almost loath to bid the rude blusterer good-by. But, to own the truth, I was little better than an icicle, and began to be suspicious that I had caught a fearful cold.

And now we were seated by the brisk fireside of the old farmhouse, the same fire that glimmers so faintly among my reminiscences at the beginning of this chapter. There we sat, with the snow melting out of our hair and beards, and our faces all ablaze, what with the past inclemency and present warmth. It was, indeed, a right good fire that we found awaiting us, built up of great, rough logs, and knotty limbs, and splintered fragments of an oak-tree, such as farmers are wont to keep for their own hearths, since these crooked and unmanageable boughs could never be measured into merchantable cords for the market. A family of the old Pilgrims might have swung their kettle over precisely such a fire as this, only, no doubt, a bigger one; and, contrasting it with my coal-grate, I felt so much the more that we had transported ourselves a world-wide distance from the system of society that shackled us at breakfast-time.

Good, comfortable Mrs. Foster (the wife of stout Silas Foster, who was to manage the farm at a fair stipend, and be our tutor in the art of husbandry) bade us a hearty welcome. At her back—a back of generous breadth—appeared two young women, smiling most hospitably, but looking rather awkward withal, as not well knowing what was to be their position in our new arrangement of the world. We shook hands affectionately all round, and congratulated ourselves that the blessed state of brotherhood and sisterhood, at which we aimed, might fairly be dated from this moment. Our greetings were hardly concluded when the door opened, and Zenobia—whom I had never before seen, important as was her plan in our enterprise—Zenobia entered the parlor.

This (as the reader, if at all acquainted with out literary biography, need scarcely be told) was not her real name. She had assumed it, in the first instance, as her magazine signature; and, as it accorded well with some imperial which her friends attributed to this lady's figure and deportment, they half-laughingly adopted it in their familiar intercourse with her. She took the appellation in good part, and even encouraged its constant use; which, in fact, was thus far appropriate, that our Zenobia, however humble looked her new philosophy, had as much native pride as any queen would have known what to do with.

"You are a king by your own fireside, as much as any monarch in his throne."

MIGUEL DE CERVANTES

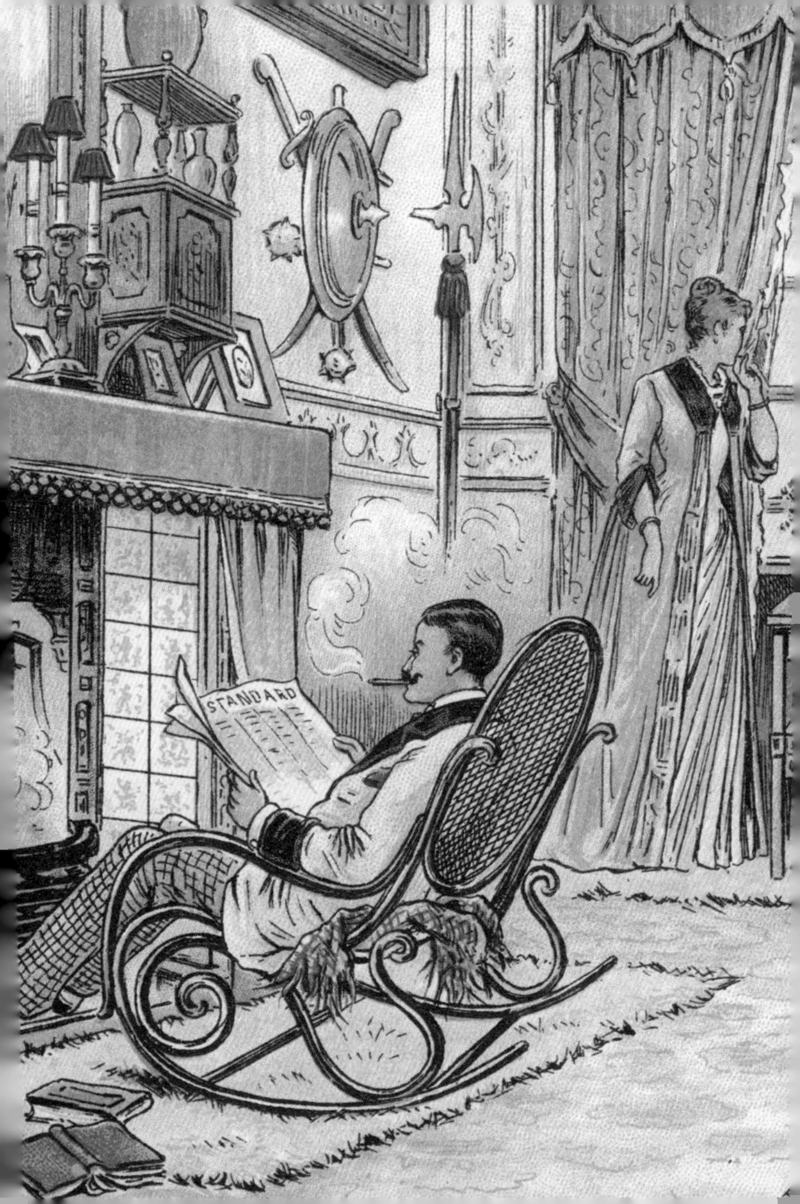
STANDARD

Cleaning the Grate

"An Ever-dirty Hearth, and a grate always choked with cinders and ashes, are infallible evidences of bad housekeeping."

from *The American Woman's Home*, Catherine E. Beecher and Harriet Beecher Stowe

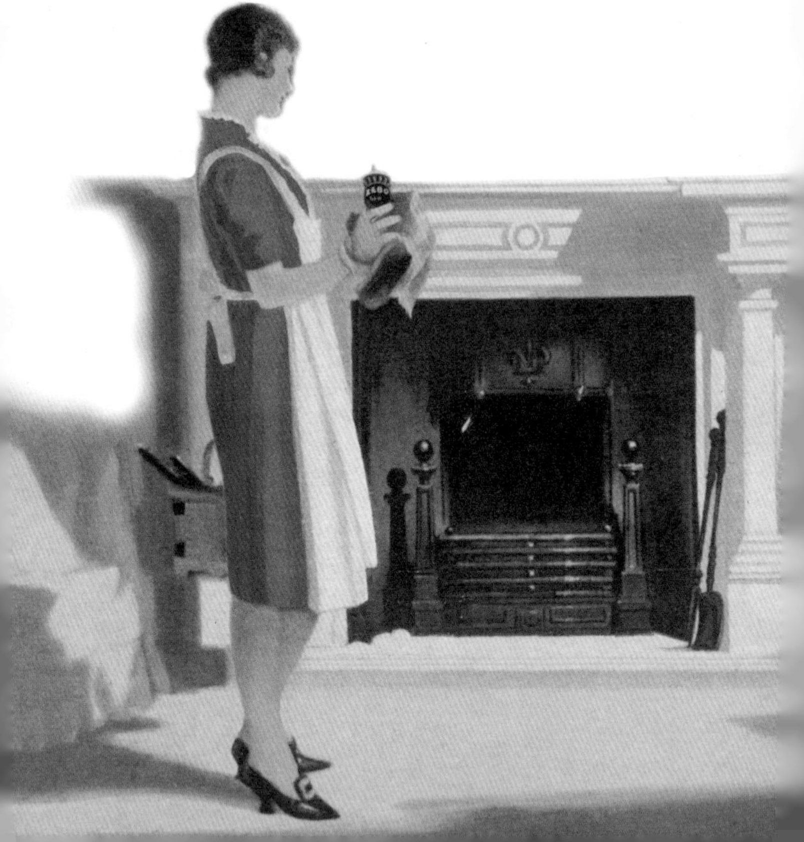

Women in the United States and Britain in the 1860s were well equipped to properly clean and maintain their fireplaces. This is because two very comprehensive books that were to become classics of the home and garden genre were published during that decade. First in the stores was Mrs. Isabella Beeton's *The Book of Household Management*, published in England in 1861. Sisters Catherine E. Beecher and Harrier Beecher Stowe then followed with *The American Woman's Home* in 1869.

The following instructions, tips, and recipes for cleaning the grate come from these two classic housekeeping works and from the 1884 edition of *Enquire Within Upon Everything*, another popular and important book of domestic information and advice.

"When bright grates are once neglected, small rust-spots begin to show themselves, which a plain leather will not remove; the following method of cleaning them must be resorted to:—First, thoroughly clean with emery-paper; then take a large smooth pebble from the road, sufficiently large to hold comfortably in the hand, with which rub the steel backwards and forwards one way, until the desired polish is obtained. It may appear at first to scratch, but continue rubbing, and the result will be success."

from *The Book of Household Management*, Mrs. Isabella Beeton

☞ "Hearths and jambs, of brick, look best painted over with black lead, mixed with soft-soap. Wash the bricks which are nearest the fire with redding and milk, using a painter's brush. A sheet of zinc, covering the whole hearth, is cheap, saves work, and looks very well. A tinman can fit it properly.

"Stone hearths should be rubbed with a paste of powdered stone, (to be procured of the stone-cutters,) and then brushed with a stiff brush. Kitchen hearths, of stone, are improved by rubbing in lamp-oil."

from *The American Woman's Home*, Catherine E. Beecher and Harrier Beecher Stowe

Mark Twain perhaps describes the same "redding technique" mentioned above in his famous novel *The Adventures of Huckleberry Finn*. Huckleberry described the big brick fireplace that was being "kept clean and red by pouring water on them and scrubbing them with another brick" in the Grangerford house.

"Brunswick Black for Varnishing Grates. Melt four pounds of common asphaltum, and add two pints of linseed oil, and one gallon of oil of turpentine. This is usually put up in stoneware bottles for sale, and is used with a paint brush. If too thick, more turpentine may be added."

from *Enquire Within Upon Everything*

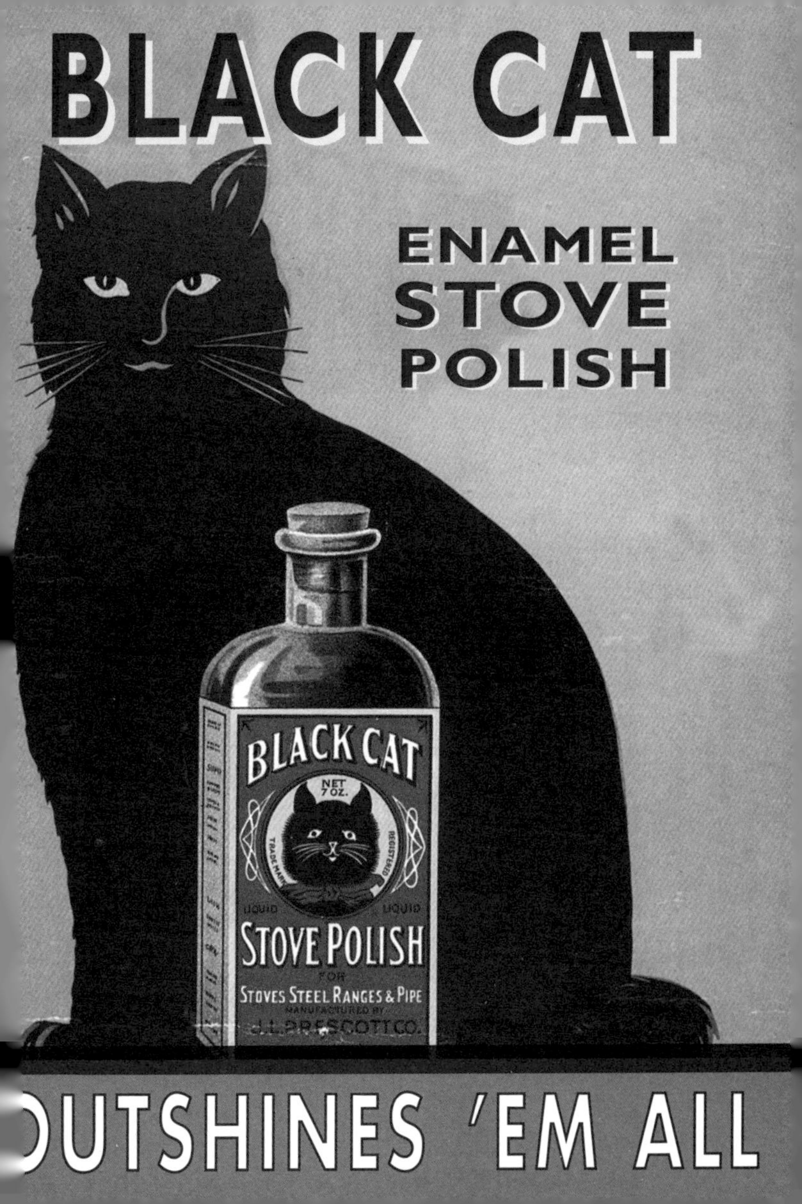

BLACK CAT
ENAMEL
STOVE
POLISH
BLACK CAT
NET
7 OZ.
TRADE MARK
REGISTERED
LIQUID
LIQUID
STOVE POLISH
FOR
STOVES STEEL RANGES & PIPE
MANUFACTURED BY
J.L.PRESCOTT CO.
OUTSHINES ’EM ALL

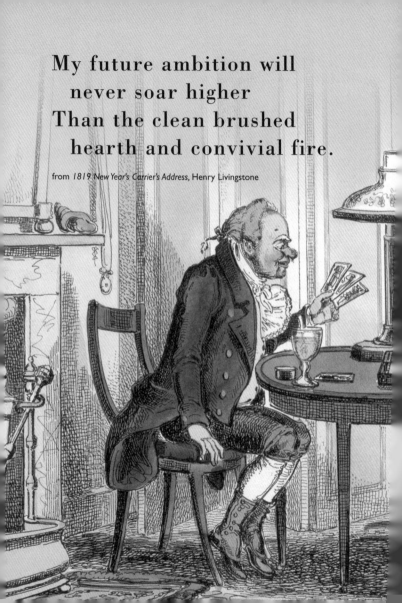

My future ambition will
never soar higher
Than the clean brushed
hearth and convivial fire.

from *1819 New Year's Carrier's Address*, Henry Livingstone

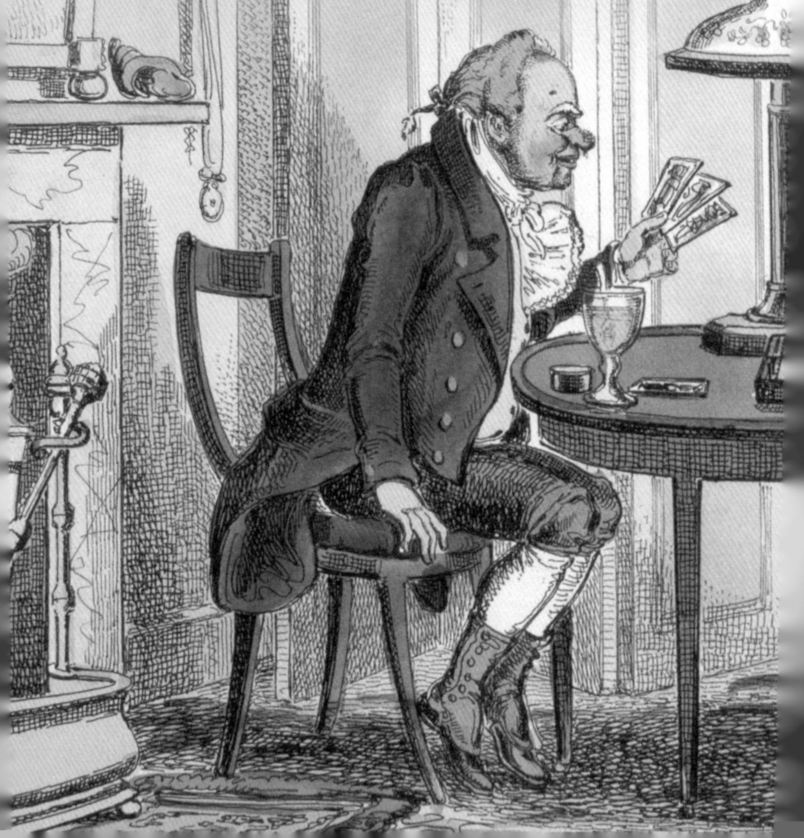

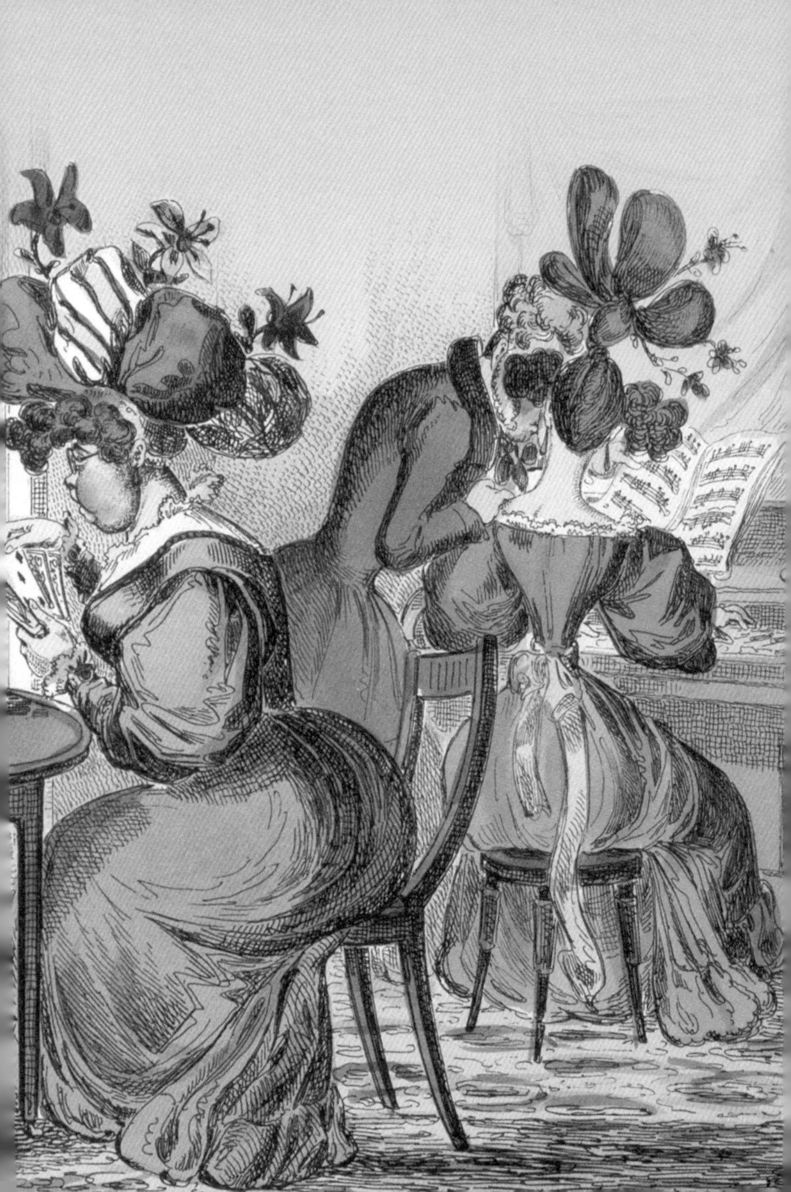

Little Orphant Annie

by

JAMES WHITCOMB RILEY

Little Orphant Annie 's come to our house to stay,
An' wash the cups and saucers up, an' brush the crumbs
    away,
An' shoo the chickens off the porch, an' dust the hearth,
    an' sweep,
An' make the fire, an' bake the bread, an' earn her board-
    an'-keep;
An' all us other children, when the supper things is done,
We set around the kitchen fire an' has the mostest fun
A-list'nin' to the witch-tales 'at Annie tells about,
An' the Gobble-uns 'at gits you
    Ef you
      Don't
        Watch
        Out!

Onc't they was a little boy wouldn't say his pray'rs—
An' when he went to bed at night, away up stairs,
His mammy heerd him holler, an' his daddy heerd him bawl,
An' when they turn't the kivvers down, he wasn't there at all!
An' they seeked him in the rafter-room, an' cubby-hole,
     an' press,
An' seeked him up the chimbly-flue, an' ever'wheres,
     I guess;
But all they ever found was thist his pants an' roundabout!
An' the Gobble-uns 'll git you
     Ef you
       Don't
         Watch
          Out!

An' little Orphant Annie says, when the blaze is blue,
An' the lampwick sputters, an' the wind goes woo-oo!
An' you hear the crickets quit, an' the moon is gray,
An' the lightnin'-bugs in dew is allsquenched away,
You better mind yer parents, and yer teachers fond and dear,
An' churish them 'at loves you, an' dry the orphant's tear,
An' he'p the pore an' needy ones 'at clusters all about,
Er the Gobble-uns 'll git you
     Ef you
       Don't
         Watch
          Out!

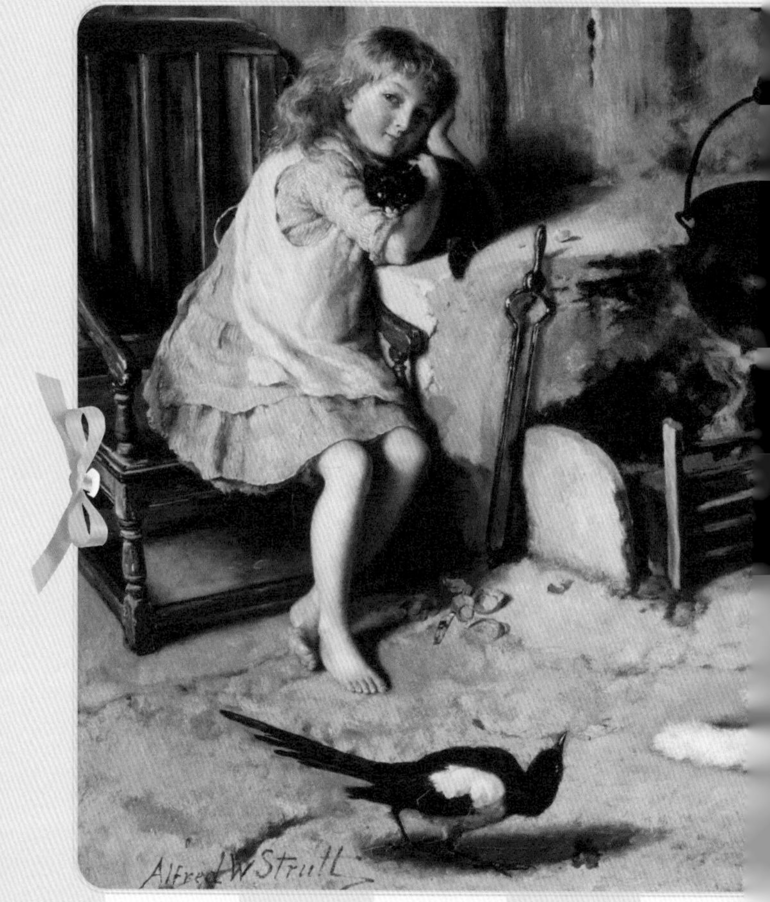
Alfred W Strutt

"An' all us other children, when the supper things is done,
We set around the kitchen fire an' has the mostest fun."

A Bath in Front of the Fire

In the days before every house had a bathroom, most people, when they wished to undress and wash their whole body, were content with sitting in a bath in front of the fire.

The most popular form of portable bath was the tin or enamel hipbath, in which the bather could sit up but not lie back. In larger houses, the hipbath was brought into the bedroom, probably from a cupboard on the landing, and placed on towels in front of the bedroom fire. In small houses and cottages the hipbath was placed in front of the kitchen hearth.

The sponging bath, also designed to be brought into bedrooms, was much shallower, designed rather like a very large, round pie dish. It was often designed with an inverted rim and with a lip for pouring off the dirty water before the bath was lifted up.

Another form of portable bath, the plunge bath, was, by the end of the nineteenth century, much larger than it had been a few decades before. By the 1880s the plunge bath was the standard-shaped bath installed in dressing rooms and bathrooms with pipes connected to the water system and the plumbing.

In wealthy households, it was the job of the lowliest of the housemaids to toil up and down the stairs with great jugs of hot water, and then to bail out the bath.

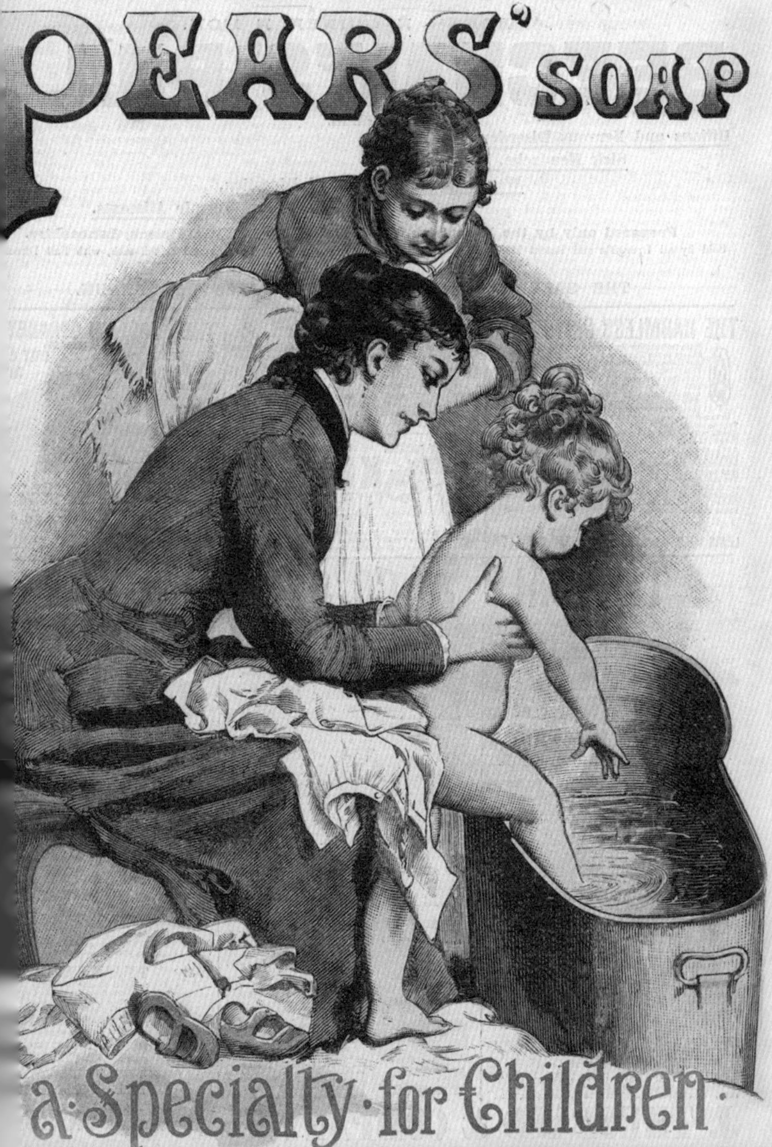
PEARS' SOAP
a·Specialty·for Children·

Housemaid's Fireside Duties

In the nineteenth century, any household with wealth and social status in England had at least one domestic servant. Housemaids, in particular, were an essential part of any smooth-running home. In *The Book of Household Management*, Mrs. Beeton provided this guide for every mistress to follow:

"The first duty of the housemaid in winter is to open the shutters of all the lower rooms in the house, and take up the hearth-rugs of those rooms which she is going to 'do' before breakfast. In some families, where there is only a cook and housemaid kept, and where the drawing-rooms are large, the cook has the care of the dining-room, and the housemaid that of the breakfast-room, library, and drawing-rooms. After the shutters are all opened, she sweeps the breakfast-room, sweeping the dust towards the fire-place, of course previously removing the fender. She should then lay a cloth (generally made of coarse wrapping) over the carpet in front of the stove, and on this should place her housemaid's box, containing black-lead brushes, leathers, emery-paper, black lead, and all utensils necessary for cleaning a grate.

"She now sweeps up the ashes, and deposits them in her cinder pail, which is a japanned tin pail, with a wire sifter inside,

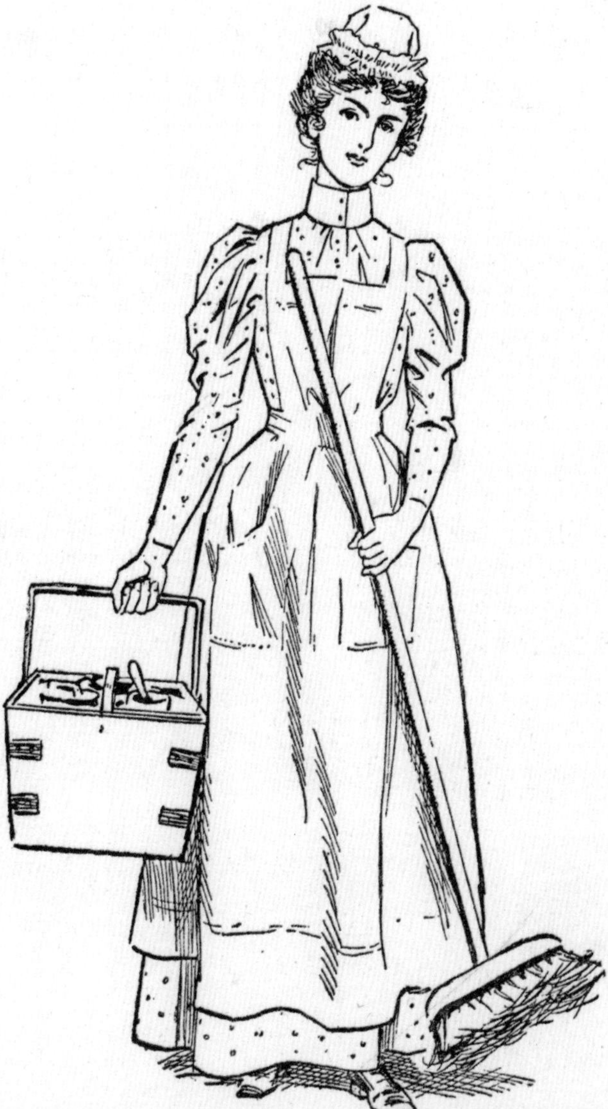

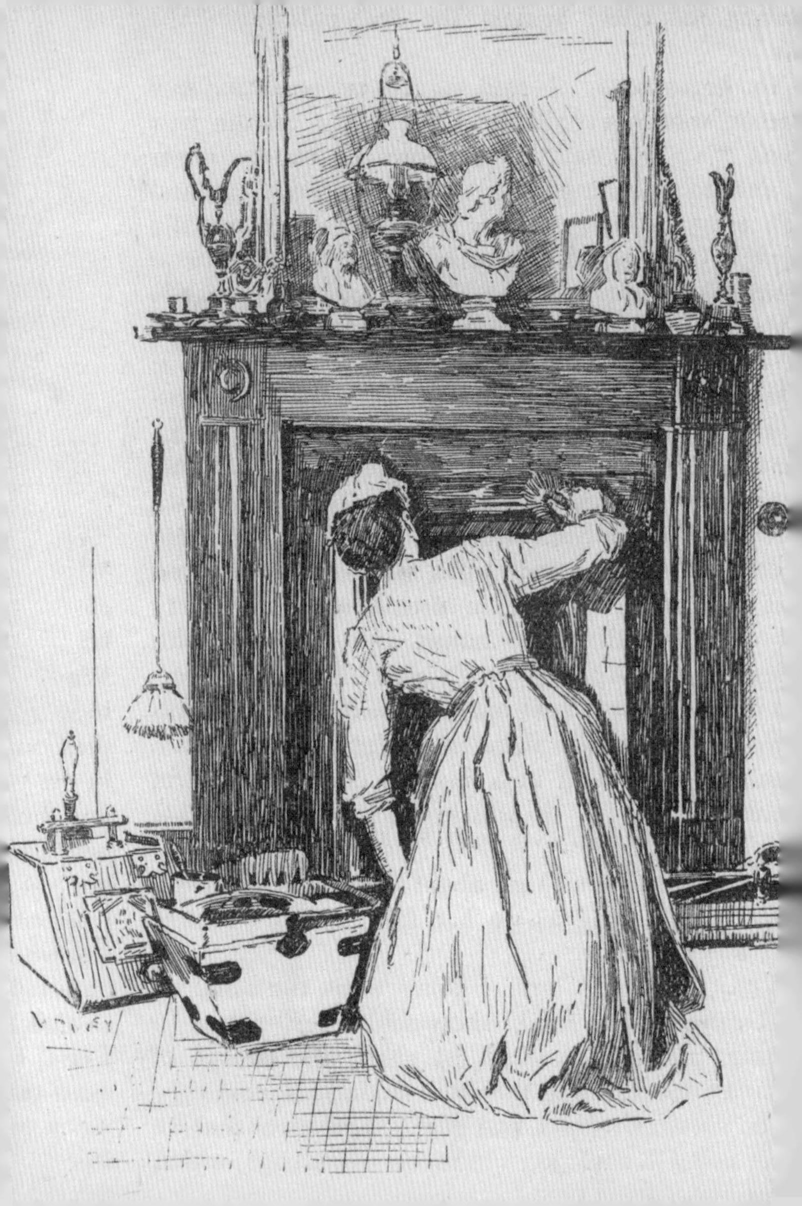

☞ and a closely-fitting top. In this pail the cinders are sifted, and reserved for use in the kitchen or under the copper, the ashes only being thrown away. The cinders disposed of, she proceeds to black-lead the grate, producing the black lead, the soft brush for laying it on, her blacking and polishing brushes, from the box which contains her tools. This housemaid's box should be kept well stocked. Having blackened, brushed and polished every part, and made all clean and bright, she now proceeds to lay the fire....

"Bright grates require unceasing attention to keep them in perfect order. A day should never pass without the housemaid rubbing with a dry leather the polished parts of a grate, as also the fender and fire-irons. A careful and attentive housemaid should have no occasion ever to use emery-paper for any part but the bars, which, of course, become blackened by the fire....

"The several fires lighted, the housemaid proceeds with her dusting, and polishing the several pieces of furniture in the breakfast parlour, leaving no corner unvisited.... She now proceeds to the dressing-room, and lights her mistress's fire, if she is in the habit of having one to dress by. Her mistress is called, hot water placed in the dressing room for her use, her clothes—as far as they are under the housemaid's charge—are put before the fire to air, hanging a fire-guard on the bars where there is one, while she proceeds to prepare the breakfast."

Well-Used Tea Leaves

In the days before tea bags, tea leaves, once used, were seldom just thrown in the trash. Poorer families often dried the tea leaves and either reused them or gave them away to families even poorer than themselves. In bigger houses, a much more satisfactory use was found for them. In the days before the vacuum cleaner, getting rid of the inevitable coal dust from the fire was a never-ending task. While the housemaid could carefully use her duster to pick up the dust on tables, shelves, and ornaments, she needed something much better to catch the dust on carpets. Sweeping a broom across the carpet would just result in clouds of horrid black coal dust rising up and settling on everything in the room.

The answer to her problem was damp tea leaves, carefully saved from every pot of tea made in the house. The housemaid would sprinkle damp tea leaves all over the carpet, take up her carpet broom, with its long, stiff bristles, and sweep up the tea leaves, working toward the center of the room. The dust her broom disturbed would be caught in the damp tea leaves. Once all the tea leaves were in a pile in the center of the carpet they could easily be shoveled up into a bucket and removed. This task left the room clean, fresh and, as Mrs. Beeton pointed out, with a slightly fragrant smell of tea about it.

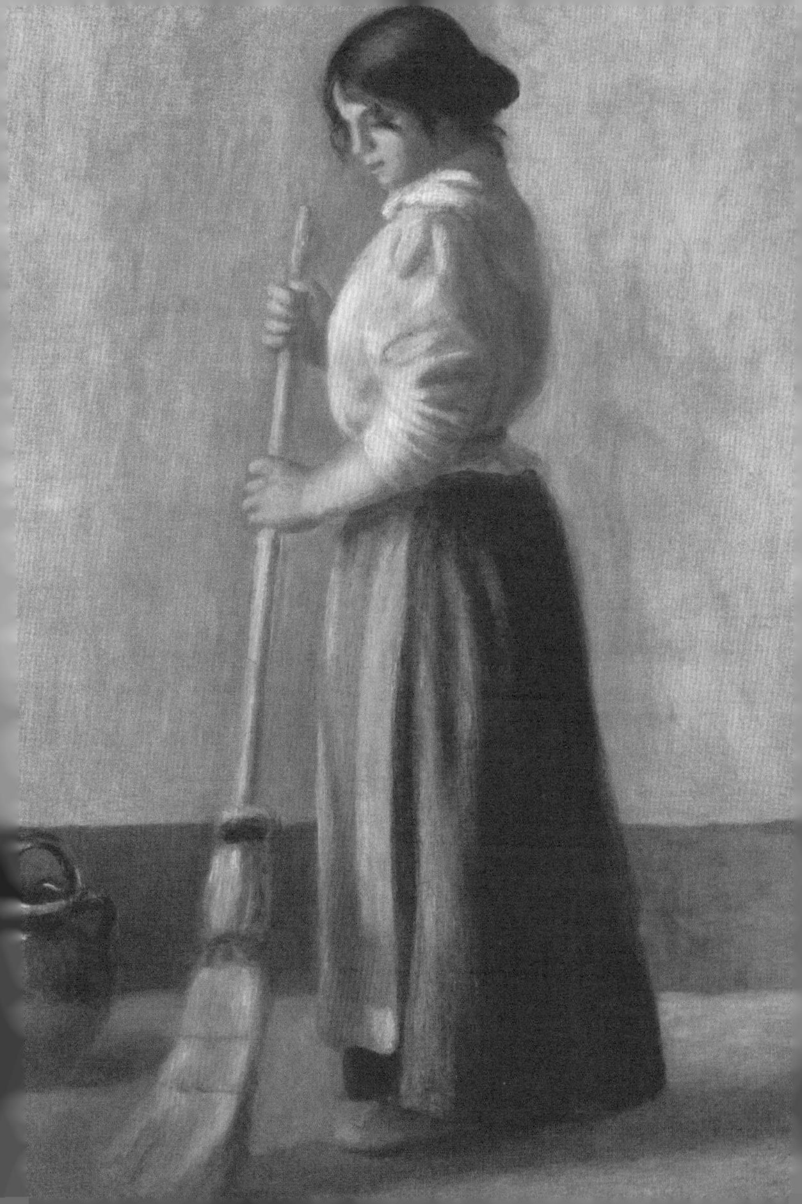

Drying the Washing

Even with the heat of a roaring fire to help dry the laundry, winter wash days were tiresome ordeals before the advent of modern washing machines and dryers. Traditionally, the laundry was done on Mondays. After everything had been washed and put through the wringer, the kitchen would be filled with garments hanging on overhead clotheslines and racks, or airing on a clotheshorse in front of the fire.

Next came the ironing. Usually this was done the day after washday, using a flat iron. The iron was heated on top of the stove, or on top of hot coals on the fireplace. The trick was to have at least two irons so when one began to cool, it could be reheated on the fire while the other one was used.

Once heated, the iron had to be cleaned before starting because of the dirt from the fire. Most housewives used a special cloth for this, and made a few strokes with each hot iron so no black spots from the coals would get on the clothes.

Often, people didn't have a special ironing board, so they put folded sheets on the kitchen table and used that as the ironing surface. One ingenious way of making ironing easier was using a piece of waxed paper to "slick up" the bottom of the flat irons. By running the iron quickly over the paper, it made the iron glide more smoothly over the cloth.

Safety Tips: Gas Fires

Modern gas heaters are clean and convenient and can flood a room with a burst of instant, glowing warmth without all the trouble of hauling in logs or coal. However, while they are easy to use, gas fires must always be properly supervised and maintained. The following are a useful set of basic safety guidelines, but it is recommended that you also always seek the advice of a qualified professional regarding your gas fire.

- **Have your fire professionally installed and regularly serviced.**

- **Make sure that you read the manufacturer's instructions thoroughly and adhere to them.**

- **Good ventilation is crucial. Always ensure there is plenty of air flow—and never seal up doorways and windows.**

- **The fire surface is very hot—keep all combustible materials at least 3ft/1m away from it.**

- **Don't discard any items, including cigarette ends, into a gas fire—this can affect combustion and produce dangerous pollutants.**

- **Stay alert to gas hazards such as leaks, and report all leaks or gas smells immediately.**

- Check the flame on your fire: normally it should be clear blue (unless it is a decorative gas fire.) If the flame is yellow or sooty, that is a danger sign—call the engineer.

- Call the engineer also if the pilot light goes out unexpectedly, or it "pops" or "bangs" when lighting.

- Check for signs of heat damage such as discoloration of the walls or heater panels.

- A faulty gas heater may give off carbon monoxide, which is highly dangerous; it can cause serious illness or even death. Symptoms of carbon monoxide poisoning include:

> Tiredness
> Shortness of breath
> Headaches
> Dizziness
> Nausea
> Weakness
> Confusion
> Chest pain

If you suspect there is carbon monoxide escaping from your fire, open all your windows and doors, turn off the appliance, and go outside quickly to breathe in fresh air. Call the engineer at once, and check with your doctor if you feel unwell.

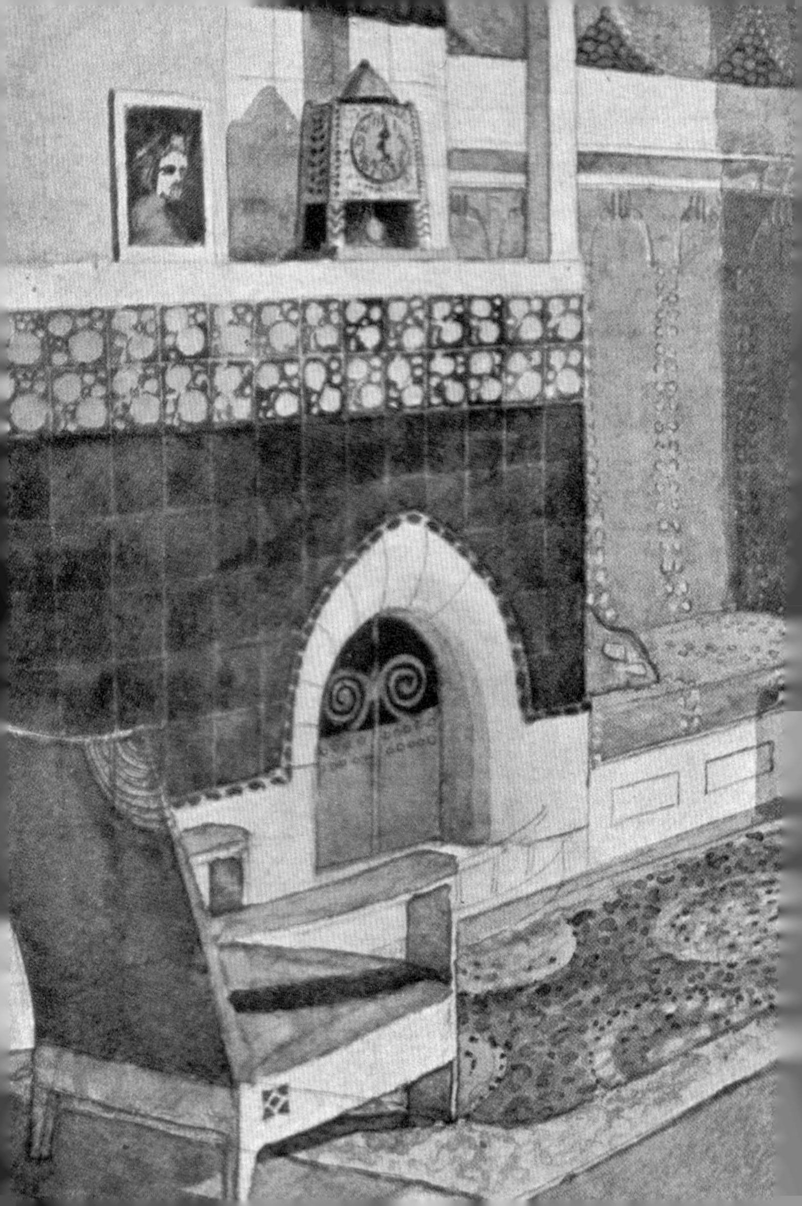

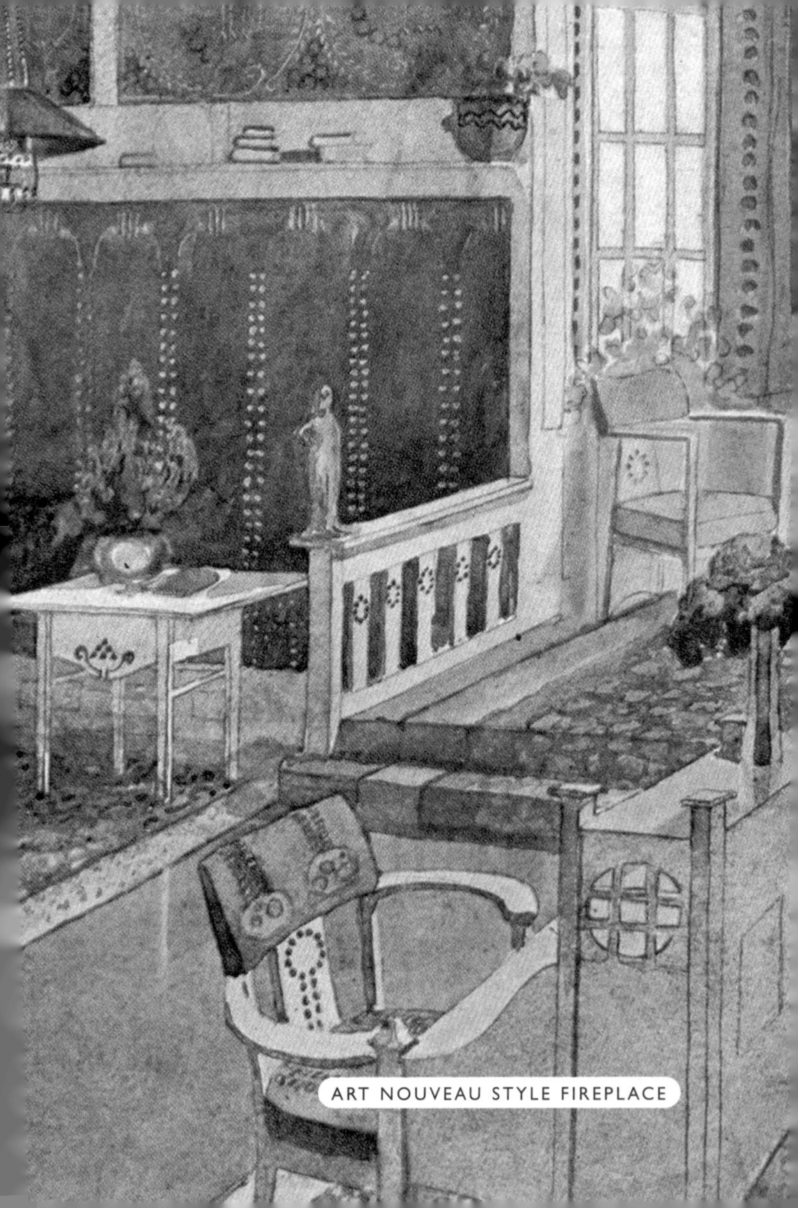

ART NOUVEAU STYLE FIREPLACE

Picture Credits

THE BRIDGEMAN ART LIBRARY
The British Museum, London: page 98; Private Collections: pages 109, 151; Lefèvre Fine Art Ltd., London: page 297.

CORBIS
Pages 140, 229, 235, 236;
© Albright-Knox Art Gallery, Buffalo, NY/Corbis: pages 242–243;
© Archivo Iconografico, S.A./Corbis: pages 230–231;
© Bettmann/Corbis pages: 17, 157, 165, 257, 259;
© Blue Lantern Studio/Corbis: page 188;
© Christie's Images/Corbis: page 288–289;
© Gianni Dagli Orti/Corbis: page 85;
© John Heseltine/Corbis: page 215;
© Historical Picture Archive/Corbis: pages 40–41, 118–119, 145–146, 208–209, 263, 270–271, 284–285, 300–381;
© Hulton-Deutsch Collection/Corbis: pages 10–11;
© Massimo Listri/Corbis: pages 239, 264;
© Lucidio Studio, Inc./Corbis: page 127;
© Swim Ink/Corbis: pages 161, 178;
© Elizabeth Whiting & Associates/Corbis: pages 133 (Dennis Stone), 267 (Rodney Hyett).

GETTY IMAGES
Pages 30–31, 38, 46–47, 158, 177, 222.

MARY EVANS PICTURE LIBRARY
Pages 6, 20, 24–25, 36–37, 43, 50–51, 59, 69, 72, 77, 78, 80–81, 83, 104, 124–125, 135, 139, 167, 170, 172–173, 181, 183, 197, 199, 200, 210–211, 212–213, 216–217, 219, 220–221, 233, 240, 253, 269, 278, 280, 291, 293, 294, 298.

THE PICTURE DESK
© The Advertising Archive Ltd.: pages 23, 87, 101, 113, 123, 225, 227, 283;
© The Art Archive: page 255; Marc Charmet: page 143; Harper Collins Publishers: pages 154–155; Private Collection/Joseph Martin: pages 102–103; Private Collection/Dagli Orti: pages 192–193.

POWERSTOCK
Pages 186–187.

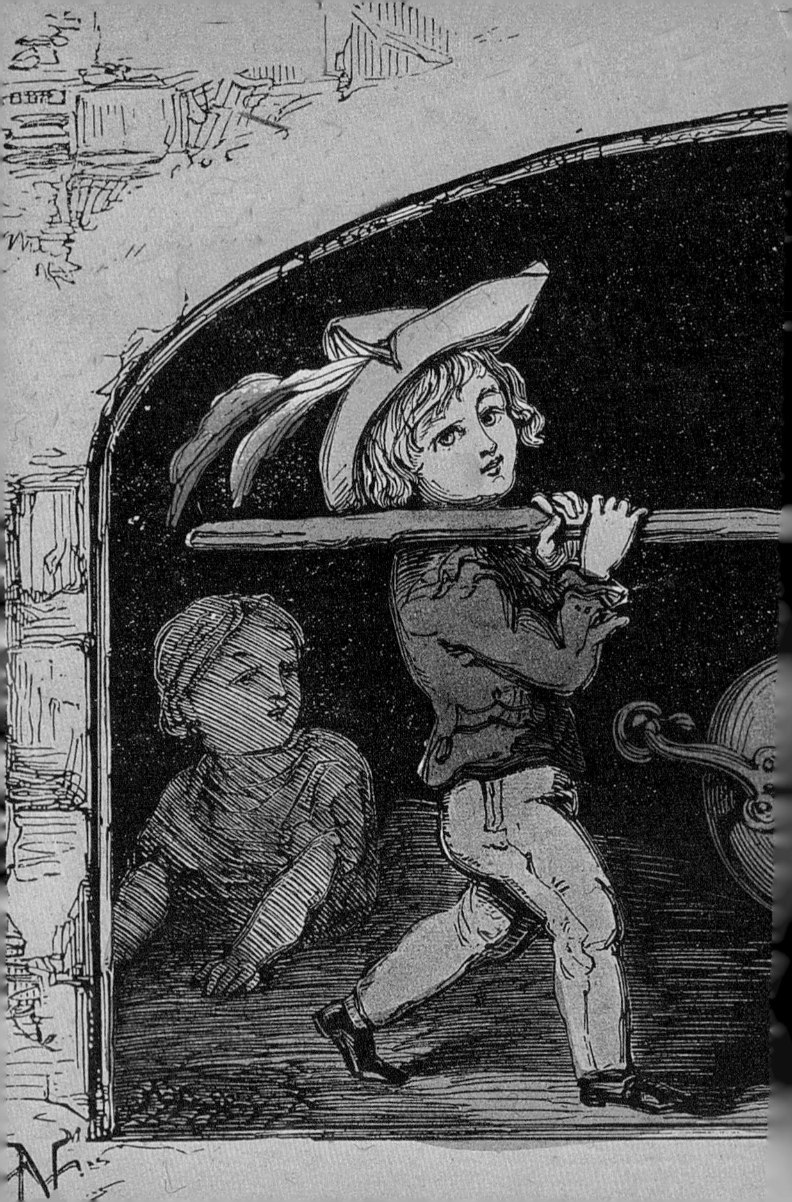